ROYAL HISTORICAL SOCIETY
GUIDES AND HANDBOOKS
No. 12
TEXTS AND CALENDARS II
AN ANALYTICAL GUIDE
TO SERIAL PUBLICATIONS
1957-1982

ROYAL HISTORICAL SOCIETY
GUIDES AND HANDBOOKS

MAIN SERIES

1. *Guide to English commercial statistics 1696–1782.* By G. N. Clark and Barbara M. Franks. 1938.
2. *Handbook of British chronology.* Edited by F. M. Powicke, Charles Johnson and W. J. Harte. 1939. 2nd edition, edited by F. M. Powicke and E. B. Fryde, 1961.
3. *Medieval libraries of Great Britain. A list of surviving books.* Edited by N. R. Ker. 1941. 2nd edition, 1964.
4. *Handbook of dates for students of English history.* Edited by C. R. Cheney. 1945. Reprinted, 1982.
5. *Guide to the national and provincial directories of England and Wales, excluding London, published before 1856.* By Jane E. Norton. 1950.
6. *Handbook of oriental history.* Edited by C. H. Philips. 1951.
7. *Texts and Calendars. An analytical guide to serial publications.* By E. L. C. Mullins. 1958. Reprinted (with corrections), 1978.
8. *Anglo-Saxon Charters. An annotated list and bibliography.* By P. H. Sawyer. 1968.
9. *A Centenary Guide to the publications of the Royal Historical Society 1868–1968 and of the former Camden Society 1838–1897.* By Alexander Taylor Milne. 1968.
10. *Guide to the local administrative units of England.* Volume I. *Southern England.* By Frederic A. Youngs, Jr. 1979. 2nd edition, 1981.
11. *Guide to bishops' registers of England and Wales. A survey from the middle ages to the abolition of episcopacy in 1646.* By David M. Smith. 1981.

SUPPLEMENTARY SERIES

1. *A Guide to the papers of British Cabinet Ministers, 1900–1951.* Compiled by Cameron Hazlehurst and Christine Woodland. 1974.
2. *A Guide to the reports of the U.S. Strategic Bombing Survey.* I *Europe.* II *The Pacific.* Edited by Gordon Daniels. 1981.

TEXTS AND CALENDARS II
AN ANALYTICAL GUIDE
TO SERIAL PUBLICATIONS
1957–1982

BY

E. L. C. MULLINS

LONDON
OFFICES OF THE ROYAL HISTORICAL SOCIETY
UNIVERSITY COLLEGE LONDON, GOWER STREET
LONDON WC1E 6BT

1983

British Library Cataloguing in Publication Data

Mullins, E L C
  Texts and calendars II: an analytical guide to
  serial publications, 1957–1982—(Royal
  Historical Society guides and handbooks; no. 12)
  1. Great Britain—History—Sources—Bibliographies
  I. Title   II. Series
  016.941   Z2017
  ISBN 0-86193-100-9

Made and Printed in Great Britain by Butler & Tanner Ltd., Frome and London

PREFACE

IN *Texts and Calendars* (1958, reprinted with corrections 1978) are listed the publications issued in general collections or in series by official bodies and private societies wholly or partly devoted to the printing—in transcript or calendar form—of sources for the history of England and Wales. Apart from a few eighteenth-century works which were included for reasons indicated in its preface, the earliest volumes listed were issued in 1802, the latest in March 1957. The present work continues *Texts and Calendars* for twenty-five years: the last additions to its lists were made in October 1982. By intent and in execution it closely resembles the earlier work, and little need here be said by way of qualification or addition to the limitations and practice described in the earlier preface. Its chief concern is with texts and calendars for English and Welsh history; publications which cannot be so described, such as catalogues, indexes, lists, and expository studies, are generally excluded unless they form part of numbered series. Like its predecessor, it is also to serve as a catalogue of one section of the library of the Royal Historical Society, and for this reason it continues to list several series—the English Place-name Survey is one, the inventories of the Royal Commissions on Historical Monuments are others—which might have been excluded from the earlier volume if the sectional boundaries of the library had been more sharply defined.

The collections and series listed in *Texts and Calendars* comprise the admissible publications of nine official bodies and sixty-three private societies. Three of those official bodies and twenty of those private societes had ceased to publish. Consequently, the Cantilupe Society is not to be found in the present volume; the Caxton, English Historical, and Parker societies do not occur; no new titles can be added to the Cymmrodorion Record Series; other Welsh societies were woefully short-lived; and no further text or calendar has issued from the Council for the Preservation of Business Archives. Inspection of the table of contents will bring to mind other absentees; it will also show that during the twenty-five years covered by this volume no less than seven entirely new record series were initiated by existing societies, and that new record societies were founded for the countries of Cambridge, Derby, Dorset, Rutland (yes Rutland), Suffolk, and Pembroke, and for the city of London and its environs.

Users of *Texts and Calendars* will find the lay-out of this supplement familiar. By and large, the titles and attributions of the publications listed are given as they are shown on their title-pages; beneath, in reduced type, notes by the compiler endeavour to amplify the title-page information and to make clear (when clarification seems called for) the nature and dates of the documents printed and the manner in which their editors have presented them. To this extent *Texts and Calendars II* is in line with its predecessor, but it goes further: the notes now attempt to indicate the scope of the introductory matter and also, when it can be done without distortion and in brief, the conclusions which may have been reached. By employing in these notes the original writers' own words in direct, or more commonly unacknowledged, quotation the compiler has sought to avoid expressions which could be construed as value judgments on the texts edited and the quality of the editing. One further point: since the introductory matter is referred to in the notes it has seemed permissible to exclude from the titles such phrases as 'with introduction and notes' and to show the exclusion by marks of omission.

For most of the collections and series in the present work the sequences of numbers allocated as an indexing aid and printed in the right-hand margins began in the earlier *Texts and Calendars*: they continue without interruption. Reference from one publication to another is in the form 'see ... below' or 'contd. from ... above' when the publication referred to is in the present work, and without 'below' and 'above' when it is in the earlier volume. Abbreviations have been used sparingly: the meaning of two only may not be immediately recognizable: HMC JP identifies works issued by the Historical Manuscripts Commission in its Joint Publications series; *T & C* identifies *Texts and Calendars*. Attention is drawn to the explanatory note preceding the index and to the two lists at the end of the volume, the first of corrections to *T & C*, the second of publications listed here but not included in the library of the Royal Historical Society.

In his earlier preface the compiler admitted that 'ingenious confusion' had on occasion defeated him: to his embarrassment he has been defeated again, this time more seriously. The list given in *Texts and Calendars* for the Surrey Record Society shows that its Publication 34, issued in 1933, concluded the first portion of the Society's edition of the Chertsey abbey cartulary: cumulated with two preceding instalments (Publications 5 and 27) it made up the Society's Volume 12 and was listed in *Texts and Calendars* as the twelfth in a series which, by the end of March 1957, had attained to Volume 23. The list for the present work, beginning with Volume 24, was already in page-proof when the compiler was informed that, correct though it was as a numerical sequence, it was incomplete as a record of the Society's output since 1957: missing from it were two further instalments of the Chertsey abbey cartulary. Issued in 1958 and 1963, they form the second volume of the cartulary and complete the edition. Unhappily for the bibliographic amateur, the designations borne by them in the Society's own enumeration of its works are 'Volume 12 continued' and 'Volume 12 concluded'. Catalogued and shelved as components of the twelfth item in a series which he had previously described, they eluded the compiler's attention. A real bibliographer would not have been so easily gulled. The brief notice printed herein (at **63**.12) is all that could be inserted at the eleventh hour; it falls far short of what otherwise would have been said of an editorial achievement as notable for the importance and scholarship of its introductory matter as for the tenacity which brought about its completion after nearly half a century.

The compiler gratefully acknowledges the assistance he received in the course of his work. Mr. P.W. Ford and Professor P.H. Hardacre were among the first to supply corrections to the earlier volume and suggestions for the second; Professor Alan Harding, Miss Elizabeth Crittall, Dr. R.F. Hunnisett, and Dr. Ian Roy responded nobly to cries for help; Mr. Norman Evans scrutinized and amended the entries proposed for the Public Record Office; and by her vigorous criticism of the entries drafted for the Historical Manuscripts Commission Miss Sonia Anderson brought about a re-consideration which vastly improved the whole section. Yet great though his obligation to individuals undoubtedly is, the compiler of a work such as this must owe an even greater debt to the libraries and librarians upon whose services he has depended. Dr. Williams's Library—always a present help for historians in trouble—again allowed access to an unbroken run of Alcuin Club publications, and during several months spent in the Guildhall Library of the Corporation of London the daily wants of a demanding reader were cheerfully and expertly supplied. Greater still, however, is his debt to the Institute of Historical Research in the University of London, his academic home in one sense or another for the past forty-five years. Its Secretary and Librarian, Mr. William Kellaway, has provided most of the corrections listed at the end of this book, and if it were possible it would be offered to him and his staff—Miss Rosemary Taylor, Mr. Clyve Jones, Mr. Robert Lyons, Dr. Keith Manley, and Mr. D.J. Munro (whose care of the Society's library does not go unnoticed)—in gratitude. The last acknowledgment must be to Dr. Greenway, the Society's assistant literary director, for her precise attention to typescript and proofs: only if some errors remain will the compiler be able to claim *Texts and Calendars II* as recognizably his.

30 May 1983   E.L.C.M.

CONTENTS

CONTENTS

xi

PART 1
OFFICIAL BODIES

3. PUBLIC RECORD OFFICE TEXTS AND CALENDARS

Calendar of the general and special assize and general gaol delivery commissions on the dorses of the patent rolls. Richard II, 1377–1399. Nendeln: KTO Press, 1977 [1976].   **3.6**

By A. H. Watford and C. A. F. Meekings, the latter responsible for the scheme of calendaring and subject indexing, the circuit tables, the formulary (which gives examples of the various commissions in full, their form on the rolls, and the form adopted in the calendar) and the notes (drawing attention to the 'readily available surviving assize, special assize and gaol delivery enrolments and files that record business done under the calendared commissions'). Entered in HMSO, *Sectional list 24* as vol. vii of the patent rolls of Rich. II.

Calendar of the patent rolls preserved in the Public Record Office. Elizabeth I. 1939–   ; in progress.   **3.16**

i : Yrs. 1–2, 1558–60. By J. H. Collingridge. Includes the two supplementary (pardon) rolls for 1 Eliz. Modifications in the system of calendaring are explained in the preface. (1939).
ii : Yrs. 3–5, 1560–3. By J. H. Collingridge and R. B. Wernham. (1948).
iii : Yrs. 6–8, 1563–6. By J. H. Collingridge and R. B. Wernham, indexed by N. J. Williams. (1960 [1961]).
iv : Yrs. 9–11, 1566–9. By J. H. Collingridge, indexed by A. W. Mabbs. (1964).
v : Yrs. 12–14, 1569–72. By J. H. Collingridge and C. S. Drew, edited and indexed by N. J. Williams assisted by R. D. Farmer. (1966).
vi : Yrs. 15–17, 1572–5. By N. J. Williams, indexed by Mrs. J. M. Davids. (1973 [1974]).
vii: Yrs. 18–20, 1575–8. Edited by J. H. Collingridge and indexed in part by Mrs. J. M. Trier. (1982).

Close rolls (supplementary) of the reign of Henry III preserved in the Public Record Office. 1244–1266. Edited by Ann Morton. 1975.   **3.17**

Transcript, Latin, of the three earliest in the class of Supplementary Close Rolls (C 55). The other 15 rolls in the class are calendared in **3.**21, 22, 24, 30. Entered in HMSO, *Sectional list 24* as vol. xv of the close rolls of Hen. III.

Calendar of the close rolls preserved in the Public Record Office. Henry VII. 2 vols., 1955 [1956]–63.   **3.27**

i : Yrs. 1–15, 1485–1500. By K. H. Ledward.

3

ii: Yrs. 16-24, 1500-9. By R. E. Latham.

Calendar of the fine rolls preserved in the Public Record   3.28
Office. 22 vols., 1911-62[63].

xxi : Edw. IV, Edw. V, Rich. III, 1471-85. By P. V. Davies, indexed by
J. G. Wickham. (1961).

xxii: Hen. VII, 1485-1509. By P. V. Davies, indexed by C. W. Berry.
(1962 [1963]).

Calendar of the liberate rolls preserved in the Public Record   3.29
Office. Henry III. 6 vols., 1916-64 [1917-65].

i : Yrs. 11-24, 1226-40. By W. H. Stevenson, indexed by C. T. Flower,
the preface by C. Johnson. (1916 [1917]).

ii : Yrs. 25-29, 1240-5. By J. B. W. Chapman, indexed by D. L. Evans.
(1930 [1931]).

iii: Yrs. 30-35, 1245-51. By J. B. W. Chapman, indexed by D. L. Evans.
(1937).

iv: Yrs. 36-44, 1251-60. By J. B. W. Chapman, indexed by Mrs. S. B.
Storey. (1959 [1960]).

v : Yrs. 45-51, 1260-7. By J. B. W. Chapman, indexed by Mrs. S. B.
Storey. (1961 [1962]).

vi: Yrs. 52-56, 1267-72, with appendices, 1220-67. By R. E. Latham,
based on the calendar by J. B. W. Chapman. Appendix I includes all
writs of liberate entered on exchequer rolls and neither printed in 1.24
nor calendared in this series. Appendix II, by Mrs. S. B. Storey, consists
of contrabrevia or copies of writs of computabitur selected from the
only known file of its kind. (1964 [1965]).

Calendar of inquisitions *post mortem* and other analogous   3.33
documents preserved in the Public Record Office. 1904- ;
in progress.

xv : 1-7 Rich. II, 1377-84. By M. C. B. Dawes, A. C. Wood, Miss D. H.
Gifford and others. (1970).

xvi: 7-15 Rich. II, 1384-92. By M. C. B. Dawes, indexed by Mrs. M. R.
Devine, Mrs. H. E. Jones and Mrs. M. J. Post. (1974 [1975]).

Calendar of inquisitions miscellaneous (Chancery) preserved   3.35
in the Public Record Office. 7 vols., 1916-68[69].

i : Hen. III and Edw. I, 1219-1307. By G. J. Morris, Harley Rodney, S.
R. Scargill-Bird and others, indexed by C. Hilary Jenkinson, the preface
by H. C. Maxwell Lyte. Further introductory matter in vol. iv. Additional inquisitions in vol. ii (appendix). (1916).

ii : Edw. II-22 Edw. III, 1307-49. By Harley Rodney, J. G. Morris and
S. R. Scargill-Bird, indexed by A. E. Bland. (1916).

iii : 22-51 Edw. III, 1348-77. By Harley Rodney and J. B. W. Chapman,
indexed by H. C. Johnson. (1937).

iv : 1-11 Rich. II, 1377-88. By J. B. W. Chapman, revised by H. C.
Johnson, indexed by R. F. Hunnisett. (1957).

v : 11-16 Rich. II, 1387-93. By J. B. W. Chapman, revised by H. C.
Johnson and R. F. Hunnisett, indexed by R. F. Hunnisett. Two inquisitions dated 19 Rich. II, 1396, have been noticed. (1962 [1963]).

vi : 16–23 Rich. II, 1392–99. By J. B. W. Chapman, revised and indexed by R. F. Hunnisett. (1963).
vii: Hen. IV and Hen. V, 1399–1422. By J. B. W. Chapman, revised and indexed by R. F. Hunnisett. (1968 [1969]).

Curia regis rolls [vols. i–vii 'of the reigns of Richard I and John', vol. viii onwards 'of the reign of Henry III'] preserved in the Public Record Office. 1922–   ; in progress.   3.38

Transcript, Latin. The introduction on the history of the rolls, by C. A. F. Meekings, begun in vol. xi, and the notes on justices by the same, are contd. in the following vols.

xii : Hilary and Trinity, 9 Hen. III, 1225; Michaelmas, 9–10 Hen. III, 1225; Hilary and Easter, 10 Hen. III, 1226. One membrane for Easter term 1225 was discovered too late for inclusion. Transcribed in part by L. C. Hector, the text completed and indexed by Sir Cyril Flower. (1957).

xiii: Easter and Trinity, 11 Hen. III, 1227; Hilary and Easter, 12 Hen. III, 1228; Michaelmas, 12–13 Hen. III, 1228; Hilary, Easter and Trinity, 13 Hen. III, 1229; Hilary, 14 Hen. III, 1230. Transcribed by L. C. Hector, Charles Johnson and Sir Cyril Flower; edited and indexed by Sir Cyril Flower. (1959 [1960]).

xiv: Trinity, 14 Hen. III, 1230; Michaelmas, 14–15 Hen. III, 1230; Hilary, Easter and Trinity, 15 Hen. III, 1231; Easter, 16 Hen. III, 1232; Michaelmas, 16–17 Hen. III, 1232. Transcribed by L. C. Hector, Charles Johnson, H. C. Johnson and Sir Cyril Flower; edited and indexed by Sir Cyril Flower. Appendix (by C. A. F. Meekings) of nine writs (five original and four judicial) for Trinity, 14 Hen. III. (1961 [1962]).

xv : Hilary and Easter, 17 Hen. III, 1233; Michaelmas, 17–18 Hen. III, 1233; Trinity, 18 Hen. III, 1234; Easter, 20 Hen. III, 1236. Also coram rege rolls, Trinity, 18 Hen. III, 1234–Easter, 21 Hen. III, 1237. Transcribed in the main by L. C. Hector; edited and indexed by Sir Cyril Flower, the indexes revised by Mrs. S. B. Storey and Miss A. N. Marr. The introduction is expanded to describe the circumstances of the appointment of William de Ralegh as justice, and the court coram rege with its records in his time. Supporting appendices set out the dates, places and business of coram rege sessions, the details of the King's itinerary, and the dates of charters attested by Ralegh and the household stewards, and of royal letters authorized by them or made in their presence. (1972).

xvi: Hilary, 22 Hen. III, 1238; Trinity, 23 Hen. III, 1239; Easter, 26 Hen. III, 1242. Also coram rege rolls, Easter, 21 Hen. III, 1237–Easter, 22 Hen. III, 1238 (incorporating cases on Eton College ms. 280); Michaelmas, 24–25 Hen. III, 1240–long vacation, 25 Hen. III, 1241; Hilary–long vacation, 25 Hen. III, 1241, and records of cases sent to the court coram rege in Michaelmas, 25 Hen. III, 1240. Edited by L. C. Hector, acknowledging the vol. to be, like others in this series, 'the work of many hands'. The expanded introduction again covers the court coram rege, its sessions and business, the King's itinerary, and attestations and authorizations, for the period 1 June 1237–9 May 1242. (1979).

Calendar of state papers, colonial series, preserved in the Public Record Office. 1860– ; in progress.   **3.54**

America and West Indies:

Addenda, 1688–1696. (Kraus reprint, 1969).

xliii: 1737. By K. G. Davies. The records of the colony of Georgia, omitted from earlier vols., are included for 1737 onwards. Other classes now included, and changes in the principles of calendaring, are described in the introduction, and there is a list of the records from which the calendar has been compiled. In the appendices: a register of South Carolina land grants in 1737, lists of persons attending meetings of the common council of Georgia and meetings of the trustees, and a summary table for the year showing the number and tonnage of ships entering and clearing from British ports in America and the West Indies. (1963).

xliv: 1738. By K. G. Davies. As the preceding, and continuing the three appendices. (1969).

Calendar of treasury books preserved in the Public Record Office. 33 vols. in 64, 1904–69.   **3.57**

Following the pattern of earlier vols. (see *T & C* 1958, 1978), pt. 1 in the vols. listed below contains the introduction to the vol., the statement of national revenue and expenditure, and extracts from the departmental declared accounts; this pt. is not indexed; the calendar and its index are contained in the subsequent pt. or pts. The calendar for the entire series was prepared by William A. Shaw (see vol. xx, pt. 1); he also wrote the introductions covering vols. i–xxv and abstracted most of the accounts. In vol. xxv, pt. 1, the statement of revenue and expenditure and the abstract of the declared accounts were the work of F. H. Slingsby, who became responsible for all the subsequent introductions, all the declared accounts, and most of the statements of revenue and expenditure. In vol. xxxi, pt. 1, and vol. xxxii, pt. 1, the statements of revenue and expenditure were prepared by A. J. W. McDonald.

xxv, pt. 1 : Introduction, with accounts, 1710–11; pt. 2: Minutes, warrants, etc., Jan.–Dec. 1711, with index. (1952, 1961).

xxvi, pt. 1 : Introduction, with accounts, 1711–12; pt. 2: Minutes, warrants, etc., Jan.–Dec. 1712, with index. (1954).

xxvii, pt. 1 : Introduction, with accounts, 1712–13; pt. 2: Minutes, warrants, etc., Jan.–Dec. 1713, with index. (1955 [1956]).

xxviii, pt. 1: Introduction, with accounts, 1713–14; pt. 2: Minutes, warrants, etc., Jan.–July 1714, and William Lowndes's secret service accounts, 8 Mar. 1702–27 July 1714, with index. (1955 [1956], 1969).

xxix, pt. 1 : Introduction, with accounts, 1714–15, (1957 [1958]); pt. 2: Minutes, warrants, etc., Aug. 1714–Dec. 1715, (1957 [1958]); pt. 3: Index, (1959).

xxx, pt. 1 : Introduction, with accounts, 1715–16, (1958); pt. 2: Minutes, warrants, etc., Jan.–Dec. 1716, with index, (1957 [1959]).

xxxi, pt. 1 : Introduction, with accounts, 1716–17, (1960) [1961]); pt. 2:

6

Minutes, warrants, etc., Jan.-Aug. 1717, (1957 [1958]); pt. 3: Warrants, etc., Aug.-Dec. 1717, with the report (including regimental accounts) of the 1715 commission for army debts, and index, (1957 [1958]).
xxxii, pt. 1 : Introduction, with accounts, 1717-18, (1962); pt. 2: Minutes, warrants, etc., Jan.-Dec. 1718, with index, (1957 [1958]).

Calendar of entries in the papal registers relating to Great Britain and Ireland. Papal letters. 1893-   ; in progress.   **3.70**

xiv: 1484-92, for the pontificate of Innocent VIII and drawn from his Vatican and Lateran registers. Prepared by J. A. Twemlow, indexed by John Brady and R. L. Storey. Responsibility for subsequent vols. assumed by the Irish Manuscripts Commission. (1960 [1961]).

xv : 1484-1492, Innocent VIII, Lateran registers. Edited by Michael J. Haren. Notable innovations include an account of the workings of the papal chancery under Innocent VIII, by Leonard E. Boyle, the general editor of the series, and, by the editor of the vol., a formulary of complete transcripts, Latin, of the main types of letters and collections of legal clauses with their accompanying schedules. A list of bulls lost from the Lateran registers of Innocent VIII is appended to the calendar. (Dublin 1978).

Acts of the privy council of England. 14 vols., 1921-64.   **3.78**

Completing the full transcript from 1542 begun in **3.77** (32 vols., 1890-1907). Vols. are not numbered.

[xliv]: 1628, July-1629, Apr. Prepared by R. F. Monger. (1958).
[xlv] : 1629, May-1630, May. Preparation begun by R. F. Monger, completed by P. A. Penfold. Includes tables (contd. in the following) showing dates of council meetings and the attendances of councillors. (1960 [1961]).
[xlvi]: 1630, June-1631, June. Prepared by P. A. Penfold. (1964).

The seven registers for the years 1631-37, with their contemporary indexes of names and the indexes of subjects added to the registers in Victorian times, were reproduced on micro-opaque cards issued in 1962. These cards are no longer available. The registers are contd. to 30 Aug. 1645 in the following facsimile edition (slightly reduced) in book form. The contemporary indexes of names and the Victorian indexes of subjects are reproduced in vols. ii, iv, vii, xi and xii.

Privy council registers preserved in the Public Record Office, reproduced in facsimile. 12 vols., 1967-8.   **3.79**

i   : 1 June-31 Oct. 1637. (1967).
ii : 1 Nov. 1637-28 Feb. 1638. (1967).
iii : 1 Mar.-9 Aug. 1638. (1967 [1968]).
iv : 12 Aug.-19 Dec. 1638. (1968).
v   : 4 Jan.-10 Apr. 1639. (1968).
vi : 12 Aug.-19 July 1639. (1968).
vii : 21 July-30 Oct. 1639. (1968).
viii: 1 Nov. 1639-24 Jan. 1640. (1968).
ix : 26 Jan.-27 Mar. 1640. (1968).
x   : 1 Apr.-27 June 1640. (1968).

xi : 1 July–25 Sept. 1640. (1968).
xii : 6 Oct. 1640–30 Aug. 1645. (1968).

Treaty rolls preserved in the Public Record Office. 1955 **3.80**
[1956]–   ; in progress.

Transcripts, Latin or French, of the rolls in the series C 76, except that some of the docs. which are in Rymer's *Foedera* have been briefly calendared.

i : 1234–1325, rolls 1–10. Edited by Pierre Chaplais. (1955).
ii: 1337–9, rolls 11–13. Edited by John Ferguson, assisted by Pierre Chaplais, Miss P. M. Barnes, Mrs. H. E. Jones, and Mrs. M. J. Post. (1972).

Calendar of state papers preserved in the Public Record Office, **3.81**
domestic series, James II. 3 vols., 1960–72.

Edited by E. K. Timings, the text of all vols. in large measure prepared by Francis Bickley.

i : Feb.–Dec. 1685. Completed by the editor with the assistance of J. D. Cantwell and A. J. W. McDonald, indexed by J. D. Cantwell. (1960).
ii : Jan. 1686–May 1687. Completed and indexed by J. D. Cantwell. (1964).
iii: June 1687–Feb. 1689. Completed by J. D. Cantwell, indexed by A. J. W. McDonald. (1972).

Gascon rolls preserved in the Public Record Office, 1307– **3.82**
1317. Edited by Yves Renouard under the supervision of Robert Fawtier. 1962.

Transcripts, Latin or French, of the rolls for the first ten years of Edw. II, of 31 items belonging to the reign of Edw. I, and of six docs. concerning Aquitaine during the period 1307–17 in other classes in the P.R.O. In the introduction, itineraries of Edw. II in France, 1308 and 1313, and biographical lists of his principal officers in Aquitaine during the period. Published jointly by the P.R.O. and the Comité des travaux historiques, continuing the series of *Rôles Gascons*, of which it is vol. iv.

Diplomatic documents preserved in the Public Record Office. **3.83**
Vol. i: 1101–1272. Edited by Pierre Chaplais. 1964.

Transcripts, Latin or French, of docs. relevant to the study of English diplomacy, selected in the main from the class of Ancient Correspondence, together with the Diplomatic Documents of the Chancery and Exchequer and a few stray docs. from other classes. Comprises 'not only the original treaties and formal instruments delivered by foreign contracting parties to English Sovereigns but all records of what may be called the medieval 'Foreign Office'' (HMSO, *Sectional list 24*). Letters relating to Scotland and Wales and those concerned with the internal administration of Gascony have been deliberately omitted.

List and analysis of state papers, foreign series, Elizabeth I, **3.84**
preserved in the Public Record Office. 1964–   ; in progress.

Continues in a new form the *Calendar of state papers, foreign series, of the*

8

reign of Elizabeth set out at **3.53**. The new form comprises a list, cataloguing the vols. which contain papers for the period covered, an analysis, providing a consolidated summary, in more or less narrative form, of all the information about any particular event or topic that is to be found in the State Papers Foreign as a whole, and an index. Vols. i-iii below were edited by R. B. Wernham.

i : 1 Aug. 1589–30 June 1590. (1964).
ii : 1 July 1590–31 May 1591. (1969).
iii: 1 June 1591–30 Apr. 1592. (1980).

Calendar of memoranda rolls (Exchequer) preserved in the Public Record Office. Michaelmas 1326–Michaelmas 1327. 1968 [1969].   **3.85**

By R. E. Latham. Combines the memoranda rolls of the lord treasurer's remembrancer and the king's remembrancer, the entries grouped in thirteen sections and each section described in the introduction. Full transcripts, Latin, of typical entries illustrative of the sections and sub-sections are appended. Includes transcripts of two docs. listing recipients of the king's livery in 2 and 4 Edw. III and serving to identify persons mentioned in the rolls.

Secret writings in the public records, Henry VIII–George II. Edited by Sheila R. Richards. 1974.   **3.86**

One hundred docs., all but one of which are written wholly or partly in cipher, now deciphered and printed in full, the exception being a draft so set out as to provide a key. Ranging in date from 1519 to 1738, the docs. indicate the types of information conveyed in cipher. Several docs. concern or are written to Mary, queen of Scots; many illustrate aspects of the civil war; the majority, letters to and reports from English envoys, deal with foreign affairs. Brief summaries of docs. in languages other than English.

Calendar of London trailbaston trials under commissions of 1305 and 1306. Edited by Ralph B. Pugh. 1975 [1976].   **3.87**

English abstract of the London section of the roll (Just. 3/39/1) in the P.R.O., with extended transcripts, Latin, of two specimen entries. The introduction ventures some general conclusions after dealing briefly with the origins of trailbaston, the first London and Middlesex commissions, the justice named for the Home circuit, the sessions of the court, its procedure, the offences tried by it, and its judgments and penalties.

Calendar of assize records, Elizabeth I. Edited by J. S. Cockburn. 5 vols., 1975–80.   **3.88**

For the Home circuit:

i : Sussex indictments. (1975).
ii : Hertfordshire indictments. (1975 [1976]).
iii: Essex indictments. (1978 [1979]).
iv: Kent indictments. (1979 [1980]).
v : Surrey indictments. (1980).

Calendar of assize records, James I. Edited by J. S. Cockburn. **3.89**
5 vols., 1975–82.

For the Home circuit:

i : Hertfordshire indictments. (1975 [1976]).
ii : Sussex indictments. (1975 [1976]).
iii: Kent indictments. (1980).
iv: Surrey indictments. (1982).
v : Essex indictments. (1982).

A general introductory vol. is planned.

Records of the wardrobe and household. Edited by Benjamin **3.90**
F. Byerly and Catherine Ridder Byerley. 2 vols., 1977–   .

i : 1285-1286. Transcript, Latin, of the book of the controller of the wardrobe for 14 Edw. I together with all the surviving household rolls which relate solely to that year, for robes, wages and fees for knights, wages for serjeants, receipts, jewels, falconry, hunting, purchases for the great wardrobe, and daily expenses. Shows the itinerary of the king and queen in England and in France. The introduction treats of the system of household accounting, the officials of household and wardrobe, and the responsibilities and functioning of their departments.

Calendar of signet letters of Henry IV and Henry V, 1399– **3.91**
1422. Edited by J. L. Kirby. 1978 [1979].

Comprising all the letters, copies, enrolments and drafts which are known to have survived among the public records and in other repositories and collections. Full transcripts, some French, some English, of specimen letters illustrate the form of the originals and the method of calendaring. The introduction treats of the signet before 1399 and under Hen. IV and Hen. V; it is preceded by a list of chancellors, keepers of the privy seal and secretaries in the period covered.

Medieval legal records edited in memory of C.A.F. Meekings. **3.92**
General editors R. F. Hunnisett and J. B. Post. 1978.

C. A. F. Meekings [*d.* 20 Jan. 1977]: a memoir. By L. C. Hector. **3.92***a*

Legal writings of C. A. F. Meekings. [A list.] **3.92***b*

Changes in the assize utrum between the constitutions of Clarendon and **3.92***c*
Bracton. Edited by Alexandra Nicol. [Transcripts, Latin, of two cases from the eyre rolls of 1227 and 1232, preceded by a discussion of the changed function of the assize and the rôle of the laymen.]

Highway robbery and trial by battle in the Hampshire eyre of 1249. Edited **3.92***d*
by M. T. Clanchy. [Transcript, Latin, with translation, of parts of the eyre roll, including the whole of one of its original membranes now separated from it. The pleas (concerning the robbery of foreign merchants in the 'pass' of Alton) contain details of trial by combat by approver, the corruption of jurors and the involvement of the knightly class in crime. These matters are discussed at length in the introduction, as also are the drawing (reproduced) of the combat at the head of the separated membrane KB 26/223 and Matthew Paris's account, a synopsis of which is appended.]

Oldcotes v. d'Arcy. Edited by P. A. Brand. [Transcripts, Latin, partly French, for the most part from de banco, coram rege and assize rolls, recording the principal stages in the complex litigation occasioned between 1274 and 1309 by the agreement which required Roger d'Arcy to make Ingram of Oldcotes a knight and to bear the costs. The saga is related with far-ranging detail in the introduction and its notes and appendices.] **3.**92*e*

Letters to John Mettingham, 1296. Edited by Franklin J. Pegues. [Transcripts, French, of 30 letters addressed to the chief justice and enrolled ('an administrative innovation') on his copy of the plea roll for the Michaelmas term. The letters are dominated by the concerns of the coast-guard system and make essentially the same request or petition: that persons in the king's service 'be kept faultless from judicial obligations, either in general terms or for specific assignment dates and actions'.] **3.**92*f*

A coroners' roll of the liberty of Wye, 1299–1314. Edited by R. F. Hunnisett. [Transcript, Latin, of the 'only coroners' roll so far known to have survived from a liberty other than a borough as a result of a general eyre'. The claim of the abbots of Battle to appoint their own coroners for Wye, the make-up of the roll, the identity of the coroner, the inquests entered on the roll, and the fact that the whole roll is uncancelled, are among the problems considered in the introduction.] **3.**92*g*

Early trailbaston proceedings from the Lincoln roll of 1305. Edited by Alan Harding. [Transcript, Latin, of 'a coherent group which in substance are fully representative of the offences which the trailbaston commission was created to deal with, and also show most clearly the interdependence of jury presentment and private complaint which it will be suggested is the distinctive mark of the trailbaston proceedings'.] **3.**92*h*

Three courts of the hundred of Penwith, 1333. Edited by G. D. G. Hall [Transcript, Latin, of the text of the three courts held within the period 5 July–3 Oct. 1333, with some consideration of questions raised, such as the 'impression' given of a circuit of the Cornish hundreds; whether the hundred was royal or private; the types of case and result; the procedure of the hue and cry; and the jurisdiction.] **3.**92*i*

A medieval robber baron: Sir John Molyns of Stoke Poges, Buckinghamshire. Edited by Natalie Fryde. [Transcript, Latin, of part of an oyer and terminer roll of 1341, with an account of Molyn's rise to influence and wealth, his disgrace in 1340, subsequent return to royal favour, and the over-mighty lawlessness which ended only with his imprisonment and death, 1361. Appended is a list of his main estates in Dec. 1340, showing the revenue acknowledged by the custodians, 1342–5]. **3.**92*j*

The tenants of the bishops of Coventry and Lichfield and of Worcester after the plague of 1348–9. Edited by Edmund Fryde. [Transcript, Latin, of part of an L.T.R. exchequer memoranda roll, with tables for the estates of the bishops of Worcester and for the Warwickshire and principal Staffordshire properties of the bishops of Coventry and Lichfield presenting the evidence about the numbers of tenants and about their holdings, rents and other money renders in 1349 as well as **3.**92*k* in earlier and later years, the whole calling in question the contention (in J. F. D. Shrewsbury's *History of bubonic plague in the British Isles*) that the death rate in the epidemic of 1348-9 was much lower than is commonly maintained.]

Reports, writs and records in the common bench in the reign of Richard I. **3.92*l*** Edited by L. C. Hector. [Transcripts of the year book reports of six cases and of the associated common pleas writs and the entries on the de banco rolls, showing how the use of the writs can 'shorten or make unnecessary the examination of the rolls as a means of tracing the record'.]

Courts, councils and arbitrators in the Ladbroke manor dispute, 1382– **3.92*m*** 1400. Edited by J. B. Post. [Evidences and proceedings in many courts of record, compiled by John Catesby and constituting a remarkably detailed account of his and his father's complicated and successful defence of property in Warwickshire against the repeated attempts of their litigious relatives to oust them. Transcripts, French, except for the deeds in French and all the Latin entries, which have been fully calendared. Table showing the relationship of Catesby and Ladbroke.]

Clergy and common law in the reign of Henry IV. Edited by R. L. **3.92*n*** Storey. [Transcripts, Latin, from coram rege rolls and files of ancient indictments, each of the 20 cases having its own introduction, preceded by a particular survey of the judges' dealings with issues concerning church institutions and clergy.]

A Wiltshire sheriff's notebook, 1464-5. Edited by M. M. Condon. **3.92*o*** [Transcript of the notebook compiled by George Darell, the greater part of it a record, incomplete, of writs received, with notes on the officials responsible for serving the process.]

The Chancery corpus cum causa file, 10-11 Edward IV. Edited by **3.92*p*** Patricia M. Barnes. [Calendar. The introduction indicates some of the ways in which the chancery files can be used, and looks in some detail at one type of file and at the use made of the recognizance *temp*. Edw. IV–Rich. III both as a device to keep the peace and as a political tool. Two appended texts are concerned with disorder in South Wales and the dispute between the Herberts and the Vaughans. Also appended is a list of suits opened in chancery on writs sub pena, 11 Edw. IV, giving the names of plaintiffs and defendants.]

4. SCOTTISH RECORD OFFICE TEXTS AND CALENDARS

Accounts of the treasurer of Scotland. 1877– ; in progress.   **4.4**

Continues, under a more accurate English title and after an interval of over 50 years, the series *Comperta thesaurariorum regum Scotorum*. The charge (or receipts) side of each account has been translated from the original Latin and abridged, the discharge (or payments) side, in Scots, is given in full transcript except for certain regular payments to individuals which have been abridged. The glossary is combined with the index.

xii : 1566–74, transcribed in the main and edited by Charles Thorpe McInnes, with notes on the treasury administration by Athol L. Murray, the account for 1569–71 transcribed by R. S. Barclay. In the appendix, treasury precepts and receipts, 1566–7. (1970).

xiii: 1574–80, transcribed and edited by C. T. McInnes, with an introduction by A. L. Murray, indexed by Bruce Jackson and Miss M. D. Young. In the appendix, treasury precepts and receipts, 1576, a register of compositions (justice courts), 1574–6, and accounts of the mint, 1578–80.

The register of the privy council of Scotland. Third series.   **4.7**
1908– ; in progress.

xv : Jan.–Dec. 1690. Edited by Evan Whyte Melville Balfour-Melville. (1967).

xvii: Jan.–Dec. 1691. Begun by Dr. Balfour-Melville, the transcription of the *acta* completed by Miss M. R. Miller. (1970).

Calendar of the state papers relating to Scotland and Mary,   **4.14**
queen of Scots, 1547–1603, preserved in the Public Record
Office, the British Museum and elsewhere. 13 vols. in 14,
1898–1969.

xiii: 1597–1603, in 2 pts. with continuous pagination. Pt. 1: June 1597–Dec. 1599; pt. 2: Jan. 1600–Mar. 1603, with index to both pts. An extended transcript, following the pattern of previous vols. in both form and content, a few texts in Latin. Edited with introduction by J. D. Mackie, the docs. for the most part selected and transcribed by M. S. Giuseppi and in large measure indexed by Anne Stevenson (Mrs. M. Kirkpatrick). (1969).

Registrum secreti sigilli regum Scotorum. The register of the   **4.15**
privy seal of Scotland. 1908– ; in progress.

v : 1556–67, in 2 pts., each pt. separately paginated. Pt. 1: 14 Dec. 1556–13 Dec. 1565; pt. 2: 14 Dec. 1565–22 July 1567, with indexes to both pts. Transcribed and in part indexed by James Beveridge, completed and edited, with introduction, by Gordon Donaldson. (1957).

vi : 24 Aug. 1567–31 Dec. 1574, with appendix of supplementary entries derived from the register of presentations to benefices. Changes in the principles of transcribing are described in the introduction. In general, the printed entry is an abridgment, in English, of the original entry in either Latin or Scots. Edited by Gordon Donaldson. (1963).

vii: 1 Jan. 1575–31 Dec. 1580. Appendix as in preceding vol. Edited by Gordon Donaldson. (1966).

Accounts of the masters of works for the building and repairing royal palaces and castles. Edited by Henry M. Paton. 1957– ; in progress.   4.19

Transcripts, relating chiefly to Holyrood, Linlithgow, Falkland, Stirling, Tantallon and Edinburgh.

i: 1529–1615. The introduction, drawing on drafts by William MacKay Mackenzie, treats of periods of building activity, sources of income, the masters of works, overseers, master masons, master wrights, craftsmen and labourers, conditions of labour, materials, and transport. (1957).

5. IRISH RECORD OFFICE TEXTS AND CALENDARS

Calendar of the justiciary rolls or proceedings in the court of **5.3**
the justiciar of Ireland, 1 to 7 years of Edward II. [?1958].

For previously issued vols. covering the years 1295-1303 1305-7 see *T & C* (1958, 1978). All but one of the rolls (that for 6 and 7 Edw. II) perished in the destruction of the Dublin P.R.O., but calendars covering the years 1308-18 had been made. The publication of the calendars began with this vol.; the remaining unpublished calendars are listed in its preface.

6. CHRONICLES AND MEMORIALS OF GREAT BRITAIN AND IRELAND

[18] Royal and historical letters during the reign of Henry the **6.**18
Fourth, king of England and of France and lord of Ireland.
Edited by F. C. Hingeston[-Randolph]. Vol. ii: A.D. 1405–
1413, with amendments, entered in calligraphy, supplied by
the Public Record Office. 1965.

The new (1964) preface explains that this vol., without the amendments,
had been printed off and was on the point of publication when doubts
arose about the soundness of the editor's text. A check against the original
mss. revealed a large number of inaccuracies resulting from mistranscrip-
tion or careless proof-reading, most of them of a minor character. Complete re-setting does not seem to have been considered, the choice seemingly being between issuing the vol. (with a long list of errata and with 62
pages of cancels) and suppressing it. The second course was adopted and
the whole impression cancelled. Eight copies were preserved 'as a literary
curiosity' and from one of these copies, with all the editor's errors ('more
numerous than serious') unobtrusively corrected in manuscript, the
present edition has been photographically reproduced. It includes a glossary of English and Scotch words, and the index to both vols.

7. ROYAL COMMISSION ON HISTORICAL MANUSCRIPTS

REPORTS AND CALENDARS SERIES

Twenty-third report of the royal commission on historical manuscripts, 1946–1959. 1961. 7.23*a*

Refers to 7.95 (vol. iii), 102 (vol. iv).

Includes the programme of work in progress, designed to conclude the series of printed calendars, and introduces the plan for joint publication with record societies. Appendix I records the progress of the National Register of Archives; appendix II contains summaries of all the separately numbered reports added to the National Register of Archives between Sept. 1957 and Oct. 1959.

Twenty-fourth report ... 1960–1962. 1962. 7.23*b*

Refers to 7.91 (vol. v), 95 (vol. iv), 101 (vol. v), and to part of the index of personal names (7.24*b*).

Reports progress of the joint publication plan. Appendices as in 7.23*a* and a revised list of locations.

Twenty-fifth report ... 1963–67. 1967. 7.23*c*

Refers to 7.25 (vols. xix, xx, xxi), 80 (vol. iv), 95 (vols. iv, v), 101 (vols. v, vi), 104 (vol. ii), and to 7.24*b*.

Lists the first twelve joint publications and vols. accepted for future publication. Appendices as in 7.23*a*, and revised list of locations as in 7.23*b*.

Introduces the plan to begin a new series of publications dealing with the 19th century, starting with the privately preserved papers of prime ministers. In an appended memorandum John Brooke suggests that the needs of historians 'will best be met by the production of *lists* of complete ms. collections, or of clearly-defined parts of collections, and *edited texts* of the most significant groups of papers within those collections'. The memorandum 'offers a programme for putting this suggestion into effect'.

Twenty-sixth report ... 1968–81. (In the press). 7.23*d*

Refers to 7.25 (vols. xxi–xxiv), 80 (vol. v), 106, 107 (vols. i–iv), 108 (vol. i), and to 7.24*b* (vol. i).

Describes the activities of the Commission since 1967, with sections on the collection of information, publication, general advisory functions, repositories for historical records, and sales and dispersals of manuscript collections. In the appendices are described or listed (i) the financial provision for the Commission and its authorized staff complement, (ii) the major unpublished lists compiled by the Commission's staff or received from private sources, (iii) the vols. published, (iv) the collections of manuscript material accepted for the nation in lieu of tax 1973-81, and (v) sales of major collections of family and personal papers, all appendices except the fourth being concerned with the period covered by the report.

Guide to the reports of the royal commission on historical manuscripts, 1870-1911. 2 vols. (called pts.) in 3, 1914-38. — 7.24*a*

i : Topographical. Title-page reads 'A guide to the reports on collections of manuscripts of private families, corporations and institutions in Great Britain and Ireland issued by the royal commissioners for historical manuscripts'. (1914).

ii: Index of persons. Edited by Francis Bickley. 1: A—Lever; 2: Lever—Z. Continuous pagination. (1935-8).

Guide to the reports ... 1911-1957. Edited by A. C. S. Hall. 2 vols. (called pts.) in 4, 1966-73. — 7.24*b*

i : Index of places. (1973).

ii: Index of persons, described as 'a composite index of all persons mentioned in the Indexes to these Reports'. Errors in the separate indexes have, as far as possible, been corrected and omissions repaired, and many persons previously unidentified have been identified. 1: A—Foullon; 2: Foulwyll—Orme; 3: Ormesby—Z. Continuous pagination. (1966).

Guide to the location of collections described in the Reports and Calendars series, 1970-1980. 1982. — 7.24*c*

Numbered as the third vol. (it was the first to appear) in the Commission's new series, 'Guides to sources for British History based on the National Register of Archives'; neither of the further vols. in preparation in 1982 falls within the terms of *T & C*. Introduced 'as an entirely fresh piece of research', the vol. supersedes the location lists in previous reports (see 7.22, 23*b*, 23*c*) and 'may at least have succeeded in indicating [the whereabouts] of every major item or group and also, where relevant, that of other connected groups which the reports themselves may have left unnoticed. In cases of loss or disappearance, the point at which this occurred has been identified whenever possible.' (Cited from the preface by the then secretary to the Commission, Dr. G. R. C. Davis).

9. Calendar of the manuscripts of the Most Honourable the Marquis of Salisbury ... preserved at Hatfield House, Hertfordshire. 24 vols. (called pts.), 1883-1976. — 7.25

Title-pages show slight variations, notably the use of the form 'Marquess' in all vols. after vol. xiv. The following particulars of editorial responsibility supplement, for vols. i-xviii, the details given in *T & C* (1958, 1978).

In the preparation of vols. i-iii the commissioners 'had the assistance' of S. R. Scargill-Bird, W. D. Selby, G. J. Morris and E. G. Atkinson, and of R. A. Roberts, E. Salisbury, R. F. Isaacson and H. E. Lawrance in vol.

iv. Similar acknowledgement is made to R. F. Isaacson in vols. v–vii, to R. A. Roberts in vols. v–xii (he indexed vols. viii and ix, and both edited and wrote the introductions to vols. viii–xii), and to E. Salisbury in vols. v–xiv (he indexed vols. x and xiii, and both edited and wrote the introductions to vols. xiii and xiv). Also associated with the early vols. were R. H. Brodie (vols. v–viii as well as the index to vol. v), A. Hughes (vols. vii–ix, xi and xii), C. G. Crump (vols. vii–xii), J. L. Lyle (vols. x–xii), and M. S. Giuseppi (vol. xii and as indexer of vol. vi). Miss Maud H. Roberts indexed vols. xi and xii, Miss Ethel Salisbury indexed vol. xiv. M. S. Giuseppi edited, with introductions, and Miss Marjorie Giuseppi indexed, vols. xv–xviii.

Vols. xix–xxiv, listed below, complete the calendar. The texts of vols. xix–xxii, originally prepared by M. S. Giuseppi, were revised, extended, edited with introductions, and indexed by D. McN. Lockie (vol. xix only, with some assistance on the index from J. L. Hobbs) and G. Dyfnallt Owen (vols. xx–xxii). The introductions survey the periods covered. The two vols. of addenda were the work of G. Dyfnallt Owen, his introductions being concerned in the main with Cecil's embassy to France in 1598 (vol. xxiii) and with 'the problem of the recusants', 'the freedom of the press', and 'Cecil's good works' (vol. xxiv).

xix : 1607. (1965).
xx : 1608. (1968 [1969]).
xxi : 1609–June 1612. (1970).
xxii : May 1612–Dec. 1668. (1971).
xxiii : Addenda, 1562–1605. (1973 [1974]).
xxiv : Addenda, 1605–1668. (1976).

The manuscripts of the House of Lords. New series [in continuation of 7.33 but not published by the Commission]. 12 vols., 1900–[78].   7.34

Vols. i–x are listed in *T & C* (1958, 1978).

xi : Addenda, 1514–end Aug. 1714, comprising papers inadvertently omitted from preceding vols., records formerly held by the clerks of the parliaments and recently re-acquired, and docs. given by private owners. Edited by Maurice F. Bond, some docs. fully transcribed, others calendared or listed, following the practice of earlier vols. All categories are described in the introduction. (1962).

xii: 1 Aug. 1714–21 Mar. 1718, continuing vol. x, and including the complete text of the standing orders of the Lords as laid on the table in 1715 and of the additions made to them to 1848. Edited by David J. Johnson, the docs. presented in the customary form of the series. The introduction treats of the standing orders in some detail, from the first occurrence of written and acknowledged orders in 1621, through the deliberations of the select committee appointed in 1715 to the printed edition of 1849. Other sections of the introduction deal with the development of the Parliament Office to c. 1750, the membership and functioning of the House during the years dominated by the rivalry of Whigs and Jacobites, and the records of appeal cases heard by the Lords, these latter constituting the largest class of records surviving for the period 1714–18. [1978].

58. Calendar of the manuscripts of the Marquis of Bath, preserved at Longleat, Wiltshire. 5 vols., 1904–80.

7.80

Vols. i–iii, titled as shown here, are briefly described in *T & C* (1958, 1978). Most of vol. i (1904) was seen through the press by J. J. Cartwright, the remainder of the work by J. M. Rigg, who was also 'responsible' for the introduction. Vol. ii (1907) was edited and indexed by Mrs. S. C. Lomas. The work of selecting and transcribing the letters and papers in vol. iii (1908) begun by J. J. Cartwright and completed by A. Maxwell-Lyte; the vol. was edited by J. M. Rigg, indexed by R. H. Brodie.

iv: Seymour papers, 1532–1686. Geoffrey Baskerville's draft calendar of the first 12 vols. of Seymour papers revised, enlarged and edited with an introduction by Marjorie Blatcher. Incorporates much non-political material omitted by Baskerville in accordance with his instructions. The scope of the material in the further 11 vols. and 18 boxes not calendared by him is indicated by report and selection. The introduction balances points for and against A. F. Pollard's assessment of Protector Somerset and contributes to a view of later members of the family, viz. Edward, 1st earl of Hertford, William, the 2nd earl, and William's second wife, Frances Devereux, with the winding up of whose affairs the vol. ends. Title-page reads 'Report on the manuscripts of the Most Honourable the Marquess of Bath preserved at Longleat. Vol. iv.' (1968).

v : Talbot, Dudley and Devereux papers, 1533–1659. Calendar, with many full transcripts, prepared from Geoffrey Baskerville's transcripts and edited with an introduction by G. Dyfnallt Owen. Talbot papers, 1569–1608; Dudley, 1558–1608; Devereux, 1533–1659. The introduction, after briefly setting out the provenance of the Longleat papers calendared by the Commission, outlines the 6th earl of Shrewsbury's relations with his countess and the Queen of Scots, the involvement of the 6th and 7th earls in Sir Thomas Stanhope's quarrel with Sir John Zouche, and the careers of Robert Dudley, earl of Leicester, and his stepson the 2nd earl of Essex. The title-page, apart from its use of the form 'Marquess', reverts to the wording of vols. i–iii. (1980).

67. Report on the manuscripts of Lord Polwarth, preserved at Mertoun House, Berwickshire. 5 vols., 1911–61.

7.91

Vols. i–iv are briefly described in *T & C* (1958, 1978). Vols. i–ii (1911–16), titled as shown here, were prepared and edited by Henry Paton, who was also 'responsible' for the index to vol. i; the index to vol. ii was compiled in part by John Harley and completed by Francis Bickley. The title-page of vol. iii (1931) has 'formerly preserved in Mertoun House, Berwickshire' and 'Edited by the Rev. Henry Paton, M.A.'; he also compiled the index. Vol. iv has 'Report ... of the Right Honourable Lord Polwarth, C.B.E., formerly preserved at ... and now in H.M. General Register House, Edinburgh', with the same editorial attribution as for the preceding vol.; it was seen through the press by J. C. Walker, and indexed by Miss E. S. G. Potter (Mrs. Sheehan) who also contributed the introduction.

v : 1725–80. Correspondence, transcribed for the most part. The title repeats the essential wording used for vol. iv, omitting the owner's

C.B.E. and the editor's M.A., naming the repository 'the Scottish Record Office, Edinburgh', and adding the words 'with an introduction by J. D. Mackie . . .'. Unlike its predecessors, the vol. is little concerned with foreign affairs; instead, it gives 'an intimate view of the machinery whereby Scotland was governed . . . and of the interaction between Scottish and English politics during this period'. The range and interest of the papers are demonstrated in the introduction. The index was 'prepared' by R. F. Monger. An appended note by Sir James Fergusson of Kilkerran gives a brief account of the Marchmont and Polwarth papers in the Scottish Record Office. (1961).

71. **Report on the manuscripts of Allan George Finch, esq.,**   **7.95** **of Burley-on-the-Hill, Rutland. 5 vols., 1913– .**

Vols. i–ii are briefly described in *T & C* (1958, 1978). On the title-pages of subsequent vols. the owner's name is preceded by 'the late'. Vols. i and ii were prepared and edited by Mrs. S. C. Lomas, who also indexed vol. i; vol. ii was indexed by Miss Edith Williamson.

iii: 1691, with addenda 1667–90. Continues the calendar, with substantial extracts, of the correspondence and other docs. accumulated by Daniel Finch, 2nd earl of Nottingham, during his first term as secretary of state, and includes items omitted from previous vols. Text in part prepared by Mrs. S. C. Lomas, completed and edited with an introduction by Francis Bickley, indexed by A. C. S. Hall. The introduction (52 pp.) digests in narrative form the many matters which came within the secretary's concern. In the appendices, docs. relating to Jacobite conspiracies, docs. containing information about France, and minutes of the committee or cabinet council appointed to advise the Queen during the King's absences from England in 1690 and 1691. (1957).

iv: 1692, with five items of addenda 1690 and 1691, and a few papers of which the dating is conjectural. Edited by Francis Bickley, with a narrative introduction (38 pp.) as before, and indexed by A. C. S. Hall. (1965).

v : In preparation. Will conclude the series. Planned to contain Nottingham's correspondence down to his removal from office at the end of 1693, with some supplementary naval and military papers, the reports of his secret agents in France and the correspondence relating to their organization.

75. **Report on the manuscripts of the Marquess of Down-**   **7.99** **shire, preserved at Easthampstead Park, Berks. 6 vols. in 7.** **1924– .**

Vols. i–iv are briefly described in *T & C* (1958, 1978). Vol. i was prepared, edited and indexed by E. K. Purnell; pagination of the two pts. is continuous. Vol. ii, edited in part by E. K. Purnell (*d.* 1933), was completed and revised by A. B. Hinds, who also prepared the introduction and the index. Vols. iii and iv, based to some extent on transcripts by the late E. K. Purnell, were edited by A. B. Hinds, who also prepared the respective introductions and indexes, but his index to vol. iv was reduced for reasons of economy and to some extent recast by R. L. Atkinson.

v : Sept. 1614–Aug. 1616. In preparation.

vi: Sept. 1616–1618. In preparation. Will conclude the series.

77. Report on the manuscripts of Lord De Lisle and Dudley, 7.101
preserved at Penshurst Place. 6 vols., 1925–66.

Vols. i–iv are briefly described in *T & C* (1958, 1978). Vol. i was prepared,
edited with an introduction, and indexed by C. L. Kingsford. Vol. ii, also
edited by C. L. Kingsford (*d.* 1926), was provided with an introduction
by William A. Shaw, and completed for press by Miss E. Salisbury; the
index, begun by Miss M. G. Smieton, was completed by H. C. Johnson.
Dr. Shaw's introduction to vols. iii and iv, both of which he edited, is in
vol. iv; he also indexed vol. iii. The index to vol. iv was compiled by R. W.
N. B. Gilling 'but owing to his absence on other duties' its revision was
carried out by R. L. Atkinson and the editor. Vols. v and vi, described
below, bear the title 'Report on the manuscripts of the Right Honourable
Viscount De L'Isle, V.C., preserved at Penshurst Place, Kent.'

v : Sidney papers, 1611–26, being mainly the correspondence of Robert,
Viscount Lisle, 1st earl of Leicester, edited in part by William A. Shaw,
his material and draft introduction revised and extended by his successor as editor, G. Dyfnallt Owen, indexed by C. G. Holland. The
introduction treats of the seeds of the Anglo-Dutch wars; Grotius and
the *mare liberum*; the herring fishery dispute with Holland; the Green-
land whale fishery; the Levant and East India trade; the dyed cloth
trade with Holland; the merchant adventurers' staple in Zeeland and
Middelburg; the honour of the flag; James I and the religious disputes
in the Netherlands: the case of Conrad Vorstius; and the surrender of
the cautionary towns, Flushing and Brill. (1962).

vi: Sidney papers, 1626–98, from the correspondence of and concerning
the family, selected, transcribed, edited with introduction, and indexed
by G. Dyfnallt Owen. The material 'suffices to throw interesting light'
on the part played by the 2nd earl of Leicester 'as a diplomat in the
prosecution of the ineffectual foreign policy of Charles I', especially in
relations with Denmark and France, to both of which countries the earl
went as ambassador. Among appended docs. are inventories of Penshurst in 1627 and 1677, a diary of events, 1636–50, the earl's journal,
1646–61, and a lease and inventory of Leicester House dated 1670.
(1966).

80. Calendar of the manuscripts of Major-General Lord 7.104
Sackville, K.B.E., C.B., C.M.G., preserved at Knole, Sevenoaks, Kent. 2 vols., 1940 [1942]–66.

i : Cranfield papers, 1551–1612, being the early papers of Lionel Cranfield
and his family, 1551–96, his mercantile correspondence, 1596–7, and
general papers, 1597–1612, abstracted or transcribed, frequently with
extensive annotation, by A. P. Newton, and including genealogical
tables showing Cranfield's descendants, the Cranfields and Randalls,
1521–1617, and the Sackville family descent *c.* 1520–1940. Indexed by
Maud Statham. (1940 [1942]).

ii: Letters relating to Lionel Cranfield's business affairs overseas, 1597–
1612, prepared for publication and edited by F. J. Fisher, indexed by
J.L. and Alice Doreen Kirby. A prefatory note records the intention
not to issue a calendar of accounts and other papers relating to Cranfield's business affairs overseas and of letters relating to his transactions

in England. This vol. bears the title 'Calendar of the manuscripts of the Right Honourable Lord Sackville of Knole, Sevenoaks, Kent'. (1966).

PRIME MINISTERS PAPERS SERIES

The prime ministers' papers, 1801–1902: a survey of the pri-   7.106
vately preserved papers of those statesmen who held the office
of prime minister during the 19th century. By John Brooke.
1968.

Partly a guide to where collections are to be found and to what they contain, partly a preliminary to the series itemized below. The survey counts as private papers 'all documents which do not remain among the records of a government department' and embraces papers 'from any period of the Prime Minister's life' and correspondence on any subject. It is not claimed that the survey is complete.

Under the name of each prime minister are listed the principal collections of his papers, a minimum of ten items being generally required to warrant inclusion. Next follows a list of his principal correspondents, indicating where his letters to them are to be found. Wherever possible, some indication is given of the number of items in the collections and the terminal dates of the correspondences. Printed works reproducing correspondence or papers on an extensive scale are listed for each prime minister.

W. E. Gladstone. Edited by John Brooke and Mary Sorenson.   7.107
4 vols., 1971–81.

i : Autobiographica. (1971).

Prints in full, with Gladstone's spelling and punctuation, and in an order based approximately on the events to which they relate, the mss. docketed by him 'Autobiographica', together with one or two related pieces, all in BL Additional mss. 44790 and 44791. Appendices contain supplementary material which is mentioned by Gladstone or which he intended to introduce into his projected autobiography, viz. his letters to William Windham Farr, 1826–32; his correspondence with his father about a choice of career, 1830–2; his anti-Reform handbills of 1831; a specimen of his verse, 'To violets in a Vaudois valley', Mar. 1832; his correspondence with Peel about his proposed resignation in 1842; his 'Twenty-seven propositions relating to current questions in theology'; his alternative versions of 'recorded errors'; and his list of his critics, 1894–5.

ii : Autobiographical memoranda, 1832–1845. (1972).

Gladstone's accounts of events or conversations, made by him for his own use, not intended for publication, supplementing his diary, and for the most part dealing with politics or religious affairs, only occasionally with his personal life. Omitted are 'the themes or essays which he wrote on aspects of theology, politics, literature, history, and other subjects', all 'important for the intellectual history of his age and as a revelation of his thought' but too extensive for inclusion.

iii: Autobiographical memoranda, 1845–1866. (1978).

Includes additions and corrections to vol. i; Gladstone's notes on Hodder's *Life of Shaftesbury* (1886); his notes on Martin's *Life of the Prince Consort*, vol. ii (1876); two memoranda by Gladstone on the income tax; and extracts from Palmerston's diary relating to the formation of his ministry, Jan. 1855.

iv: Autobiographical memoranda, 1868–1894. (1981).

Includes, in the appendices, Gladstone's memoranda on the Conservative party, and E. W. Hamilton's account of the formation of Gladstone's third ministry, 29 Jan.–6 Feb. 1886. An essay by R. J. Olney returns the autobiographical writings, in quantity only a small fraction of Gladstone's surviving archive, to their place in the history of the papers as a whole, 1822–1970. Sources used for vols. i–iv are listed at the end.

Wellington   7.108

i : Political correspondence, 1833–November 1834. Edited by John Brooke and Julia Gandy. (1975 [1976]).

Issued as the first vol. of a projected edition of Wellington's political correspondence to 1846. 'The word "political" has been given a wide interpretation. Thus correspondence dealing with military affairs ... has been included if these were likely to have political repercussions ... Letters dealing with strictly military business ... have been omitted. Correspondence dealing with Oxford University, the Cinque Ports, etc. has been included or omitted on the same principles. ... Letters from Wellington found in other collections have also been included.'

ii: Political correspondence, November 1834–April 1835. Edited by R. J. Olney and Julia Melvin. In preparation.

Palmerston.   7.109

i : Private correspondence with Sir George Villiers (afterwards fourth earl of Clarendon) as minister to Spain, 1833–1837. Edited by Roger Bullen and Felicity Strong. In preparation.

JOINT PUBLICATIONS SERIES*

1. Missenden cartulary, pt. iii. See **36.**12   7.110
2. Tutbury cartulary. See **62.**75
3. Constable's correspondence. See **100.**4
4. Letter books of Sir Samuel Luke. See **35.**42

---

*This series 'was initiated to help local and other record societies to produce editions of historical texts of importance for the study of national history'. The vols. selected for inclusion were published simultaneously by the Commission and by the society concerned. Full and correct titles are given in the entries indicated; the place of each in the Joint Publications series is shown by the addition, within square brackets, of HMC JP followed by its series number.

5. Cinque ports, white and black books. See **47**.22
6. Shrewsbury mss. See **93**.1
7. Talbot papers. See **93**.4
8. Correspondence of Rev. J. Greene. See **65**.23
9. Register of Wolstan de Bransford. See **69**.47
10. Oxfordshire inventories. See **58**.44
11. Dale cartulary. See **93**.2
12. London commissary court, testamentary records, i. See **12**.82
13. London commissary court, testamentary records, ii. See **12**.86
14. (Not used)
15. (Not used)
16. Bedfordshire sessions. See **35**.48
17. Blyth cartulary. See **57**.27
18. Buckinghamshire musters. See **36**.17
19. Ledger of John Smythe. See **42**.28
20. Wells chapter act book. See **61**.73
21. Southampton terrier. See **45**.15
22. John Lydford's book. See **40**.44
23. Cuxham manorial records. See **58**.50
24. Kniveton leiger. See **93**.7
25. Stafford archdeaconry visitations. See **62**.81
26. Doddridge correspondence. See **55**.29
27. Register of Adam de Orleton. See **69**.53

8. ROYAL COMMISSION ON HISTORICAL MONUMENTS (ENGLAND)*

An inventory of historical monuments in the county of Dorset.   **8.10**
5 vols. in 8, 1952–75.

  i : West. (1952).
  ii : pts. 1–3: South-east. (1970).
  iii: pts. 1–2: Central Dorset. (1970).
  iv: North Dorset. (1972).
  v : East Dorset. (1975).

This is the first inventory completed by the Commission in which monuments of the 18th century and first half of the 19th century have been
included. Every vol. prints the text of the pertinent commission, the
official report, an illustrated inventory, a sectional preface under subject
headings calling attention to particularly interesting examples in the inventory, a list of monuments thought especially worthy of preservation, a
glossary of terms used, one or more distribution maps, and an index. The
first vol. (issued as *An inventory of the historical monuments in Dorset*)
should include an inserted addendum of seven pages, inclusive of plate
and plans, issued post-1969, supplementing the account of the early
church at Sherborne given in the sectional preface to the vol. An introduction to the topography, settlement, building materials etc. of the
county occurs in vol. ii, pt. 1, and by a liberal interpretation of the terminal
date (1850) there is in pt. 3 of the same vol. a brief section on the early
railway bridges, buildings, sheds and tracks. Vol. v includes blazons of all
arms earlier than 1850 mentioned in the five vols. of the inventory. The
Commission draws attention to the fact that its archives 'remain perma-
nently accessible to accredited persons who may wish to consult them,
due notice having been given to the Secretary'.

An inventory of the historical monuments in the city of Cam-   **8.11**
bridge. 1 vol. in 2, and case of maps. 1959.

An inventory of the historical monuments in the city of York.   **8.12**
1962–   ; in progress.

  i : Eburacum. Roman York. (1962).
  ii : The defences. (1972).
  iii: South-west of the Ouse. (1972).

---

*All publications described below adhere in the main to the practice set out in the
note to **8.10**, commonly with a glossary and one or more maps in every volume.

iv: Outside the city walls east of the Ouse. (1975).
v : The central area. (1981).

Included in vol. i are special articles on glass and jet, gypsum burials and some skeletal remains in Roman York. The introduction to vol. ii reviews the history and development of the defences from the post-Roman period to 1970, examines briefly the arrangements for maintaining and manning the defences, considers details (especially of the walls) and makes comparisons between the defences of York and those of other towns. The castle is not treated in detail since its building history in given in *The history of the king's works*, i (1963) and the VCH vol. for the *City of York* (1961). An account of the growth and development of the city to 1069 precedes the sectional preface in vol. iv.

An inventory of historical monuments in the county of Cambridge. 1968– ; in progress.   **8.13**

i : West Cambridgeshire. (1968).
ii: North-east Cambridgeshire. (1972).

An inventory of the historical monuments in the county of Northampton. 1975– ; in progress.   **8.14**

i : Archaeological sites in north-east Northamptonshire. (1975).
ii : Archaeological sites in central Northamptonshire. (1979).
iii: Archaeological sites in north-west Northamptonshire. (1981).

Ancient and historical monuments in the county of Gloucester. 1976– ; in progress.   **8.15**

i: Iron Age and Romano-British monuments in the Gloucestershire Cotswolds. (1976).

An inventory of historical monuments [in] the town of Stamford. 1977.   **8.16**

Ancient and historical monuments in the city of Salisbury. 1980– ; in progress.   **8.17**

i: Covers the area of the former municipal borough, exclusive of the cathedral close and its walls and gates. Includes Old Sarum castle (with transcript, Latin, of contract for repairs, 7 Oct. 1366) and cathedral, and all monuments and constructions from the Norman conquest to 1850.

9. ROYAL COMMISSION ON HISTORICAL MONUMENTS (WALES)

An inventory of the ancient monuments in Caernarvonshire. **9.3**
3 vols., 1956–64.

In all vols, the inventory, arranged by parishes, aims to comprehend all monuments earlier in date than 1750; after 1750 'the standard of . . . interest which a structure must display in order to qualify for inclusion increases steadily. . . . Nothing later than 1850 is included.' Monuments 'thought especially worthy of preservation' are listed in the commissioners' reports, and matters of particular interest are referred to in introductory notes. Every vol. has its own glossary and index as well as maps, plans and plates, a list of 'finds', and an account of the roads (communications) of the area.

    i : East: The cantref of Arllechwedd and the commote of Creuddyn. Treated at length in the prefatory matter are the Craig Lwyd group of axe factories (with an appendix listing all known or suspected implements of Craig Lwyd rock found in Wales, England and Scotland). Noted, briefly, are large sheepfolds and peat houses. (1956).

    * ii : Central: The cantref of Arfon and the commote of Eifionydd. Includes a table of changes in parish boundaries. (1960).

    iii: West: The cantref of Lleyn, together with the general survey of the county, describing the physical background and treating in sequence the prehistoric ages, the Roman occupation (especially hut settlements, native life, mining and metal working), and all subsequent periods until c. 1800. Sections of the survey are devoted to ecclesiastical architecture (inclusive of dissenters' chapels and sepulchral memorials, and listing parish registers); fortifications of all kinds (with an appendix of masons' marks and graffiti); domestic architecture; heraldry (with an armorial); holy wells, and building materials. (1964).

An inventory of the ancient monuments in Glamorgan. **9.4**
1976– ; in progress.

    i : Pre-Norman. In 3 'pts.', each 'pt.' separately paginated, with maps, plans and plates, and its own glossary and index. Entries are arranged not by parishes but according to types of monument; lists of parishes, civil and ecclesiastical, show the incidence of the monuments. Lists of 'finds' have been omitted. The commissioners' report, repeated in all 'pts.', includes a list of monuments thought 'especially worthy of preservation'. In all 'pts.' C. H. Houlder was responsible for describing the background, and A. H. A. Hogg the communications. The authorship

28

and compilation of other sections within the 'pts.' were allocated as shown:

Pt. i : The stone and bronze ages. C. H. Houlder (caves; neolithic burial and ritual structures) and W. E. Griffiths (bronze age burial and ritual structures; cooking mounds). (1976).

Pt. ii : The iron age and the Roman occupation. A. H. A. Hogg (hill forts and related structures; hut settlements) and W. E. Griffiths (Roman remains). (1976).

Pt. iii: The early Christian period. A. H. A. Hogg (dykes), D. B. Hague (monastic sites), and W. G. Thomas (monastic sites; inscribed and sculptured stones). (1976).

ii : Ecclesiastical monuments. In preparation.

iii: Medieval secular monuments. In preparation.

iv: Domestic architecture from the Reformation to the industrial revolution. 1981–   ; in progress.

Pt. i : The greater houses. An introductory survey, in three sections, deals with the geographical and historical background, the architectural history, and building construction, ornament and decoration. A notable innovation is the use of distribution maps showing the location of known houses of sheriffs and deputy-lieutenants and other social features in order to provide 'a quick reference to the changing fortunes of individual families'. Among indications of status mapped in this way are dovecotes, deer parks, fishponds, gatehouses and heraldic ornament, 'all more or less the exclusive preserve of the landowning class'. (1981).

Pt. ii: The lesser houses. In preparation.

v : Industrial and later structures. In preparation.

Pt. i : The Swansea canal.

PART 2
NATIONAL SOCIETIES

10. ALCUIN CLUB, COLLECTIONS

40. Anglican liturgies of the seventeenth and eighteenth cen- **10.40**
turies. By W. Jardine Grisbrooke. 1958.

Texts of the Scottish liturgy of 1637, Jeremy Taylor's liturgy, three
liturgies of Edward Stephens, the liturgy of William Whiston, the liturgy
of John Henley, the nonjurors' liturgies of 1718 and 1734, the liturgy of
Thomas Rattray, and the Scottish communion office of 1764, with a
commentary on every text and, in the appendix, a text reconstructed from
a Book of Common Prayer containing, in the hand of William Sancroft,
amendments proposed during the revision of 1661–2.

41. The use of lights in Christian worship. By D. R. Dendy. **10.41**
1959.

42. Documents of the baptismal liturgy. By E. C. Whitaker. **10.42**
1960.

Brings together some forty translations, not all of them by the author,
covering 'most of the principal and substantial documents from which our
knowledge of the Church's baptismal rite is to be drawn and its history
constructed'.

43. The liturgy in English. Edited by Bernard Wigan. 1962. **10.43**

Intended to take the place of J. H. Arnold's out-of-print *Anglican liturgies*
(1939) and to widen its scope. The texts printed, beginning with the
liturgy of the first English Prayer Book (1549), include more of the Anglican liturgies that existed in 1939 and several new liturgies issued since
then. Among the latter are some liturgies which, though composed in
English, are not Anglican, as well as liturgies which, though Anglican,
have not before been printed in English.

44. St. Augustine's lectionary. By G. G. Willis. 1962. **10.44**

Derived almost entirely from references to the lessons in St. Augustine's
sermons. Includes a preliminary chapter on lectionary systems before St.
Augustine (with a skeleton lectionary of the Church of Milan, drawn from
the writings of St. Ambrose), a commentary on St. Augustine's lectionary,
and a section on some later lectionaries.

45. The influence of the synagogue upon the divine office. By **10.45**
C. W. Dugmore. 1964.

A reprint of the first (1944) edition, omitting the original preface and
introduction.

46. Essays in early Roman liturgy. By G. G. Willis. 1964.   **10.46**

The solemn prayers of Good Friday.
Ember days.
What is *mediana* week?
The offertory prayers and the canon of the Roman mass.
Cursus in the Roman canon.
The connection of the prayers of the Roman canon.

47. Christian initiation: baptism in the medieval west. A study   **10.47**
in the disintegration of the primitive rite of initiation. By J. D.
C. Fisher. 1965.

48. Baptismal anointing. By Leonel L. Mitchell. 1966.   **10.48**

49. The ordination prayers of the ancient western churches.   **10.49**
By H. B. Porter, Jr. 1967.

50. Further essays in early Roman liturgy. By G. G. Willis.   **10.50**
1968.

Roman stational liturgy.
The variable prayers of the Roman mass.
The consecration of churches down to the ninth century.
St. Gregory the Great and the Lord's Prayer in the Roman mass.
Early English liturgy from Augustine to Alcuin.

51. Christian initiation: the Reformation period. Some early   **10.51**
reformed rites of baptism and confirmation, and other contemporary documents. By J. D. C. Fisher. 1970.

52. Christian initiation: rites of baptism and confirmation   **10.52**
since the Reformation period. By Peter J. Jagger. 1970.

53. The Anglican ordinal, its history and development from   **10.53**
the Reformation to the present day. By Paul F. Bradshaw.
1971.

54. The liturgy of comprehension, 1689: an abortive attempt   **10.54**
to revise the Book of Common Prayer. By Timothy J. Fawcett.
1973.

Seeks 'to make available an accurate working text of the Proposals of the
Commissioners ... in 1689, on the revision of the Book of Common
Prayer'. Includes a transcript of the diary of the proceedings kept by John
Williams, bishop of Chichester.

55. Martin Bucer and the Book of Common Prayer. By E. C.   **10.55**
Whitaker. 1974.

Latin text, with facing English translation, of Bucer's *Censura* or critical
examination of the 1549 Prayer Book, together with a translation of the
last section of his tract *De ordinatione legitima*, setting out an ordination
rite.

11. BRITISH ACADEMY, RECORDS OF SOCIAL AND ECONOMIC HISTORY
(new series)

1. **Charters of the honour of Mowbray, 1107–1191. Edited by D. E. Greenway. 1972.** **11.10**

Transcripts, Latin, with brief English abstracts, of the charters of Nigel d'Aubigny in full and of those charters issued by other members of the Mowbray family 'that have not been printed before or have appeared in editions that are either unsatisfactory or difficult to obtain. Charters already satisfactorily edited are calendared and their witnesses noted.'

The introduction describes the fief—'one of the greatest honours of the [Anglo-Norman] realm'—created for Nigel, the losses of land, status and security suffered by his heir, Roger de Mowbray, the feudal structure of the honour, its economy and administration. Detailed descriptions of seals (some illustrated). Pedigrees of the 11th-century families of Aubigny and Mowbray. Glossary. Maps.

2. **The lay subsidy of 1334. Edited by Robin E. Glasscock. 1975.** **11.11**

The basic lists, county by county for almost the whole of England, of the places taxed in 1334, together with their tax quotas, compiled from two or more subsidy rolls (in the case of Cumberland, Northumberland and Westmorland the rolls for the fifteenth and tenth of 1336).

The introduction, after describing the lay subsidies of the early 14th century, the fifteenth and tenth of 1334, and the types of property and particular areas exempted from the 1334 tax, considers the 1334 tax quotas, what they represent, and their uses in historical inquiry. Maps.

3. **The diary of Ralph Josselin, 1616–1683. Edited by Alan Macfarlane. 1976.** **11.12**

Transcript, superseding the earlier edition (see **33.15**). The diary deals summarily with Josselin's life to Aug. 1644 and then becomes more detailed, with several entries a week. The period 1646–53 is especially well covered and accounts for two-fifths of the whole.

The previous use made of the diary is described in the introduction, which also assesses its accuracy and coverage, and indicates its main themes. Genealogical tables show the kinship of major families (Constable, Cooke, Eldred, Haines, Harlakenden, Honywood, Josselin, Little, Mildmay). Also biographical notices of Earls Colne families and individuals. Maps.

4. **Warwickshire grazier and London skinner, 1532–1555: the account book of Peter Temple and Thomas Heritage. Edited by N. W. Alcock. 1981.** 11.13

Transcript of the book kept by the founder of the landed family, the Temples of Stowe, in which is included the select set of accounts recorded from 1532 to 1540 by his cousin Heritage, a London skinner. In his book, Temple noted 'every detail of his farming and personal income and expenditure during the very period that saw his metamorphosis from insignificance to wealth'. Because the ms. is 'extraordinarily disordered' the entries have been brought together by subject, in chronological order, and presented as the core of an historical commentary and biography.

The main part of the vol. is preceded by a review setting the scene for the accounts, concentrating particularly on the family background and Temple's early life, as well as on the history and topography of Burton Dassett, where he farmed. The concluding section covers his later life and 'aims in particular to show how his grazing profits were put to use'. Between these two, the accounts are arranged according to their concern with (i) farming, viz. cattle, sheep, wool, stock, hay, pasture letting, and arable, (ii) rents and estate administration, viz. Hertfordshire property, Stepney, Coventry, Dassett bailiff's accounts and memoranda, and wood sales, and (iii) personal matters, such as household expenses, New Year's gifts, servants, building work, and finance.

5. **Charters and custumals of the abbey of Holy Trinity, Caen. Edited by Marjorie Chibnall. 1982.** 11.14

Concerned with the English estates only. Transcripts, Latin, the charters (with brief English abstracts) selected as 'particularly relevant to the custumals and the administration of the property' in the 12th and 13th centuries. All early leases are included. The surveys and custumals are for Felsted, Pinbury, Tarrant, Minchinhampton, Horstead, 'Dineslai' (which 'cannot possibly be identified as Tilshead' but 'could have been' Dinsley, later Temple Dinsley, in Hitchin, Herts.), and Avening.

Although known as a cartulary, the ms. from which most of the texts here printed are derived contains but few charters; its great interest lies in the series of 12th-century surveys of French and English properties preserved in it. Part of the introduction lists and annotates its contents; the remainder studies the English properties of the abbey, their surveys, charters and custumals, the administration of the English lands through agents in England (notably Simon of Felsted and his son William who both—as well as their descendants—did well for themselves at the expense of the abbess), and the evidence of the surveys for the stability as well as the distintegration of the demesne in the 12th century. Some early abbesses are listed in an appendix. Glossary. Maps.

12.   BRITISH RECORD SOCIETY LIMITED, INDEX LIBRARY

77. Index to wills proved in the prerogative court of Canter-   **12.77**
bury. Vol. xi: 1686–1693. Edited by C. Harold Ridge. 1958.
Continues the series begun with **12.10**. Contd. in **12.80** below.

78. Index to wills at Chelmsford (Essex and East Hertford-   **12.78**
shire). Edited by F. G. Emmison. Vol. i: 1400–1619. 1958.
A composite index to all extant wills prior to 1620 in the Essex Record
Office proved in the archdeaconry court of Essex from 1400, the archdeaconry court of Colchester from 1500, the archdeaconry court of Middlesex (Essex and Herts. jurisdiction) from 1554, the commissary court of
London (Essex and Herts. jurisdiction) from 1441, the peculiar of Writtle
with Roxwell from 1607, and the peculiar of Good Easter from 1613. The
title used here is derived from the half-title and title-page. Contd. in the
following and **12.84** below.

79. Index to wills at Chelmsford (Essex and East Hertford-   **12.79**
shire). Vol. ii: 1620–1720. 1961.
For the courts as above, with additionally the peculiar of the deanery of
Bocking from 1627 and the peculiar of the liberty of the Sokens from 1644
(Kirby-, Thorpe-, and Walton-le-Soken).

80. Index to wills proved in the prerogative court of Canter-   **12.80**
bury. Vol. xii: 1694–1700. Edited by Marc Fitch. 1960.

81. Index to administrations in the prerogative court of Can-   **12.81**
terbury. Vol. iv: 1596–1608. Edited by Marc Fitch. 1964.
Continues the series begun with **12.68**. Contd. in **12.83** below.

82. Index to testamentary records in the commissary court of   **12.82**
London (London division) now preserved in Guildhall
Library, London. Edited by Marc Fitch. Vol. i: 1374–1488.
1969. [HMC JP 12].
Contd. in **12.86** below.

83. Index to administrations in the prerogative court of Can-   **12.83**
terbury. Vol. v: 1609–1619. Edited by Marc Fitch. 1968.

84. Index to wills at Chelmsford (Essex and East Hertford-   **12.84**
shire). Vol. iii: 1721–1858. 1969.
For the eight probate courts as in **12.**79 above.

85. Index of cases in the records of the court of Arches at   **12.85**
Lambeth Palace library, 1660–1913. Edited by Jane Houston.
1972.
Includes a summary list of the records of the court.

86. Index to testamentary records in the commissary court of   **12.86**
London (London division). Vol. ii: 1489–1570. 1974. [HMC
JP 13].

87. Index of the probate records of the court of the archdeacon   **12.87**
of Berkshire. Vol. ii: 1653–1710. Compiled by Jasmine S.
Howse. 1975.
Continues **12.**8 but on a different plan, as the title indicates, and is 'a
complete record of all the archidiaconal probate documents which have
survived for the years it covers'. The introduction, by D. M. Barratt,
shows where wills and administrations of other Berkshire persons are to
be found. Map showing the pre-1858 testamentary jurisdictions in the
county.

88. Index of the probate records of the court of the archdeacon   **12.88**
of Ely, 1513–1857. Compiled and edited by Clifford A. Thurley and Dorothea Thurley. 1976.
The introduction, by Heather E. Peek, indicates where probate records
for other Cambridgeshire persons are to be found. Map showing the pre-
1858 testamentary jurisdictions in the county.

89. Index to testamentary records in the archdeaconry court   **12.89**
of London now preserved in Guildhall Library, London. Vol.
i: (1363)–1649. Edited by Marc Fitch. 1979.

90. Index of the probate records of the court of the archdeacon   **12.90**
of Suffolk, 1444–1700. Compiled by M. E. Grimwade. Edited
by W. R. and R. K. Serjeant. Vol. 1: A–K. 1979.
Map showing the pre-1858 testamentary jurisdictions of the county. Continuous pagination.

91. Index of the probate records ... archdeacon of Suffolk,   **12.91**
1444–1700. Vol. 2: L–Z. 1980.

92. Administrations and inventories of the archdeaconry of   **12.92**
Northampton (now preserved in the County Record Office

at Northampton). Pt. ii: 1711–1800. Extracted by the late
Henry Isham Longden [d. 1942]. Edited by Clare Baggott.
1980.

Includes a quite uncommon find of 170 administrators' accounts,
separated from their letters of administration, covering the period 1665 to
1685 and properly belonging to 12.70.

14. CANTERBURY AND YORK SOCIETY

54. Registrum Thome Bourgchier, Cantuariensis archiepis- **14.54**
copi, A.D. 1454–1486. Transcribed and edited by F. R. H. Du
Boulay. 1957.

> Common-form entries (testamentary commissions, institutions, etc.) cal-
> endared. The introduction, besides describing the register and its contents
> (with particular attention to the institutions and ordinations), enlarges on
> the printed lives of the archbishop and shows that there is evidence enough
> 'to make possible the suggestion that he was more than the "clever time-
> server" who survived political storms through easy political virtue'.

55. The registers of Roger Martival, bishop of Salisbury, **14.55**
1315–1330. Vol. i: The register of presentations and institutions to benefices. Edited by Kathleen Edwards. 1959.

> Abstract, in English, with full Latin transcripts of unusual entries, entries
> in full letter form, vicarage ordinations, and confirmations of heads of
> religious houses. Contd. in **14.**57, 58, 59, 68 below.

56. The *acta* of the bishops of Chichester, 1075–1207. Edited **14.56**
... by H. Mayr-Harting. 1964.

> Transcripts, Latin mainly from cartulary copies. The introduction treats
> of the bishop's household and chancery, the cathedral chapter, the arch-
> deacons, the administration of the diocese, and the forgeries of Lewes
> priory. Appended are itineraries of the bishops of the period and a list of
> the cathedral clergy.

57. The registers of Roger Martival ... Vol. ii: The register of **14.57**
divers letters (first half). Edited by C. R. Elrington. 1973.

> Transcript, Latin, somewhat shortened. Concluded, with indexes, in the
> following. Pagination is continuous.

58. The registers of Roger Martival ... Vol. ii (bis): The **14.58**
register of divers letters (second half). Edited by C. R. Elrington. 1972.

59. The registers of Roger Martival ... Vol. iii: Royal writs. **14.59**
Edited by Susan Reynolds. 1965.

> Abstracts, in English, with a formulary and full Latin transcripts of entries
> or parts of entries not in common form.

60. The register of Edmund Lacy, bishop of Exeter, 1420–   **14.60**
1455. *Registrum commune*. Edited by G. R. Dunstan. Vol. i.
1963.

Transcript, Latin, some texts in French, common-form entries calendared. In this vol. are the vicar-general's register, 1420–21, ending with a manumission dated 1432, and the bishop's register to 26 Mar. 1436. Contd. in **14.**61, 62, 63, 66 below. All vols. issued jointly with the Devon and Cornwall Record Soc. See **40.**31 below.

61. The register of Edmund Lacy . . . *Registrum commune*. Vol.   **14.61**
ii. 1966.

26 Mar. 1436–27 Mar. 1448.

62. The register of Emund Lacy . . . *Registrum commune*. Vol.   **14.62**
iii. 1967.

23 Apr. 1448–18 Sept. 1455, followed by miscellaneous processes, compositions, injunctions, indentures, etc.

63. The register of Edmund Lacy . . . *Registrum commune*. Vol.   **14.63**
iv. 1971.

Wills proved in the bishop's court and ordinations. In the appendix, docs. entered in and not properly belonging to the register of institutions.

64. The register of John Pecham, archbishop of Canterbury,   **14.64**
1279–1292. Vol. i. Edited by the late F. N. Davis and others.
1969.

Transcript, Latin, of all those entries omitted from C. Trice Martin's three vols. in the Rolls Series (see **6.**77), in the order in which they are bound, with references to the Rolls Series edition, so that the two editions together provide a printed version of the whole register. The parts comprising this vol. and including the archbishop's itinerary were published in 1908 and 1914; it ends in the middle of the Michaelmas ordinations of 1287. Contd. in the following.

65. The register of John Pecham . . . Vol. ii. Edited by Decima   **14.65**
Douie. 1968.

Completes this edition, with a catalogue of Pecham's letters found in other sources and abstracts of their contents, and a mandate to the dean and chapter of Lichfield, 19 Nov. 1280.

   The register is introduced as of interest not merely as the earliest surviving register for Canterbury 'but because it represents an advance over earlier and even certain contemporary ones such as those of Lincoln, Worcester and Hereford in format and in arrangement'. Many important administrative docs. and others of great historical interest are not in the register. Stylistically its most striking characteristic is 'its use of the cursus probably introduced by the Italian notary, John of Bologna'. Other notaries are identified. The household, besides being efficient and distinguished, is described as most remarkable for its cosmopolitanism.

66. The register of Edmund Lacy ... Vol. v. 1972. **14.66**

Indexes and brief introduction outlining the bishop's life, describing the registers, and offering 'some crude statistics' on the numbers of clerks 'who did not complete the progression from the first tonsure to the priesthood'. Also additions and corrections to vols. i–iv, together with additions and corrections to the earlier, incomplete edition of which only 2 pts. with continuous pagination were issued (1909, 1915), pt. 1 having the register of institutions, edited by F. C. Hingeston-Randolph, and pt. 2 (published by the Devon and Cornwall Record Soc. in conjunction with William Powell and Co. of Exeter) the first 234 folios of the *registrum commune*, transcribed and summarized by Charles Gordon Browne, edited and annotated by Oswald J. Reichel. Neither pt. of the earlier edition is indexed; stocks of both pts. were destroyed by bombing during 1939–45; no further pts. were issued.

67. Canterbury professions. Edited by Michael Richter, with a palaeographical note by T. J. Brown. 1973. **14.67**

A complete textual edition, Latin, of episcopal professions of obedience to the archbishops, the last by Edmund de Lacy, bishop of Exeter, 31 Oct. 1420. In the appendices, forms of professions, specimens of the *decretum* in England, a form of examination of the bishop-elect, two docs. concerning a transfer of obedience from Cluny to Canterbury *c.* 1148, and an indult from Innocent IV assuring Archbishop Boniface that the bishops consecrated by the Pope nevertheless owed obedience to Canterbury. The introduction deals with the history of the episcopal profession of obedience in Canterbury province.

68. The registers of Roger Martival ... Vol. iv: General introduction to the registers, by Kathleen Edwards, and the register of inhibitions and acts, edited by Dorothy M. Owen. 1975. **14.68**

The introduction shows the bishop and his clerks at work, how the registers were kept, apparent innovations due possibly to the bishop's initiative, the importance of his chancellor, Robert Worth, and the work of the registrar, notaries public and other secretarial staff. The registers and other archives are considered, as also is their place of custody, and the physical appearance of the four surviving registers is described in detail. Itinerary of the bishop. Corrigenda to vols. i–iii.

In the edited text, all inhibitions and relaxations have been calendared; other entries apart from repeated commissions and citations are transcribed, Latin, with brief English headings.

69. The register of Thomas Rotherham, archbishop of York, 1480–1500. Edited by Eric E. Barker. Vol. i. 1976. **14.69**

The register of vicars-general followed by the archbishop's own. Since the whole register is in 'well-established common form' all entries except those in English have been calendared. Two further vols. planned.

70. The register of William Melton, archbishop of York, 1317–1340. Vol. i. Edited by Rosalind M. T. Hill. 1977. **14.70**

Transcript, Latin, common-form entries and entries already in print calendared. This vol. has the register for the archdeaconry of Richmond, suffragans, and peculiars of Howden, Howdenshire, Allerton and Allertonshire. Contd. below. Further vols. planned.

71. The register of William Melton ... Vol. ii. Edited by David Robinson. 1978.   14.71

For the archdeaconry of Cleveland, the transcriptions somewhat abridged.

72. The register of Robert Hallum, bishop of Salisbury, 1407–17. Edited by Joyce Horn. 1982.   14.72

Entries in English and French fully transcribed, all other entries calendared in English. Contains institutions, wills, licences, letters, commissions, royal writs, judicial *acta*, and some entries not belonging to Hallum's episcopate. In the appendices, institutions and exchanges which appear to have taken place but of which there is no record in the register, original docs. of Hallum's chancery not in the register, an itinerary, examples of Hallum's literary style, and a calendar of docs. related to (and including) his will.

The brief introduction sets out the little that is known of Hallum's family, and summarizes his career as a canon lawyer, the events leading to his appointment to Salisbury, and the distinguished learning, oratory, and zeal for reform shown by him as leader of the English delegation at the council of Constance. Also touched on are diocesan administration, the composition of his household, his relations with the chapter and the city, and the working of his chancery.

15. CATHOLIC RECORD SOCIETY, PUBLICATIONS, RECORDS SERIES

50. The Mawhood diary. Selections from the diary note- **15.50**
books of William Mawhood, woollen-draper of London, for
the years 1764–1790. Edited by E. E. Reynolds. 1956.

Transcript of all passages referring to the Catholic life of the time. Includes genealogical table and biographical notices of the diarist and his
family.

51. The Wisbech stirs, 1595–1598. Edited by P. Renold. 1958. **15.51**

Transcripts of 38 docs., all annotated, illustrating the quarrels among the
Catholics imprisoned in Wisbech castle, the Latin docs. with English
translation.

52. The letters and despatches of Richard Verstegan, *c.* 1550– **15.52**
1640. Edited by Anthony G. Petti. 1959.

Transcripts of all known letters and despatches by Verstegan spanning
the period 1591–1617, with English translations of Spanish copies and
Italian extracts from them.

53. Miscellanea. Recusant records. Edited by Clare Talbot. **15.53**
1961.

Transcripts, with translations where necessary, of a book of recusants,
1582, and numerous other lists among the Cecil papers at Hatfield; petitions from or concerning recusants, also at Hatfield; reports on and lists of
recusants in the Yelverton mss.; Gatehouse bills; York castle recusant
lists; the case of Mrs. Dorothy Scrope, 1609; West Riding presentments
of recusants, 1597; the examination of William Singleton at Durham,
1626, with letters concerning him; the northern book of compositions for
recusancy, 1629–32, and other docs. concerning the northern commission.

54. The *Responsa scholarum* of the English college, Rome. **15.54**
Edited by Anthony Kenny. Pt. 1: 1598–1621. 1962.

Transcripts, Latin, somewhat shortened, of the autobiographical statements written by the majority of students entering the college, with
English summaries. Contd. in the following. Pagination is continuous.
The indexes, compiled by E. E. Reynolds, include in pt. 2 an index of the
students' names (Latin forms) in **15.**37, 40.

55. The *Responsa scholarum* ... Pt. 2; 1622–1685. 1963. **15.55**

56. Miscellanea. Edited by E. E. Reynolds. 1964.   **15.56**

The recusancy papers of the Meynell family of North Kilvington, North Riding of Yorks., 1596–1676. Edited by Hugh Aveling. [Thomas Meynell's book of evidences, written between c. 1613 and 1631, with transcripts of numerous other docs., 1569–1676, including wills, inventories and sequestration papers, illustrating the operation of the recusancy laws. Omits the medieval Meynell docs. copied into the book. The introduction gives an account of the family, describes the estate, and in some 25 pp. sets out the recusancy of Thomas (1564?–1653) and his heir Anthony (1591–1669).]

Papers from Lambeth Palace library. Edited by Carson I. A. Ritchie. [Letters selected from the correspondence file, 1693–5, of Bishop John Leyburn, vicar apostolic, with the cipher code, and other letters of 1697 removed from the post and sent to Archbishop Tenison by W. H. Spence, a government spy.]

Register of Marnhull, 1772–1826. Edited by R. E. Scantlebury. [Baptisms. In the introduction, biographical accounts of the Catholic family of Hussey of Marnhull, Dorset, from c. 1650, and of the clergy who served the mission there.]

57. Recusant roll no. 2, 1593–1594. An abstract, in English,   **15.57**
... by Hugh Bowler. 1965.

In the introduction, 'a lengthy discussion of the anti-recusancy laws and a technical study of the system by which they were implemented'. In the appendix, the text of the statute of 1586–7 from *Statutes at large* (1770). For roll no. 1 see **15.18**; for subsequent rolls see **15.61** below.

58. Letters of William Allen and Richard Barret, 1572–1598.   **15.58**
Edited by P. Renold. 1967.

Transcripts, English, Latin, Spanish, with translations and notes, of letters and papers supplementary to the collection of Cardinal Allen's correspondence etc. assembled by T. F. Knox and to the smaller group edited in **15.9**, with all known letters of Dr. Barret, Allen's successor as president of Douay college. The introductory outline of Barret's life emphasizes 'his constant pre-occupation with the extremely straitened financial position of the College' and concludes that 'more trustworthy evidence' is needed before he can 'justly be condemned as an unsuitable successor to Allen'.

59. Isle of Wight registers. Newport, 1792–1887; Cowes,   **15.59**
1796–1856. Transcribed ... by R. E. Scantlebury. 1968.

Baptisms, confirmations, marriages, deaths. Latin. In the introduction, pedigrees of Urry of Sheat, Browne of Brenchley (Kent), Iden of Stoke (Kent) and Heneage of Hainton and Cadeby; notices of the clergy who served Cadeby; extracts from the receipts and payments ledgers of James Windsor Heneage, 1759–86; and transcripts of letters to his wife Elizabeth, *née* Browne, builder of the Newport and Cowes churches. Notices of the clergy (to c. 1950) of Newport and Cowes precede the respective registers.

60. Recusant documents from the Ellesmere manuscripts. Edited by Anthony G. Petti. 1968. **15.60**

Transcripts of close on 200 items, grouped under 47 main headings, spanning the years 1577–1716, dealing mainly with the periods 1581–1613 and 1674–1708.

61. Recusant roll no. 3 (1594–1595) and recusant roll no. 4 (1595–1596). An abstract, in English, by Hugh Bowler. 1970. **15.61**

In the introduction, the results of the investigation to discover the number of new land-seizures made in the exchequer accounting years covered by rolls 1–4.

62. The letter book of Lewis Sabran, S.J. (rector of St. Omers college), October 1713 to October 1715. Edited by Geoffrey Holt. 1971. **15.62**

In the introduction, an outline of Fr. Sabran's life, a list of his published works, some consideration of the relative value of currencies mentioned in the letter book, a summary description of the organization of the Society of Jesus at the time, and the names of the St. Omers community in 1712 and 1714.

63. Douai college documents, 1639–1794. Edited by P. R. Harris. 1972. **15.63**

Contains a fragmentary diary, 1639–43; lists of persons, 1660–79; Edward Dicconson's diary, 1704–7 and 1714; lists of provosts and deans, c. 1718–74; a list of persons at the college in 1738 and of arrivals until 1782; the prefect of studies book, 1750–94, and Henry Tichborne-Blount's diary, 1770–81.

Includes an appendix of brief biographical notices of priests connected with the college, 1750–94, and, in the introduction to the prefect of studies book, a sketch of the life lived at the college and of the course of studies pursued there, as well as a summary account of the last months of the college and the return to England.

64. Spain and the Jacobean Catholics. Edited by Albert J. Loomie. Vol. i: 1603–1612. 1973. **15.64**

Docs. selected from the files of the Spanish crown's highest consultative body, the Council of State (Secretaría de Estado), to illustrate its deliberations concerning English catholicism, the Spanish texts in full with English translation. Contd. in **15.68** below.

The introduction analyses the 'emergent policy of the Spanish crown' in a period which 'coincides with the paramount role of Sir Robert Cecil in virtually all aspects of domestic and foreign policy'. Shown are 'both the place of the Catholic problem in Spanish diplomacy and the wide variety of expedients adopted by Philip's court and his envoys to produce a change in the lot of the recusants'. 'Within these documents there is indicated nearly every form of peaceful intervention at hand to the early 17th century diplomat.' The formation of the Council, the range of its authority, and its procedures, are briefly described. Also includes a bibliography of printed collections relevant to the study of Anglo-Spanish diplomatic activities.

65. Post-Reformation catholicism in Bath. Edited by J. An-   **15.65**
thony Williams. Vol. i. 1975.

An introductory outline, 1558–*c*.1850, followed by the accounts (in the Archives nationales, Paris) of Bell-tree lodging house and mission, 1746–61; docs. in the P.R.O. relating to the Gordon riots in Bath, June–Nov. 1780; and the journal kept by Fr. Peter Augustine Baines, O.S.B., 1817–19. Contd. in the following.

66. Post-Reformation catholicism in Bath. Vol. ii: Registers,   **15.66**
1780–1825. 1976.

Baptisms, marriages, deaths, converts. Includes baptisms at Horton, 1772–87.

67. Elizabethan casuistry. By P. J. Holmes. 1981.   **15.67**

Two collections of cases of conscience, probably used in the training of seminary priests, the 'Douai–Rheims' cases from several sources and the 'Allen–Persons' cases almost entirely from Lambeth Palace ms. 565, both collections in English translations.

The brief introduction demonstrates the two considerations which moved the leaders of English catholicism when they drew up these texts: 'the obligation on Catholics to avoid heresy and shun heretics' and 'the need for Catholics to adapt themselves … in order to survive'. Illustrations are given of how laymen and clergy might bend the rules and apply the doctrine of equivocation. Monastic lands might be bought and sold, provided that the ownership was recognized as belonging to the monasteries, and that 'profit above a reasonable level' was used to further the Catholic cause.

68. Spain and the Jacobean Catholics. Vol. ii: 1613–1624.   **15.68**
1978.

The introduction is concerned in the main with the activities in London of Diego Sarmiento de Acuña, Count Gondomar, and his confidants and sympathizers, the 'Spanish faction'. Spanish representatives in London and their assistants are listed, and as in vol. i the ms. sources and relevant printed collections are described. Included in the appendix of docs. pertaining to the Iberian peninsula are 'the unusual original directives of James I concerning the Anglican services he desired to be conducted for Prince Charles during his visit to the Catholic court at Madrid in 1623'.

69. St Omers and Bruges colleges, 1593–1773: a biographical   **15.69**
dictionary. By Geoffrey Holt. 1979.

The names and other particulars of some 4,300 boys educated at one or other of the colleges, recovered from printed works and ninety ms. sources.

18.   ENGLISH PLACE-NAME SOCIETY

39. —— —— Gloucestershire. Pt. ii: The north and west **18.**39
Cotswolds. 1964.

40. —— —— Gloucestershire. Pt. iii: The lower Severn val- **18.**40
ley, the forest of Dean. 1964.

41. —— —— Gloucestershire. Pt. iv: Introduction, biblio- **18.**41
graphy, analyses, index, maps. 1965.

42. The place-names of Westmorland. By A. H. Smith. Pt. i: **18.**42
Introduction, river- and lake-names, road-names, the barony
of Kendal. 1967.

43. —— —— Westmorland. Pt. ii: The barony of Westmor- **18.**43
land, analyses, index, maps. 1967.

44. The place-names of Cheshire. By J. McN. Dodgson. Pt. **18.**44
i: County name, regional- and forest-names, river-names,
road-names, the place-names of Macclesfield hundred. 1970.

45. —— —— Cheshire. Pt. ii: The place-names of Bucklow **18.**45
hundred and Northwich hundred. 1970.

46. —— —— Cheshire. Pt. iii: The place-names of Nantwich **18.**46
hundred and Eddisbury hundred. 1971.

47. —— —— Cheshire. Pt. iv: The place-names of Broxton **18.**47
hundred and Wirral hundred. 1972.

48. —— —— Cheshire. Pt. v (1:i): The place-names of the **18.**48
city of Chester. The elements of Cheshire place-names (A –
Gylden). 1981.

Contd. in **18.**54 below.

49. The place-names of Berkshire. By Margaret Gelling. Pt. **18.**49
1: County, district, road, dyke and river-names; the hundreds
of Ripplesmere, Bray, Beynhurst, Cookham, Charlton, War-
grave, Sonning, Reading, Theale, Faircross. 1973.

Pagination of this and the two following is continuous.

50. —— —— Berkshire. Pt. 2: The hundreds of Kintbury **18.**50
Eagle, Lambourn, Shrivenham, Ganfield, Ock, Hormer,
Wantage, Compton, Moreton. 1974.

With index to pts. 1 and 2. Index map and distribution maps in end
pocket.

51. —— —— Berkshire. Pt. 3(i): The Old English charter   **18.**51
boundaries of Berkshire. Pt. 3(ii): Introduction to 'Theplace-
names of Berkshire', and analyses of material in pts. 1 and 2.
1976.

With maps illustrating the charter boundaries in slip-case.

52. The place-names of Dorset. By A. D. Mills. Pt. i: The Isle   **18.**52
of Purbeck, the hundreds of Rowbarrow, Hasler, Winfrith,
Culliford Tree, Bere Regis, Barrow, Puddletown, St. George.
1977.

53. —— —— Dorset. Pt. ii: The hundreds of Cogdean,   **18.**53
Loosebarrow, Rushmore, Combs Ditch, Pimperne, Badbury,
Cranborne, Wimborne St. Giles, Knowlton, Monkton Up
Wimborne. 1980.

54. —— —— Cheshire. Pt. v (1:ii): The elements of Cheshire   **18.**54
place-names (haca – yolden). The personal-names in Cheshire
place-names. 1981.

108. The travels of Leo of Rozmital through Germany, Flan-   **20.108**
ders, England, France, Spain, Portugal and Italy, 1465–1467.
Translated ... and edited by Malcolm Letts. 1957.

From the German account by Gabriel Tetzel, arranged in chapters, each
chapter followed by supplementary passages from the Latin versions
(printed in 1577, 1843 and 1951) of the lost account in Czech by Václav
Šašek, both Rozmital's companions. The travellers crossed to England in
Feb. 1466 and were received luxuriously by Edw. IV. Court etiquette is
described, as also are the places they saw (among them Canterbury,
London, Windsor, Reading, and Andover) and the English countryside.
Appendices treat of disposable decorations (such as the collars of SS
distributed by Hen. VI), Bohemian manners (from the 15th-century
account in Latin by Johannes Butzbach), the safe-conduct and commen-
dation granted to Rozmital's party by Edw. IV, and the safe-conduct (in
Catalan) granted by John II of Aragon.

109. Ethiopian itineraries *circa* 1400–1524, including those   **20.109**
collected by Alessandro Zorzi at Venice in the years 1519–24.
Edited by O. G. S. Crawford. 1958.

Zorzi's Italian text, with facing translation by C. A. Ralegh Radford,
sketch-maps by Frank Addison, a bibliography of books, articles and
maps, a gazetteer of names on Fra Mauro's map, a genealogy for the
Habab tribe, and notes by R. A. Skelton on an Ethiopian embassy to
western Europe in 1306. The introduction summarizes and comments
upon the itineraries and gives an outline of European interest in Ethiopia
in earlier centuries.

110. The travels of Ibn Baṭṭūṭa, A.D. 1325–1354. Translated,   **20.110**
with revisions and notes, from the Arabic text edited by C.
Defrémery and B. R. Sanguinetti, by H. A. R. Gibb. Vol. 1.
1958.

Travels through north-west Africa, Egypt, Syria, Mecca, as dictated to
the secretary Ibn Juzayy. Contd. in **20.**117, 141 below. Pagination is
continuous.

111. English privateering voyages to the West Indies. 1588–   **20.111**
1595. Edited by Kenneth R. Andrews. 1959.

Docs. (some summarized entirely or in part) relating to 25 voyages, drawn
mainly from the records of the High Court of Admiralty, with selections

from narratives printed by Hakluyt and from a quantity of translations by Miss I. A. Wright of originals (1593-5) in the Archivo General de Indias in Seville intended for her projected fourth vol. on English West Indies voyages (see **20.**66, 71, 99). Referred to are the voyage of the *Drake*, the *Examiner*, the *Hope* and the *Chance* (1588), of the *Black Dog* (1588-9), of John Chidley (1589), of the *Bark Young* (1590); the expeditions of 1591; the voyage of Benjamin Wood (1592), of Christopher Newport (1592), of William King (1592); the voyages of William Parker (1592 and 1593); the voyage of Sir John Burgh (1593), of James Langton (1593-4), of the *Centaur* and the *Edward Bonaventure* (1594); the voyages of the *Golden Dragon* and the *Prudence*, the *Affection* and the *Jewell* (1594); the voyages of William Parker (1594 and 1595); the voyage of John Ridlesden (1595), of the *Rose Lion* (1594-5), and of Amyas Preston and George Sommers (1595).

The introduction describes the jurisdiction, business, and records of the court, and sets out many aspects of privateering in general during the Spanish war and, more particularly, in the West Indies. See also **20.**142 below.

112. The tragic history of the sea, 1589–1622: narratives of **20.**112 the shipwrecks of the Portuguese East Indiamen *São Thomé* (1589), *Santo Alberto* (1593), *São João Baptista* (1622), and the journeys of the survivors in South East Asia. Edited from the original Portuguese by C. R. Boxer. 1959.

The narratives by Diogo do Couto, João Baptista Lavanha and Francisco Vaz d'Almada, translated from the original editions of accounts which were subsequently included in the *História trágico-marítima* edited by Bernando Gomes de Brito at Lisbon in 1735-6. The writers and their narratives are considered in the introduction.

Other matters treated in the introduction and appendices include the round voyage made by the Indiamen between Lisbon and Goa, the ships and their crews, the navigational aids (rutters and instruments), pay and allowances, overcrowding and overloading, provisions, allotment of deck and cargo space, allowance of liberty chests, and the rate of shipwreck. Maps. Glossary. See also **20.**132 below.

113. The troublesome voyage of Captain Edward Fenton, **20.**113 1582–1583. Narratives and documents edited by E. G. R. Taylor. 1959.

Transcripts of all the surviving records of the voyage 'for China and Cathay' sponsored by the Privy Council and intended to establish the first English trading base in the Far East. Includes Fenton's sea journal and extracts from the private diary kept by his chaplain Richard Madox.

The introduction sets out the plan and preparation of the voyage, and its progress (to Sierra Leone, to Brazil, and the return to England). Other sections of the introduction are concerned with the officers and crew, navigation, piracy and privateering, and the aftermath of recrimination and enquiry. Plates (many of them reproducing charts and drawings in Madox's diary).

114. The Prester John of the Indies. A true relation of the 20.114
lands of the Prester John, being the narrative of the Portuguese
embassy to Ethiopia in 1520 written by Father Francisco Alvares. The translation of Lord Stanley of Alderley (1881)
revised and edited with additional material by C. F. Beck-
ingham and G. W. B. Huntingford. Vol. 1. 1961.

Chapters 1–88 of Alvares's account of the mission of Dom Rodrigo de
Lima, from his landing at Massawa on the west coast of the Red Sea in
Apr. 1520 to his re-embarking there six years later, the first European
embassy known to have reached the Ethiopian court and returned in
safety. Contd. in the following. Pagination is continuous.

The introduction, after setting out the events which caused the mission
to be sent and the history of Alvares's text in its several editions, evaluates
the translation by Lord Stanley (see 19.64): his 'errors were few, and few
of his errors were important . . . a creditable attempt to make sense of what
is at times an extremely obscure text'. This edition seeks to improve the
rendering of certain sentences, to bring Stanley's Victorian English 'closer
to the homely confused style of Alvares', to modify his exclusive reliance
on one particular version, and to annotate the text—'a formidable task to
which Stanley made almost no contributions'. Alvares's reliability is assessed, much corroborative evidence being drawn from Ethiopian chronicles and land charters, the latter 'a class of document which is most
unusual outside Europe and is similar in form and content to the Saxon
land charters of England'. A note explains the transliteration of the
Ethiopic alphabet. Maps, plates, and text-figures.

115. The Prester John of the Indies. Vol. 2. 1961. 20.115

Chapters 89–142, with the narrative of the return to Portugal. The
appendices, by G. W. B. Huntingford, comprise a translation of a 17th-
century Ethiopian description of Aksum; accounts of the rock-cut
churches at Lālibalā, of the Ethiopian tábot (the altar or ark), and of the
Ethiopian calendar; a glossary of official titles and terms used by Alvares;
notes on maps (including Gastaldi's of the Nile basin, 1550, and of Ethiopia, 1564, both reproduced, the latter in end pocket); and a gazetteer.

116. The history of the Tahitian mission, 1799–1830, written 20.116
by John Davies, missionary to the South Sea islands, with
supplementary papers from the correspondence of the missionaries. Edited by C. W. Newbury. 1961.

Chapters 6–12 and 14–20 of Davies's unpublished 'History', drawn in
large measure from copies of missionary letters and journals of which he
was custodian in the 1830s, his chapters 1–5 (on the earlier years of
European penetration) summarized in the editor's introduction, and chapter 13 omitted as already in print (see pp. 119–60 of 20.52). The editor's
'epilogue', continuing the history of the mission to 1860, includes part of
Davies's 'Conclusion' and the supplementary correspondence. An appended table sets out the origins and genealogy of the Pomare dynasty.
Also appended is a note on missionary codes of law, together with a list of
the codes and regulations of Eastern Polynesia.

117. The travels of Ibn Baṭṭūṭa, A. D. 1325-1354. Vol. 2. 1962.   **20.**117

Through southern Persia, Iraq, southern Arabia, east Africa, the Persian Gulf, Asia Minor, and south Russia. Appended is 'a preliminary survey' of the chronology of the travels in Asia Minor and south Russia, made necessary because the narrative 'involves a number of serious inconsistencies, if not downright impossibilities' and is in one instance 'a complete fiction'.

118. The travels and controversies of Friar Domingo Navar-   **20.**118
rete, 1616-1686. Edited from manuscript and printed sources by J. S. Cummins. Vol. 1. 1962.

A translation of the autobiographical portions of the *Tratados historicos*, i.e. the sixth book, with interpolated references to his travels and experiences brought together from other parts of the *Tratados* and his unpublished works, based upon the 1704 translation by Awnsham and John Churchill. This vol. is concerned with his travels in China and the outward journey.

The introduction describes Navarrete's life (1618-86) and work, his character, and his attitude to non-Europeans; summarizes the origin and nature of the Jesuit-Dominican controversy over the Chinese rites, Navarrete's attitude to it, and its development down to the papal Instruction of 1939; examines his relations with the Jesuits; lists and comments on his writings and the controversies they gave rise to; and remarks on the Churchills' edition of the *Tratados*.

Vol. 2, below, completing the selection, includes Navarrete's account of his journeys to and stays in Fu-Chien (1659), Chê-Kiang, Peking, Canton, Macao and Malacca (1670), and on via Madras and Goa to Madagascar, Lisbon, Rome and Madrid. Ends with his account of the island of Santo Domingo (1681) and appendices on, *inter alia*, the detention of the missionaries in Canton, 1666-70, and his relations with François Pallu, bishop of Heliopolis, and Richard Cony, governor of St. Helena. Maps and plates. Pagination is continuous.

119. The travels and controversies of Friar Domingo Navar-   **20.**119
rete. Vol. 2. 1962.

120. The Cabot voyages and Bristol discovery under Henry   **20.**120
VII. By James A. Williamson, with the cartography of the voyages by R. A. Skelton. 1962.

Docs. from English, Portuguese and Spanish archives, transcribed or in translation, relating to the Atlantic voyages out of Bristol in 1480 and 1481; the undated discovery of the so-called Isle of Brasil by Bristol men some time before 1496; the expeditions led by John Cabot in 1496; those sent forth by the syndicates of Bristol merchants and Azorean promoters in 1501-6; and the expedition under Sebastian Cabot in 1509 or 1508-9 intended for the discovery of the north-west passage.

The introduction (170 pp.) presents a closely argued account of the voyages and the intellectual environment in which they were conceived and performed. Some earlier conclusions on the Cabot voyages the editor here disclaims or modifies in the light of later discoveries. Maps, plates.

121. *A Regiment for the Sea*, and other writings on navigation 20.121
by William Bourne of Gravesend, a gunner (*c.* 1535–1582).
Edited by E. G. R. Taylor. 1963.

Reprints (after a brief account of Bourne's life and works, and with technical introductory summaries) Bourne's two almanacks (for three years, 1571, and for ten years, 1581) and the *Regiment* (1574), together with the variants and additions in the 1580 edition. Appended are the surviving portion of John Dee's navigational tables entitled *Canon gubernauticus* (1558), the wills of Bourne (1573) and his wife Dorothy (1582), and a bibliographical description of Bourne's manuscript and printed works by D. W. Waters and R. A. Skelton. Charts, plates.

122. Byron's journal of his circumnavigation, 1764–1766. 20.122
Edited by Robert E. Gallagher. 1964.

The voyage of the *Dolphin*, captain the Hon. John Byron, possibly the third ship to have been copper sheathed. Includes the secret instructions by the Admiralty, a list of the crew, and transcripts of docs. relating to the voyage. The appendix on the Patagonians includes 'The Patagonian giants' by Helen Wallis and Horace Walpole's *Account of the giants lately discovered* (1776). In the introduction, accounts of the fitting out, the historical background, Byron's instructions, the voyage, the paying off, and the aftermath. Charts, maps, plates.

123. Missions to the Niger. Edited by E. W. Bovill. Vol. i: 20.123
The journal of Friedrich Hornemann's travels from Cairo to
Murzuk in the years 1797–98. The letters of Major Alexander
Gordon Laing, 1824–26. 1964.

The first of a series of vols. on the exploration of the Niger following its discovery by Mungo Park, in two 'books'. Book 1 consists of Hornemann's journal, as printed in 1802, with an introduction relating the formation of the African Association in June 1788, its sponsorship of the expeditions of Ledyard, Lucas and Houghton, Hornemann's introduction to and relations with the Association, the publication of his journal, and his disappearance and death. Book 2, on the re-discoverer of Timbuktu, builds up Laing's 'stirring and romantic story ... from miscellaneous material drawn from a variety of contemporary sources', chief amongst them his correspondence with Hanmer Warrington (consul-general in Tripoli), Edward Sabine and James Bandinel, and Warrington's official dispatches. This selected material, printed as written, is 'welded together with editorial matter'. Appended are two portions of Laing's journal, his 'Cursory remarks on the course of the Great River Niger', his 'Notes on Gadamis', a letter to him by his wife (*née* Warrington), and the report of his death printed in *L'Etoile*, 2 May 1827. The introduction includes sections on Laing as soldier and as explorer, his relations with Warrington and Hugh Clapperton, his qualities and achievement. Maps, plates. Other vols. in this series are at **20.**128, 129, 130 below.

124. Carteret's voyage round the world, 1766–1769. Edited 20.124
by Helen Wallis. Vol. 1. 1965.

A conflation of the journal written by Philip Carteret shortly after 1773 as a corrective to the account of his voyage published by John Hawkesworth and his previously written 'abstract', the two together forming a consecutive narrative of the voyage in his own words, with resort to others of his papers where the 'abstract' is lacking. Charts, plates.

The introduction (100 pp.) sets out the probable reasoning behind the Admiralty's despatch of the expedition commanded by Samuel Wallis in the *Dolphin* with Carteret in command of the *Swallow* as consort, and describes the preparations, the choice of Wallis rather than Carteret as commander, the grievances which vitiated their relations, and the separation of the two ships in the entrance to the Strait of Magellan ('an accident which neither man resisted too strenuously ... their ships unsuitable as consorts, and their temperaments incompatible'). The separation 'made possible two sets of discoveries instead of one', Carteret's voyage across the Pacific resulting in 'the first rediscovery by a European of the legendary islands of Mendaña and Quirós', i.e. Egmont Island or Santa Cruz. The events there and their consequences are described, as are his relations with the Dutch at Celebes, his meeting with Bougainville, and arrival at Spithead.

Vol. 2, below (pagination is continuous), contains transcripts of docs., 1756–69, relating to the preparations, the voyage to and across the Pacific, the transactions with the Dutch, and the voyage home. The aftermath is treated in a further group of docs., 1770–1811, with its own introduction, describing and assessing the results of the voyage and its significance, the injustice done by Hawkesworth to the commanders of the voyages related by him, Carteret's later life, his defects and qualities.

125. Carteret's voyage round the world. Vol. 2. 1965.   **20.**125

126. La Austrialia del Espíritu Santo. The journal of Fray   **20.**126
Martín de Munilla O. F. M. and other documents relating to
the voyage of Pedro Fernández de Quirós to the South Sea
(1605–1606) and the Franciscan missionary plan (1617–1627).
Translated and edited by Celsus Kelly, with ethnological introduction, appendix, and other contributions by G. S. Par-
sonson. Vol. 1. 1966.

The *Relación* of Munilla, chaplain and vicar of the royal fleet and commissary of the Franciscans in the Quirós expedition, with introduction (133 pp.), maps, charts and plates.

Vol. 2 below (pagination is continuous) contains the *Summario breve* of Juan de Iturbe, followed by 31 further docs. in translation bearing on the preparations for the expedition, the voyage, Quirós in New Spain, negotiations for another expedition, and the missionary plan, with charts and plates. Appendix I lists the ships' companies; appendix II aims to disentangle the confusions in the naming of the islands of the Pacific, and to identify Pouro and Manicolo.

127. La Austrialia del Espíritu Santo. Vol. 2. 1966.   **20.**127

128. Missions to the Niger. Vol. ii: The Bornu mission, 1822–   **20.**128
25, pt. 1. 1966.

The pagination of this and the two following is continuous: described as 'vols.' they constitute three pts. of a single vol. in which is reprinted the *Narrative of travels and discoveries in northern and central Africa in the years 1822, 1823, and 1824 by Major Denham, F. R. S., Captain Clapperton and the late Doctor Oudney*, 2nd edition 1826, omitting its appendices XII-XVI, and with extra plates from the first edition. This pt. begins Dixon Denham's narrative. Previously unpublished docs. relating to the mission are included in the introduction (115 pp.) and in the appendix. Glossary, itineraries, maps, plates. Further itineraries, maps, plates are included in the two following pts. Pt. 3 has a general map in end pocket.

129. Missions to the Niger. Vol. iii [*recte* ii]: The Bornu mis-   **20.129** sion, 1822–25, pt. 2. 1966.

Dixon Denham's narrative, chapters III-VII and the supplementary chapter on Bornu, with additional docs.

130. Missions to the Niger. Vol. iv [*recte* ii]: The Bornu mis-   **20.130** sion, 1822–25, pt. 3. 1966.

Hugh Clapperton's narrative, with the appendix of letters, etc. brought back by Denham and Clapperton as translated from the Arabic by the then interpreter to the Colonial Office, Abraham Salamé, and additional docs.

131. The journal and letters of Captain Charles Bishop on the   **20.131** north-west coast of America, in the Pacific, and in New South Wales, 1794–1799. Edited by Michael Roe. 1967.

Recording the voyage out of Bristol begun in the *Ruby*, Charles Bishop master, in Oct. 1794 bound for the otter-fur trade of north-west America, ended in the *Nautilus* at Macao in Aug. 1799, the *Ruby* having been sold at Amboyna in Nov. 1796.

The introduction sketches the opening-up of the otter-fur trade, the impetus given to it by the arrival of James Cook off the north-west coast in 1778, the formation of the King George's Sound Company in 1785, the activities of the East India Company and Bengal Fur Society, the Nootka Sound incident from its beginning in 1789, the expedition sent out under Vancouver in 1791, and the enterprise of ship-builders and merchants like Sydenham Teast of Bristol, owner of the *Ruby*. Bishop's reports to Teast, his accounts of receipts and disbursements, and lists of his crews, form a large part of the 'memoranda' appended to his journal. The introduction concludes with a résumé of Bishop's later voyages, his settling in New South Wales, and his departure for England in 1809 as passenger, pauper and lunatic. Maps.

132. Further selections from the *Tragic History of the Sea*,   **20.132** 1559–1565. Narratives of the shipwrecks of the Portuguese East Indiamen *Aguia* and *Garça* (1559), *São Paulo* (1561), and the misadventures of the Brazil-ship *Santo António* (1565).

Translated and edited from the original Portuguese by C. R. Boxer. 1968.

The narratives by Diogo do Couto, Henrique Dias and Afonso Luís. Maps, charts, plates. See **20.**112 above.

133. The letters of F. W. Ludwig Leichhardt. Collected and newly translated by M. Aurousseau. Vol. 1. 1968.   **20.**133

Full texts and annotated calendar of all letters, together with translations of those in German, French and Italian, the aim being 'to establish an authentic text, and so to enable the man to speak for himself'. This pt. contains the letters written while he was in Germany, 1832–7, and between 1837 and his departure for Sydney in 1841, with portrait and maps. Contd. in **20.**134, 135 below. Pagination is continuous.

134. The Letters of F. W. Ludwig Leichhardt. Vol. 2. 1968.   **20.**134

The years of scientific reconnaissance, 1842–4, around Sydney and Newcastle, in the Hunter-Goulburn valley, and to the Moreton Bay district. Maps.

135. The letters of F. W. Ludwig Leichhardt. Vol. 3. 1968.   **20.**135

Major exploration, from 1844 until his disappearance in 1848, with a table of subsequent events to June 1964. Maps. Genealogical tables of Nicholson and Leichhardt families, and five additional letters, 1842–4.

136. The Jamestown voyages under the first charter, 1606–1609. Documents relating to the foundation of Jamestown and the history of the Jamestown colony up to the departure of Captain John Smith, last president of the council in Virginia under the first charter, early in October, 1609. Edited by Philip L. Barbour. Vol. 1. 1969.   **20.**136

Transcripts from many sources, decoded and translated as necessary, presented in groups, each group with its own introductory narrative, viz. (i) the preliminaries, Apr.–Nov. 1606, (ii) the original voyage, Jan.–Oct. 1607, (iii) in Virginia, 1608, and (iv) events in England, 1608–9. Map and combined list of the original planters to about 1 Oct. 1608. Contd. in the following. Pagination is continuous.

137. The Jamestown voyages . . . Vol. 2. 1969.   **20.**137

Groups (v) dissatisfaction and the second charter, 1609, (vi) Spain investigates, and (vii) Capt. John Smith's summary: *A map of Virginia* (Oxford, 1612), with its annexed second pt. attributed to eight or nine other writers. The appendices include glossaries of Indian words and phrases, personal names, and place-names.

138. Russian embassies to the Georgian kings, 1589–1605. Edited with introduction, additional notes, commentaries and bibliography by W. E. D. Allen. Texts translated by Anthony Mango. Vol. 1. 1970.   **20.**138

The embassy of Zvenigorodski and Antonov, 1589-90, the text annotated and with additional commentaries. The introduction surveys the historical and geographical backgrounds, the route through the Caucasus, the peoples of the areas, the kingdoms, and early relations with Russia and Persia. Maps, plates. Contd. in the following. Pagination is continuous.

139. Russian embassies ... Vol. 2. 1970.   20.139

The embassy of Tatischev and Ivanov, 1604-5, the text annotated and with additional commentaries as above, followed by supplementary docs. from the embassy of Sovin and Polukhanov, 1596-9, a commentary on the sources, and genealogical notes and tables on the Russian royal houses, the Ottoman sultans, the Safavid shahs, the Giray khans of the Crimea, and other rulers. Maps, plates.

140. *Sucesos de las Islas Filipinas*, by Antonio de Morga.   20.140 Translated and edited by J. S. Cummins. 1971.

The first history of the Spanish Philippines to be written by a layman. From the first edition, Mexico 1609. See **19.39**. In the introduction, a life of Morga, his reasons for writing, an evaluation of his *Sucesos*, and a bibliographical account of other editions. Maps, plates.

141. The travels of Ibn Baṭṭūṭa, A. D. 1325-1354. Vol. 3. 1971.   20.141

Turkestan, Khurasan, Sind, north-western India and Delhi, and including his account of the reign of Sultan Muhammad ibn Tughluq. Maps, plates.

142. The last voyage of Drake and Hawkins. Edited by Kenneth R. Andrews. 1972.   20.142

A sequel to **20.111** above. Transcripts or translations of docs., mainly from manuscripts, and including many from the archives at Seville, juxtaposing English and Spanish evidence for the study of the West Indian expedition of 1595-6. The docs. are arranged in groups, each group with its own introduction, viz. (i) the preliminaries, (ii) the expeditionary force, (iii) the English narratives by Thomas Maynarde, John Troughton and Sir Thomas Baskerville, (iv) events in the Canaries, (v) the Puerto Rico action, (vi) Tierra Firme, (vii) Avellaneda's expedition, and (viii) the aftermath. Appendix on 'The art of navigation in the age of Drake', by D. W. Waters. Maps, plates.

143. To the Pacific and Arctic with Beechey: the journal of Lieutenant George Peard of H.M.S. *Blossom*, 1825-1828. Edited by Barry M. Gough. 1973.   20.143

Transcript of 'a distinctly important record' of the scientific mission, with maps and plates and a list of the officers of the *Blossom* in 1825. The introduction sets out the genesis of the voyage, the preparations, the Admiralty's instructions, the voyage itself and its achievements, and includes an outline of Peard's life and naval career.

144. The Hakluyt handbook. Edited by D. B. Quinn. Vol. 1. 1974.   20.144

Essays by many hands, together constituting 'a conspectus of modern views on the significance of various aspects of Hakluyt's work' and 'the first study so far made of the extent to which Hakluyt used fully and successfully the materials available to him at the time'. Includes a chronological guide to the events of Hakluyt's life, by Alison M. and D. B. Quinn, and a concordance between *Principal navigations* (3 vols. 1598–1600) and *Principal navigations* (12 vols. 1903–5) Maps, plates. Contd. in the following. Pagination is continuous.

145. The Hakluyt handbook. Vol. 2. 1974.   **20.145**

Contains an account of the contents and sources of the three major works (*Divers voyages* and the two *Principal navigations*), by Alison M. and D. B. Quinn; a bibliography of Hakluyt's books and sources, by D. B. Quinn, C. E. Armstrong and R. A. Skelton, in three pts. viz. (i) works compiled, translated or published by him, (ii) works in which his influence is known or acknowledged, (iii) works the publication of which he may have influenced; a bibliography of secondary works on Hakluyt and his circle, by L. E. Pennington; and a list of the publications of the Hakluyt Society 1846–1973.

146. Yermak's campaign in Siberia: a selection of documents   **20.146**
translated from the Russian by Tatania Minorsky and David
Wileman, and edited with an introduction and notes by Ter-
ence Armstrong. 1975.

Accounts of the first Russian entry in force into Siberia, in the 1580s, from the Stroganov, Yesipov, Remezov and New chronicles, with royal charters and letters relating to the advance across the Urals, 1558–84.

Besides describing the chronicles and setting out the current state of Russian textual criticism concerning them, the introduction describes Muscovy's eastern frontier in the 16th century, the growth of the Stroganov family and the relationship between it and the tsar, and the campaign conducted by Yermak's adversary Kuchum in the Siberian khanate. Also considered are Yermak's identity, his fame as folk-hero (in a contribution by W. Harrison), the cossacks (in particular the Volga cossacks), the routes into Siberia, and the non-Russian peoples encountered in the advance. All the illustrations in the Mirovich version of the Remezov chronicle are reproduced in this edition, and there are general remarks upon them. Maps, plates.

20.147
147. An Elizabethan in 1582: the diary of Richard Madox,
fellow of All Souls. Edited by Elizabeth Story Donno. 1976.

Transcript, the Latin and Greek and all the cipher passages rendered into English. The diary, kept for a single calendar year by the chaplain on the *Galleon Leicester*, chronicles the initial attempt to establish a spice trade in the Moluccas. It also records the author's winding up of his affairs at Oxford, his stay in London, the slow passage from Blackwall to Southampton, and the many visits to and from persons interested in the enterprise. Includes transcripts of Madox's register or 'booke' and the diary of John Walker, chaplain on the *Edward Bonaventure*.

The introduction relates what is known of Madox's life and background, and describes the voyage, its origins and participants, its course and sequel. Charts, plates, and key to the cipher.

148. Sir Francis Drake's West Indian voyage, 1585–86. Edited by Mary Frear Keeler. 1981.   **20.148**

Previously unpublished docs. selected and 'set forth in a single volume in order that the nature and significance of the enterprise may be more fully understood', together with 'new editions of the *Primrose* journal and the *Summarie* in their early spelling'.

The introduction includes 'a brief description of the kinds of sources, in this volume and elsewhere, that are now available concerning the voyage', classified as (i) 'furnishing lists', accounts, and plans, (ii) logs and journals, (iii) despatches and newsletters, (iv) contemporary narratives, and (v) maps. Also described are the plans for the voyage; its organization as a joint-stock enterprise; the adventurers, ships, and personnel; problems of administration and authority; the several stages of the voyage; and its significance. In the appendices, a descriptive list of ships for the expedition; biographical notes on the personnel; a bibliographical note on *A summarie and true discourse*; and a note on the maps. Maps, plates.

149. François Valentijn's description of Ceylon. Translated and edited by Sinnappah Arasaratnam. 1978.   **20.149**

The first twelve chapters of Valentijn's description (culled from other writers) in vol. v of his *Oud en nieuw Oost-Indien* (1724), omitting some docs. printed elsewhere in English translation. The introduction sketches the life of the author, describes the sources used by him, and cautiously evaluates his work. Maps, plates.

150. The travel journal of Antonio de Beatis: Germany, Switzerland, the Low Countries, France and Italy, 1517–1518. Translated from the Italian by J. R. Hale and J. M. A. Lindon. Edited by J. R. Hale. 1979.   **20.150**

Kept by the chaplain and amanuensis to Cardinal Luigi of Aragon. The introduction considers European travel, the nature and sources of the Renaissance travel journal, and the travel journals of de Beatis's contemporaries. Outline family tree of the Neapolitan house of Aragon. Map, plates.

151. The Periplus of the Erythraean Sea, by an unknown author, with some extracts from Agatharkhidēs 'On the Erythraean Sea'. Translated and edited by G. W. B. Huntingford. 1980.   **20.151**

A trader's guide to the coasts of the Indian Ocean and its branches the Red Sea and the Persian Gulf, 'giving information about the ports, harbours, roadsteads, and marts, together with their imports and exports ... as well as navigational aids', written between A.D. 95 and 130. Appendices on the topography of the *Periplus*, the products of the Erythraean area (including a glossary of imports and exports, viz. clothing material, vegetable products, ivory, horn, shell, hardware, precious stones, etc.), its ethnology and history, shipping, elephant-hunting, and the Mountains of the Moon. Maps, plates.

152–5. *In the press.*

156. The three voyages of Edmond Halley in the *Paramore*,   **20.**156
1698–1701. Edited by Norman J. W. Thrower. 1981.

Transcripts of Halley's three journals (the journal for the third voyage published for the first time), reproducing as far as is typographically practicable the symbols used by him, and of 139 relevant docs., most of them previously unprinted and together forming an important and remarkably complete documentation which 'if read in conjunction with the journals greatly enriches these accounts'.

The introduction provides a life of Halley, with accounts of the three voyages, an assessment of their cartographic results, and a view of them in relation to other official English voyages of exploration in the 17th and early 18th centuries. In the appendices an admittedly incomplete list of published maps arising from Halley's three voyages in the *Paramore* serves to 'suggest something of the influence of Halley's cartography'. The description to accompany his Atlantic chart (see the following) is Appendix D. Charts, plates.

157. The three voyages of Edmond Halley . . .   **20.**157

Facsimiles of Halley's Atlantic chart (1 sheet) and of his Channel chart (2 sheets), in slip-case.

158. The expedition of the *St. Jean-Baptiste* to the Pacific,   **20.**158
1769–1770, from the journals of Jean de Surville and Guillaume Labé. Translated and edited by John Dunmore. 1981.

The 'most significant section' from the two main shipboard journals of a complex expedition: from the arrival at the Batan Islands to the departure from New Zealand at the beginning of 1770. In the appendices, extracts from Labé's journal relating the circumstances of Surville's death and the problems it caused; the full muster-roll; a consideration of the character and behaviour of Father Paul-Antoine Léonard de Villefeix, leading to the assumption that he celebrated New Zealand's first Christian service, in all likelihood on board ship in Doubtless Bay at Christmas 1769; and a note on scurvy.

The introduction considers the officers and crew; the backers; the motives and aims of the expedition; the ship, its cost and cargo; the voyage; the return home and the legal tangle which had then to be unravelled; and the results (the elimination of the non-existing Davis Land, the rediscovery of the Solomon Islands, and important contributions 'from a cultural background that was quite different from that of the English commentators and observers' to western knowledge of pre-colonial Maori life). Maps, plates.

159. The voyage of Semen Dezhnev in 1648: Bering's precur-   **20.**159
sor. With selected documents. By Raymond H. Fisher. 1981.

Aims 'to draw together what earlier scholars, mostly Russian and Soviet, have uncovered and what interpretations and explanations they have advanced' concerning the voyage 'of a party of petty entrepreneurs' around the eastern tip of Asia in the summer of 1648, anticipating by

80 years the voyage of Vitus Bering. Of this earlier voyage Semen De-zhnev, an illiterate Siberian cossack, was the surviving leader. The author writes: 'Mere compilation has not ... been my intention. I have felt free to expand some of the arguments on controversial matters, to present my own conclusions in certain instances, and to take sides on disputed points or to suspend judgement ... the final evaluation of the significance of the voyage is my own.'

160. Newfoundland discovered: English attempts at coloni-sation, 1610–1630. Edited by Gillian T. Cell. 1982. **20.160**

Transcripts of 50 docs., the primary authorities from which is derived the introductory narrative history in four chapters, viz. (i) the first colony, (ii) Richard Whitbourne, propagandist, (iii) Lord Falkland's colony, (iv) Sir George Calvert and the Ferryland colony. Maps, plates.

21. HAKLUYT SOCIETY, EXTRA SERIES

34–37. The journals of Captain James Cook on his voyages of
discovery. 4 vols. in 5, and portfolio, 1955–74.   **21.4a**

Edited from the original mss., vols. i–ii by J. C. Beaglehole with the
assistance of J. A. Williamson, J. W. Davidson and R. A. Skelton, vol. iii
by J. C. Beaglehole. Vol. iv, originally planned as a collection of essays on
particular aspects of Cook's life and achievement, could not be realized as
planned; instead, and by arrangement with its original publisher, copies
of Professor Beaglehole's life of Cook were issued in the same format as
the *Journals*. The separate and unnumbered portfolio of charts and views
drawn by Cook and his officers, reproduced from the originals, and edited
by R. A. Skelton, was issued in 1955 (second edition 1970). Vols. i, ii and
iii have two introductions, the first narrating and commenting upon the
incidents of the voyage, the second concerned with the texts. All vols.
have plates and maps.

i : The voyage of the *Endeavour*, 1768–1771. 1955.   **21.4b**

Admiralty instructions and the journal of the first voyage, with appendices containing (i) Cook's letters and reports describing the voyage, (ii)
docs. illustrating the Royal Society's interest in the voyage, (iii) drafts
and variants of the journal, (iv) extracts from an anonymous journal and
from the journals of Robert Molyneux and W. B. Monkhouse, surgeon,
(v) a roll of the ship's company, (vi) a calendar of all docs. bearing on
the voyage other than logs and journals, and (vii) extracts from contemporary newspapers. A pamphlet of addenda and corrigenda was issued
in 1968.

ii : The voyage of the *Resolution* and *Adventure*, 1772–1775. 1961.   **21.4c**

Admiralty instructions and the journal of the second voyage, with
appendices containing (i) Cook's letters and reports, (ii) docs. on the
controversy over the *Resolution*, (iii) docs. on the Board of Longitude
and the voyage, (iv) extracts from the journals of Tobias Furneaux,
commander of the *Adventure*, James Burney, Charles Clerke, and
Richard Pickersgill, (v) the journal of William Wales, (vi) verses, 'The
Antarctic muse', by Thomas Perry, (vii) rolls of the ships' companies,
and (viii) a calendar of docs., 29 Aug. 1771–3 May 1776. A pamphlet of
addenda and corrigenda was issued in 1969.

iii: The voyage of the *Resolution* and the *Discovery*, 1776–1780. 1967.   **21.4d**

In two pts., with continuous pagination. Pt. 1 has the Admiralty instructions, the journal of the third voyage, and supplementary extracts from
journals or logs by James King, Clerke, Burney, George Gilbert, and

Thomas Edgar. Pt. 2 has the appendices, containing (i) William Anderson's journal, (ii) David Samwell's journal, (iii) extracts from the journals of Clerke, Burney, John Williamson, Edgar, King, and Alexander Home on Cook as a dietician, (iv) rolls of the ships' companies, and (v) a calendar of docs., 17 Feb. 1774–29 July 1791. A pamphlet addendum to vol. iii, entitled *Cook and the Russians*, was issued in 1973 and corrected in ms. at the request of the Society in 1977.

iv: The life of Captain James Cook. By J. C. Beaglehole. 1974.   **21.**4*e*

38. The journal of Christopher Columbus. Translated by   **21.**5 Cecil Jane, revised and annotated by L. A. Vigneras with an appendix by R. A. Skelton. 1960.

Based on the translation by Cecil Jane, with recourse to the transcription of the ms. by Bartolomé de las Casas made by Cesare de Lollis and Julian Paz for the *Racolta Colombiana* in 1892. Includes Columbus's letter of Feb.–Mar. 1493 describing the results of his first voyage, and ninety illustrations from prints and maps of the period. The introduction gives a brief account of the Las Casas ms., the criticisms made of it, and its editions. The appendix studies the cartography of the first voyage.

39. The principall navigations, voiages and discoveries of the   **21.**6 English nation, by Richard Hakluyt. Imprinted at London, 1589. A photo-lithographic facsimile with an introduction by David Beers Quinn and Raleigh Ashlin Skelton, and with a new index by Alison Quinn. Small folio, 1965.

In 2 pts. with continuous pagination, the first containing Hakluyt's preliminaries, map, first and second parts, and the editor's introduction; the second the 'third and last part', the 'table alphabeticall', and the new index. The introduction assesses the character of Hakluyt's book; traces the book's inception and printing history; discusses Hakluyt's sources (medieval, published English, and unpublished contemporary); comments on Hakluyt's interest in non-literary materials, i.e. 'curiosities', drawings, and maps; and describes Hakluyt's editorial labours leading to the second edition. Bibliographical description and a provisional checklist of surviving copies.

40. The diary of A. J. Mountjoy Jephson: Emin Pasha relief   **21.**7 expedition, 1887–1889. Edited by Dorothy Middleton, with preface, prologue and epilogue compiled by the editor in collaboration with Maurice Denham Jephson. 1969.

Contains about two-thirds of the fullest extant first-hand account of the expedition led by H. M. Stanley to the relief of the governor of the equitorial province of Egypt, isolated in the northern Sudan by the rising and victory of the Mahdi. The abridgements made in this edition are stated in the preface. Narrative introduction (56 pp.), plates, maps.

41. The journals and letters of Sir Alexander Mackenzie.   **21.**8 Edited by W. Kaye Lamb. 1970.

Mackenzie's 'General history of the fur trade from Canada to the North-

West' and his journal of his expedition from Fort Chipewyan (in what is now northern Alberta) to the Pacific in 1793, the texts reprinted from the 1801 edition of the published *Voyages*, in which both were 'edited freely by William Combe', together with his unpublished and hence editorially unaltered journal of his expedition from Fort Chipewyan to the Arctic in 1789, as well as every known extant letter or fragment of a letter written by him. The introduction (52 pp.) is both a life of Mackenzie and an account of the part played by the North West Company in the development of the early fur trade of Canada. Maps, plates.

42. Ying-yai sheng-lan: 'The overall survey of the ocean's shores' by Ma Huan, 1433. Translated from the Chinese text edited by Feng Ch'eng-Chün with introduction, notes and appendices by J. V. G. Mills. 1970.   **21.9**

'The fullest and most interesting account' of China's overseas expansion in the early 15th century, by the interpreter who accompanied the envoy Cheng Ho on three of his enormous naval expeditions. The introduction includes a life of Cheng Ho, with outlines of his seven expeditions, 1405–33, and a life of Ma Huan, with an account of extant versions of his 'Overall survey', a summary of its contents, and a sketch of 'what seem to be the more important matters mentioned'.

The appendices treat of (i) southern Asian place-names as known to the Chinese in 1433, (ii) the Mao K'un map, (iii) ships, seamanship, navigation and related matters, (iv) the Lung ya strait, the course followed by Chinese merchant ships passing between the Malacca strait and the south China sea in 1433, (v) the voyage from Kuala Pasai to Beruwala, (vi) four Chinese stellar diagrams, (vii) the location of La-sa, on the coast of the Arabian peninsula, and (viii) the earliest European rutter of the voyage from Malacca to China, said to be derived from Tomé Pires and to be dated 1514. Maps, plates. Map of southern Asia in end pocket.

23. HARLEIAN SOCIETY, PUBLICATIONS

108. Merchants' marks. By the late Edward Mars Elmhirst. **23.**107
Edited by Leslie Dow. 1959.

An ordinary, claiming to be the first attempted, containing some 1281
marks found in English printed sources and ms. collections. Includes a
memoir of E. M. Elmhirst (*d.* 1957) by the editor, and a brief introduction
by Frank Girling.

109, 110. Visitation of London, 1568, with additional pedi- **23.**108
grees, 1569–90, the arms of the city companies, and a London
subsidy roll, 1589. Edited from the transcripts prepared and
annotated by the late H. Stanford London, by Sophia W.
Rawlins. 1963.

Includes a note by A. Colin Cole on the heraldry of the visitation with
illustrations of arms and crests typical of the Tudor period.

111, 112. The life of William Bruges, the first Garter king of **23.**109
arms. By the late Hugh Stanford London. With a biographical
notice of the author [1884–1959] and a bibliography of his
published writings by Sir Anthony Wagner. 1970.

In the appendices: notes on some contemporary heralds; the will (Latin)
of Richard Bruges, 1415; an abstract of the will of Richard's widow
Katherine Bruges, 1436; the will of William Bruges, 1449; William
Bruges's petition (French) to Hen. V; minutes (French, with the accompanying English version) of a chapter of English heralds held at Rouen, 5
Jan. 1420; a chronological summary of the career of John Smert, Garter
(*d.* ?1478); and summaries of chancery suits concerning Bruges and his
relations. Plates.

113, 114. Rolls of arms, Henry III. The Matthew Paris **23.**110
shields, c. 1244–59, edited by Thomas Daniel Tremlett;
Glover's roll, c. 1253–8, and Walford's roll, c. 1273, edited by
the late Hugh Stanford London; additions and corrections to
A catalogue of English rolls of arms, by Sir Anthony Wagner.
1967.

Vol. ii in the series 'Aspilogia, being materials of heraldry', published by
the Society of Antiquaries. See **23.**100.

115, 116. A catalogue of the earl marshal's papers at Arundel **23.**111

Castle. Prepared by Francis W. Steer, with a foreword by Sir Anthony Wagner. 1964.

117. The visitation of Dorset, 1677, made by Sir Edward Bysshe, knight, Clarenceux king of arms. Transcribed and edited by G. D. Squibb. 1977.   23.112

24. HARLEIAN SOCIETY, PUBLICATIONS, REGISTER SECTION

86, 87. The registers of St. Dunstan in the East, London. Pt.   **24.82**
iii: Baptisms, 1692–1758; marriages, 1692–1754; burials,
1692–1766. Transcribed by R. H. D'Elboux and Winefride
Ward. 1958.

Continues **24.**69, 81.

88. The registers of St. Margaret's, Westminster. Pt. ii: Bap-   **24.83**
tisms, Jan. 1675/6–June 1681; marriages, Jan. 1675/6–Jan.
1681/2; burials, April 1664–Feb. 1665/6. Transcribed by
Winefride Ward. 1958.

Continues **24.**64.

89. The registers of St. Margaret's, Westminster. Pt. iii: Bur-   **24.84**
ials, March 1666–March 1673; christenings, June 1681–
March 1688; weddings, February 1681–September 1699.
Transcribed by Winefride Ward. 1977.

25. HENRY BRADSHAW SOCIETY

85. Ordo breviarii fratrum minorum auctore Fratris Hay-   **25.85**
monis de Faversham (1243-4). [1961].

Issued anonymously. Contains the *ordo breviarii, ordo ad benedicendum mensam*, and *ordo missalis*. Omits the calendar, the texts of the *statuta* and certain later docs.

86. The monastic *ordinale* of St. Vedast's abbey, Arras. Edited   **25.86**
... by Louis Brou. Vol. 1. 1957.

Latin, early 14th century (Arras, Bibliothèque municipale, ms. 230(907)), with introduction (94 pp.) and notes in French. In this vol. the calendar and *temporale*. Map showing relation of the palace and cathedral to the medieval abbey buildings. Text contd. in the following, with continuous pagination.

87. The monastic *ordinale* of St. Vedast's abbey, Arras. Vol.   **25.87**
2. 1957.

Sanctorale, commune sanctorum, the *ordo* in Old French, etc.

88. The benedictionals of Freising. Edited by Robert Amiet,   **25.88**
with additional material by C. Hohler and B. J. Wigan. 1974.

Latin, 8th century (Munich, Bayerische Staatsbibliothek, Cod. lat. 6430). Introduction and notes in French.

89. The *portiforium* of Saint Wulstan. Edited by Anselm   **25.89**
Hughes. Vol. i. 1958.

Latin, with vernacular translations and prayers, c. 1065 (Cambridge, Corpus Christi College ms. 391). Presumably intended for use by St. Wulstan in the cathedral priory at Worcester and when on his travels, and apparently copied from books at or from Winchester, the text gives 'a fairly complete version of the monastic office as it was sung in England shortly before the Norman Conquest'. Concluded, with introduction, in the following.

90. The *portiforium* of Saint Wulstan. Vol. ii. 1960.   **25.90**

91. Manuale ad usum percelebris ecclesia Sarisburiensis.   **25.91**
From the edition printed at Rouen in 1543, compared with those of 1506 (London), 1516 (Rouen), 1523 (Antwerp), 1526 (Paris). By A. Jefferies Collins. 1960.

The introduction argues that 'the Canons of Salisbury ... did not fashion the Manual that lies before us single-handed'. Attention is drawn to the contributions by two 14th-century Englishmen, William of Pagula and John de Burgh, and also to the strictures pronounced by Clement May-deston, a purist in ritualism. 'The printed Sarum Manuals ... placed within the reach of most of the clergy in the Province of Canterbury a standard, not to say authoritative text, their differences being limited to unessentials.' More importantly, they provided an unmatched abundance of instructional rubric.

92. Liber regie capelle. A manuscript in the Biblioteca Pub- **25.92** lica, Evora. Edited by Walter Ullmann, with a note on the music by D. H. Turner. 1961.

An account, in Latin, of the English royal chapel—'the only detailed account which we possess of any medieval royal chapel'—by William Say in 1449, drawn from a then existing custumal or ordinal of the chapel and intended for presentation to Alfonso V of Portugal. Includes a 15th-century recension of the *Liber regalis*.

93. The missal of the New minster, Winchester. Edited by D. **25.93** H. Turner. 1962.

Latin (Le Havre, Bibliothèque municipale, ms. 330). One of 'the five fairly complete mass-books of probable English provenance remaining from before 1100, and the oldest true missal'.

94. The Bec missal. Edited by Anselm Hughes. 1963. **25.94**

A *missale plenum* of the use of the abbey of Bec, written between 1265 and 1272 (Paris, Bibliothèque nationale, ms. lat. 1105). The introduction and footnotes to the text aim to indicate the contribution of the Bec missal to the solution of English liturgical problems, particularly about 'the grouping and the ultimate origins of the various mediaeval Uses in this country'.

95. Missale de Lesnes. Edited by Philip Jebb. 1964. **25.95**

Latin, early 13th century (London, Victoria and Albert Museum, ms. L 404), written for the Augustinian abbey of St. Thomas of Canterbury at Lesnes (Lessness, Liesnes), Kent, its richness seeming to indicate that it was designed for the use of the abbot on chief feasts and other special occasions.

96. The Bridgettine breviary of Syon abbey. Edited by A. **25.96** Jefferies Collins. 1969.

Latin, with English rubrics, c. 1370 (Cambridge, Magdalene College ms. F.4.11), the rubrics 'tacitly acknowledging that mastery of Latin would be an accomplishment rare in nuns'. The introduction includes an outline history of the Order, in Sweden, and of the foundation and subsequent moves of the English house.

97. The Claudius pontificals. Edited by D. H. Turner. 1971. **25.97**

Three fragmentary pontificals, Latin, 10th, 11th and 12th centuries respectively, from B.L., Cotton ms. Claudius A. iii. Detailed descriptive introduction.

98. Expositio antiquae liturgiae gallicanae. Edited by the late **25.98** E. C. Ratcliff. 1971.

The letters of pseudo-Germanus, Latin, 9th century (Autun, Bibliothèque municipale, ms. 184), the text reconstructed in part. No critical apparatus. Introductory note by Bernard Wigan. Palaeographical note by Francis Wormald.

99. The customary of the Benedictine abbey of Bury St. Ed- **25.99** munds in Suffolk. Edited by Antonia Gransden. 1973.

Latin, written in or soon after 1234 (B.L., Harleian ms. 1005), concerned in the main with the respective rights and duties of the abbot and the obedientiaries. Includes other docs. of earlier and later dates relating to the customs of the abbey. The introduction includes an account of monastic administration and the observance of the Rule in the abbey during the 12th and 13th centuries.

100. The Cracow pontifical. Pontificale Cracoviense saeculi **25.100** XI. Edited by Z. Obertýnski. 1977.

Latin, third quarter of the 11th century (Cracow, Jagellionian Library, ms. 2057). Editorial introduction and notes in German. Forewords by Alexander Gieysztor and Jadwiga Karwasinska.

26. HUGUENOT SOCIETY OF LONDON, PUBLICATIONS, QUARTO SERIES

46. A calendar of the correspondence of J. H. Ott, 1658–1671, **26.46** in the library of the Huguenot Society of London. Edited by Leonard Forster. 1960.
Correspondence between Johann Heinrich Ott (1617–82) and the principal Calvinist theologians of his day.

47. The register of the reformed church at Le Mans, 1650– **26.47** 1685. Edited by Sir Charles Clay, with an appendix by Arthur Grimwade on Pezé Pilleau, goldsmith. 1961.
Transcript, French. Baptisms, 1669–84; marriages and burials, 1650–84. With genealogical table showing ancestry of Pezé Pilleau (d. 1776).

48. Actes du consistoire de l'église française de Threadneedle **26.48** Street, Londres. Vol. ii: 1571–1577. Edited by Anne M. Oakley. 1969.
Transcript, French. Continues **26.38**.

49. French protestant refugees relieved through the Thread- **26.49** needle Street church, London, 1681–1687. By A. P. Hands and Irene Scouloudi. 1971.

Alphabetical register, drawn from ms. and printed sources, the entries summarized, annotated and classified.

50. The archives of the French protestant church of London: **26.50** a handlist compiled by Raymond Smith. 1972.
With notes on the amalgamated churches of L'Artillerie, La Patente Spitalfields and St. Jean Spitalfields.

51. Records of the Royal Bounty and connected funds, the **26.51** Burn donation, and the Savoy church, in the Huguenot library, University College, London: a handlist compiled by Raymond Smith. 1974.
Relating to (i) funds which afforded relief to French protestant refugees and their descendants in the period 1686–1876, (ii) 26 congregations in London, two in Canterbury, and one each in Thorpe-le-Soken and Sandwich, and (iii) the Savoy church archive.

52. The French protestant hospital: extracts from the archives 26.52
of 'La Providence' relating to inmates and applications for
admission, 1718-1957, and to recipients of and applicants for
the Coqueau charity, 1745-1901. Compiled by Charles F. A.
Marmoy. Vol. i: Introduction; entries A-K. 1977.
Contd. in the following.

53. The French protestant hospital Vol. ii: Entries L-Z; 26.53
appendices. 1977.

The appendices list (i) districts and places of origin, (ii) trades and occupations, (iii) guarantors and sponsors giving financial aid to inmates, (iv)
committees, churches and societies contributing to the maintenance of
inmates.

54. A calendar of the letter books of the French church of 26.54
London from the civil war to the restoration, 1643-1659. Edited by Robin D. Gwynn. 1979.

The introduction surveys the composition, organization and history of the
French church of London in the 1640s and 1650s, as well as, though more
briefly, the French congregations at Canterbury, Dover, Norwich, Sand-
toft, Southampton, Thorney, and Whittlesey. Appended is a photographic
reproduction of the 1915 edition, in French and English, of the 1641
Discipline of the French protestant church in London.

55. The case book of 'La maison de charité de Spittlefields', 26.55
1739-41. Edited by Charles F. A. Marmoy. 1981.

Transcript of the register of recipients of 'portions' (originally of bread,
soup and meat) distributed to poor French protestants during a period
which experienced one of the hardest winters of the century. A redrawn
map of Spitalfields (based on John Rocque's of 1746) shows the area
served by 'La Soupe', the Huguenot churches of the area, and the streets
where the needy refugees most commonly lived.

27. JEWISH HISTORICAL SOCIETY OF ENGLAND*

Calendar of the plea rolls of the exchequer of the Jews pre-   **27.3**
served in the Public Record Office and the British Museum.
Vol. iv: Henry III, 1272; Edward I, 1275–1277. Edited by H.
G. Richardson. 1972.

Most entries calendared in English, with full Latin text of 'some entries
important on account of form or content'. Contains the plea rolls of Easter
term, 56 Hen. III (1272) and Hilary, 5 Edw. I (1277), and the memoranda
rolls of Hilary, 3 Edw. I (1275) and Michaelmas 3–4 Edw. I. In the
appendices, full Latin text and English translation of rolls of receipts from
the Jews of Canterbury, 35–38 Hen. III, and from Jews in the Tower of
London, 2–5 Edw. I.

Bevis Marks records. Pt. iii: Abstracts of the *ketubot* or   **27.8**
marriage-contracts and of the civil marriage registers of the
Spanish and Portuguese Jews' Congregation for the period
1837–1901, with an introduction and an index by G. H.
Whitehill. 1973.

Published jointly with the Spanish and Portuguese Jews' Congregation.
The abstracts combine the information given in the *ketubot* with that to be
found in the civil register, the civil registration being obligatory from
1837, when the Registration Act of 1836 came into force.

The introduction describes the typical *ketubah* or Hebrew–Aramaic
marriage-contract, as well as variations upon it; the procedure for marriages according to the usages of the Jews in England and Wales; the state
of the Bevis Marks congregation during the early Victorian period (1837–
60), and identifies three factors which seem to have made this period 'a
time of stagnation or even decline'. Statistical information is given regarding the number of marriages, of marriages with Ashkenazim, of marriages
with proselytes, the number of illiterates, the average age of the parties,
their addresses and occupations.

Abstracts of the *ketubot* from 1687 to 1837 were published as *Bevis
Marks records*, pt. ii, in 1949. Pt. i, containing the early history of the
congregation from the beginning until 1800, appeared in 1940. Both pts.
were published by the Board of Elders.

---

*Record publications only.

28. NAVY RECORDS SOCIETY, PUBLICATIONS

98. The private correspondence of Admiral Lord Colling- **28.**98
wood. Edited by Edward Hughes. 1957.

Letters to his unmarried sisters in Newcastle, 1776–1810, to Dr. Alexander ('Jupiter') Carlyle, 1792–1805, to Sir Edward Blackett, 1792–1804, to Mrs. Stead, 1801–9, and to Adm. Purvis, 1806–10. In the appendices, an account of the battle off Cape St. Vincent by William Christie, schoolmaster of the *Excellent*, and letters from the Duke of Northumberland, 1808–9. Excludes all letters printed in the *Memoir* (1828) and all official letters written when Collingwood was c.-in-c. Mediterranean.

99. The Vernon papers. Edited by B. McL. Ranft. 1958. **28.**99

Transcripts, shortened occasionally, of all significant docs. dealing with Vernon's command in the West Indies, 1739–42, and of a selection relating to his command in the English Channel, 1745, each section with its own introductory narrative and commentary, the West Indies section having additional introductions dealing with operations, signals and tactics, and administration, training and discipline.

100. Nelson's letters to his wife, and other documents, 1785– **28.**100
1831. Edited by George P. B. Naish. 1958.

Nelson to Lady Nelson, 1785–1800, and Lady Nelson to Nelson, 1794, 1797–1801, with docs. relating to Nelson's services, 1785–1800, and a few other docs., the latest in date being Lady Nelson's will and its codicils, the whole arranged chronologically in seven chapters, each chapter with its own introduction. Pedigrees of Nelson of Burnham Thorpe and Herbert of Nevis. Facismiles and plates. The edition for public sale (Routledge & Kegan Paul Ltd.) has more illustrations.

101. A memoir of James Trevenen. Edited by Christopher **28.**101
Lloyd and R. C. Anderson. 1959.

Trevenen, born 1 Jan. 1760, served as midshipman in 1776 with Cook on his last voyage to the South Seas, was promoted lieutenant in 1780, travelled in England and Scotland, France and Italy, and being still unemployed joined the Russian naval service, losing his life in the war with Sweden, 9 July 1790. This vol. is drawn from one of two ms. copies of the memoir written by Trevenen's brother-in-law, Adm. Sir Charles Vinicombe Penrose, the editors including everything of naval interest written by Trevenen but omitting much of Penrose's editorial matter, and supplying introductions to the British and Russian sections.

102. The papers of Admiral Sir John Fisher. Edited by P. K. Kemp. Vol. i. 1960. **28.**102

Official papers written by or at the instigation of Fisher as First Sea Lord from 21 Oct. 1904 and submitted by him to the Board of Admiralty as declarations of naval policy, preceded by the editor's general introduction. The papers are arranged in four parts, each part with its own introduction, tables, appendices and designs, viz. Fisher's scheme of reform (the whole-sale scrapping of obsolete warships, the reorganization of fleets and squadrons, and the nucleus crew system for ships of the reserve fleet), printed and circulated to the Board under the title *Naval Necessities*, I; his committee on the design of new ships; the *Dreadnought* controversy (a selection of printed papers); and his ideas about the garrisoning of Gibraltar. Contd. in **28.**106 below.

103. Queen Anne's navy: documents concerning the administration of the navy of Queen Anne, 1702-1714. Selected and edited by R. D. Merriman. 1961. **28.**103

Correspondence between the Admiralty and Navy boards and between these and the Navy Board's subsidiaries, the Victualling and Sick and Wounded boards, with letters to and from the dockyards, flag officers, captains, and other individuals, arranged (as in **28.**89) to illustrate the principal branches of naval administration. Appended are lists of the Admiralty, commissioners of the boards, ships added and removed, the navy on 1 Aug. 1714, the annual numbers of workmen in each royal dockyard, categories of tradesmen in the dockyards, and officers of the dockyards at 1 Aug. 1714.

104. The navy and South America, 1807-1823: correspondence of the commanders-in-chief on the South American station. Edited by Gerald S. Graham and R. A. Humphreys. 1962. **28.**104

Selected from the correspondence of the five commanders-in-chief and their subordinates, viz. R.-adm. Sir William Sidney Smith, V.-adm. the Hon. Michael de Courcy, R.-adm. Manley Dixon, Commodore William Bowles, and Commodore Sir Thomas Hardy, to illustrate the rôle of the Royal Navy during the movement towards South American independence and the course of the movement itself. Maps.

105. Documents relating to the civil war, 1642-1648. Edited by J. R. Powell and E. K. Timings. 1963. **28.**105

From many sources, printed as well as unprinted, chosen to 'reveal what it [the fleet] did, and the abilities of the men who led it', arranged year by year, each year preceded by a brief outline of the course of events. Docs. already in print dealing with operations off Ireland and the Channel Islands have been omitted and 'some of the less important documents printed as epitomised in the Calendar of State Papers'.

106. The papers of Admiral Sir John Fisher. Vol. ii. 1964. **28.**106

General introduction followed, in pt. 1, by Fisher's modernization and reorganization proposals as set out in his *Naval Necessities* II and III, and in pt. 2 his *War Plans*, each pt. with its own introduction.

107. The health of seamen: selections from the works of Dr. James Lind, Sir Gilbert Blane and Dr. Thomas Trotter. Edited by Christopher Lloyd. 1965.   **28.**107

> Extracts from Lind's *Treatise of the scurvy* (1753) and *Essay on the most effectual means of preserving the health of seamen* (3rd edition, 1779, with its appended papers on fever and infections); from Blane's *Observations on the diseases of seamen* (2nd edition, 1789) and dissertation on the comparative health of the navy, 1779-1814; and from Trotter's *Medicina nautica* (2nd edition, 1804).

108. The Jellicoe papers: selections from the private and official correspondence of Admiral of the Fleet Earl Jellicoe of Scapa. Edited by A. Temple Patterson. Vol. i: 1893-1916. 1966.   **28.**108

> Early career and World War I to the battle of Jutland, 31 May 1916, its preliminaries and aftermath, with diagrams. General and four sectional introductions. Contd. in **28.**111 below.

109. Documents relating to Anson's voyage round the world, 1740-1744. Edited by Glyndwr Williams. 1967.   **28.**109

> From ms. and newspaper evidence, much of it never before sufficiently investigated, supplementing or challenging accepted views on, especially, the origins of the expedition, the capture of the Acapulco treasure galleon, and the authorship of the 1748 account of the voyage, issued under the name of Richard Walter but held by the editor to be Anson's own apologia, 'ghosted' for him by Benjamin Robins. Plates.

110. The Saumarez papers: selections from the Baltic correspondence of Vice-Admiral Sir James Saumarez, 1808-1812. Edited by A. N. Ryan. 1968.   **28.**110

> Two hundred and fifty items shedding 'new light on the war at sea, as well as upon European history, in the post-Trafalgar period ... and upon the career of a distinguished officer whose unique contribution to the war was to keep open the gates of northern Europe after Napoleon had decreed that they be closed'.

111. The Jellicoe papers. Vol. ii: 1916-1935, with an appendix on the papers of Vice-Admiral J. E. T. Harper. 1968.   **28.**111

> Further selections, covering his last months at sea, his year as First Sea Lord, subsequent unemployment, the Empire mission, the Jutland controversy and his last years. The appendix contains Adm. Harper's narrative of the exchanges between himself and the Admiralty to July 1927 concerning the Admiralty's decision in 1920 to postpone indefinitely the publication of the record or account of the battle of Jutland prepared by Harper and others. Editorial introductions to all sections.

112. The Rupert and Monck letter book, 1666, together with **28.**112 supporting documents. Edited by J. R. Powell and E. K. Timings. 1969.

In two parts, each with editorial introduction, the first being the letter book of the joint admirals Prince Rupert and George Monck, duke of Albemarle, in the Dartmouth mss., the second containing 93 docs. from numerous sources elucidating the letter book and especially the division of the fleet, the Four Days' battle, and the St. James's day fight. On the two last, see the introduction to **28.**80.

113. Documents relating to the Naval Air Service. Edited by **28.**113 S. W. Roskill. Vol. i: 1908–1918. 1969.

A selection of papers from the earliest beginnings of naval aviation to the end of World War I, dealing with administrative and organizational issues, or throwing light on persons involved in the controversy over the Naval Air Service. The only operational records included are those which to the editor seemed of exceptional interest or had not been published before. General introduction and separate introductions to the five parts. Glossary of initial letter abbreviations. Appendix I: Growth of the R.N.A.S., 4 Aug. 1914–1 Apr. 1918. Appendix II: Disposition of R.N.A.S. aircraft 'as reported 30th March 1918', before their transfer to the R.A.F.

114. The siege and capture of Havana, 1762. Edited by David **28.**114 Syrett. 1970.

A documentary account of 'the largest, the most complex and perhaps the most difficult campaign undertaken by the British during the Seven Years' war'. More than 500 docs. on the preparations for the campaign, the administrative arrangements, the mobilization and deployment of person-nel and material, as well as naval strategy and operations. Maps and plates. Detailed introduction. Appended are Lt.-gen. David Dundas's narrative of the campaign and his observations on its conduct, being the first two sections of the memorandum he wrote in 1800.

115. Policy and operations in the Mediterranean, 1912–14. **28.**115 Edited by E. W. R. Lumby. 1970.

Docs. dealing with (i) the debate on strategy and the Anglo-French con-versations, 30 Apr. 1912–9 May 1914, (ii) the escape of *Goeben* and *Breslau*, 27 July–12 Aug. 1914, (iii) the court of inquiry and subsequent court martial of R.-adm. Troubridge, 7 Sept.–9 Nov. 1914 (these docs. published by special permission of the Ministry of Defence and with the consent of the Troubridge family), and (iv) operations after the escape, 13 Aug.–31 Dec. 1914. General introduction and introductions to the four parts. Maps of the shadowing and chase of the two cruisers.

116. The Jacobean commissions of enquiry, 1608 and 1618. **28.**116 Edited by A. P. McGowan. 1971.

The depositions concerning embezzlement and corruption in naval affairs laid before the commission of 1608, and the report of the commission of 1618. Introduction concludes: 'if the 1608 Commission of Enquiry had been a dismal failure, that of 1618 was an almost unqualified success'.

117. The Keyes papers: selections from the private and official **28.**117
correspondence of Admiral of the Fleet Baron Keyes of Zee-
brugge. Edited by Paul G. Halpern. Vol. i: 1914–1918. 1972.

Covering (i) Keyes' war service as commodore of the Submarine Service,
Aug. 1914–Feb. 1915, (ii) the Dardanelles expedition, Feb. 1915–Jan.
1916, (iii) his service in the Aegean, then with the Second Battle Squadron
and as second-in-command of the Fourth, Jan. 1916–Sept. 1917, and (iv)
his service as Director of Plans, Oct.–Dec. 1917, and Vice-Admiral at
Dover, Jan.–Dec. 1918. Glossary of initial-letter abbreviations. Maps.
Contd. in **28.**121, 122 below.

118. The Royal Navy and North America: the Warren papers, **28.**118
1736–1752. Edited by Julian Gwyn. 1973.

Mainly letters to or from Captain (later V.-adm. Sir) Peter Warren, with
some others in which he is prominently mentioned, all previously unprinted, selected because of their concern with the 1745 seige of Louis-
bourg and its aftermath, or with the proposed conquest of Canada in 1746.
Introduction. Biographical notices of persons mentioned. Directory of
Warren papers of related interest published elsewhere. Maps, plans,
plates.

119. The manning of the Royal Navy: selected public pam- **28.**119
phlets, 1693–1873. Edited by J. S. Bromley. 1974.

Twenty-five published pamphlets re-printed and annotated, with a
general introduction and, as appendices, *A translation of the French King's
ordinance relating to the enrolling of sea-officers, sailors, and sea-faring people*
(1689), *Marine plan* (1780), Captain Marryat, R.N., on the disposition of
a ship's company (1822), Sir John Barrow on manning the navy (1839),
part of the report of the Manning Commission (1859), the revised regulations for the Royal Naval Reserve (1873), and biographical notices of all
the authors.

120. Naval administration, 1715–1750. Edited by Daniel A. **28.**120
Baugh. 1977.

Modelled on and in continuation of **28.**103 above. Docs. selected chiefly
but not exclusively from Admiralty memorials to the King in Council,
letters to the Admiralty from flag officers and the Navy and Victualling
boards, letters from dockyard commissioners and officers to the Navy
Board, and Navy Board orders to the yards, grouped into chapters to
illustrate the most challenging problems of the era and the means chosen
to deal with them. In the appendix, lists of Admiralty Board, Admiralty
secretaries, Navy Board and Victualling Board, 1715–1750.

121. The Keyes papers. Vol. ii: 1919–1938. 1980. **28.**121

Covering the activities of Lord Keyes during the interwar period when he
was successively Rear-Admiral commanding Battle Cruiser Squadron and
deputy chief of naval staff (1919–25), c.-in-c. Mediterranean station
(1925–28), c.-in-c. Portsmouth (1929–31), and M.P. for Portsmouth
North (from Feb. 1934 onwards). Issues of major concern to him in the

1930s were the Invergordon mutiny and the control of the Fleet Air Arm. Maps.

122. The Keyes papers. Vol. iii: 1939–1945. 1981.   28.122

(i) From the outbreak of war, Sept. 1939, to the fall of France, July 1940, (ii) service as director of Combined Operations, July 1940–Oct. 1941, and (iii) the final phase, Nov. 1941–Dec. 1945, with Keyes active in the Commons and Lords, touring the Normandy beaches in July 1944, visiting in the course of a goodwill mission to Australia and New Zealand General MacArthur's advanced headquarters on New Guinea and witnessing the American invasion of Leyte in the Philippines. List of operation code names. Tables showing naval resources available to Combined Operations on 27 July 1940 and 25 Aug. 1941, and the weekly statement of landing craft and carriers at 15 Oct. 1941. Maps.

123. The navy of the Lancastrian kings: accounts and inven-   28.123
tories of William Soper, keeper of the king's ships, 1422–1427.
Edited by Susan Rose. 1982.

Readily understandable translation from the original work-a-day Latin, with appended fragmentary accounts for ship repairs c. 1417 and the duke of Bedford's expeditions of 1416; select biographies of persons mentioned in the accounts; a descriptive list of vessels in the charge of the clerk of the king's ships temp. Hen. V and Hen. VI; and a glossary of technical terms. The introduction is concerned with the life and work of William Soper (d. 1459); the owning of ships directly by the crown from the reign of John to the mid-15th century; the development of financial, constructional, and administrative procedures; the ships and their voyages.

30. PIPE ROLL SOCIETY, PUBLICATIONS*

70 (32). Feet of fines for the county of Norfolk ... 1201-1215,   **30.70**
for the county of Suffolk ... 1199-1214. Edited by Barbara
Dodwell. 1958.

> Contains, with **30.**65, all those final concords for the reign of John in the
> Public Records which have been labelled Norfolk or Suffolk, those East
> Anglian concords contained in the 'unknown' and 'divers counties' files,
> and two which had been wrongly assigned to other counties. The detailed,
> analytical introduction includes a description of the docs. and of their
> filing holes and slits.

71 (33). The *cartae antiquae*, rolls 11-20. Edited by J. Conway   **30.**71
Davies. 1960.

> Continues **30.**55. Full text, Latin, of all docs. not printed in full in official
> publications.

72 (34). Interdict documents. Edited by Patricia M. Barnes   **30.**72
and W. Raymond Powell. 1960.

> John fitz Hugh's survey, 1210, of church lands in Wiltshire seized by King
> John, and the small fragment of another relating to the same county,
> edited with a consideration of the dating and a summary of fitz Hugh's
> career by W. R. Powell, together with docs. edited by P. M. Barnes
> concerning the cathedral priory of Christ Church, Canterbury, viz. the
> exchequer inquest of 1211 into its temporalities, the claim for issues,
> 1207-8, and the claim for damages, 1207-13, with an introduction exam-
> ining in some detail 'the king's treatment of a single house ... which he
> judged guilty of usurping his rights and disobeying his command'.

73 (35). The great roll of the pipe for the sixteenth year of the   **30.**73
reign of King John, Michaelmas 1214. (Pipe roll 60). Edited
by Patricia M. Barnes. 1962.

> Transcript, Latin, with introduction.

74 (36). A medieval miscellany for Doris Mary Stenton.   **30.**74
General editors Patricia M. Barnes and C. F. Slade. 1962.

> The Anstey case. Edited by Patricia M. Barnes. [Transcripts, Latin, of   **30.**74*a*
> Richard of Anstey's account, drawn up in 1167, of the expenses incurred

---

* The 'new series' numbers are shown on the left in round brackets.

by him in establishing his claim to succeed William de Sackville, his uncle, and the papal rescript to which it was formerly sewn.]

Some charters of the earls of Chester. Edited by G. Barraclough. [Transcripts, Latin, of 14 charters earlier in date than 1215, including three which illustrate the system of 'avowries' in Cheshire.] **30.74b**

Episcopal charters for Wix priory. Edited by C. N. L. Brooke. [Transcripts, Latin, of seven episcopal charters, with a provisional list of the 12th-century forgeries and a consideration of when and where they were made.] **30.74c**

Early charters of Sibton abbey, Suffolk. Edited by R. Allen Brown. [Transcripts, Latin, of 12 charters, mostly 12th-century.] **30.74d**

Norman and Wessex charters of the Roumare family. Edited by F. A. Cazel, Jnr. [Transcripts, Latin, of eight charters, late 12th-century, two concerning Cleeve abbey.] **30.74e**

The original charters of Herbert and Gervase, abbots of Westminster, 1121–1157. Edited by Pierre Chaplais. [Transcripts, Latin, of two deeds by abbot Herbert, and of six by abbot Gervase of Blois, supporting the contentions that 'as late as the mid-twelfth century the royal chancery had not acquired the complete monopoly of the writing of royal charters' and that 'the vast majority of royal charters of the period . . . produced outside the royal *scriptorium* consist of fabrications, based on genuine grants which no longer satisfied the needs of the grantees concerned'. The appendix prints the forged 'original' foundation charter of Hurley priory, 1085–6, in parallel with the text of a copy of the genuine original, and likewise the forged 'original' and the genuine original of a charter of Stephen for Westminster abbey, 1151.] **30.74f**

Winchcombe annals, 1049–1181. Edited by R. R. Darlington. [Transcript, Latin, of one of two texts collated with the other, showing that down to 1138 the Winchcombe annalist drew on the *Chronicon ex chronicis*, introducing errors and confusions sufficient to suggest 'a high degree of incompetence'.] **30.74g**

Treaty between William earl of Gloucester and Roger earl of Hereford. Edited by R. H. C. Davis. [Transcript, Latin, of the treaty made early in the period 1147–50, basically a renewal of the treaty made by the two earls' fathers. The introduction compares the two treaties and shows that the later treaty is 'a great deal more precise' and 'that the conditions which it stipulates are all in the interest of the earl of Hereford', described by the editor as 'evidently a specialist in treaties of conditional love, having one with the earl of Gloucester, one with the earl of Leicester, and a third with Stephen'. The earlier treaty is reconsidered.] **30.74h**

Some charters relating to the honour of Bacton. Edited by Barbara Dodwell. [Transcripts, Latin, of 11 charters of the first half of the 12th century (six from the registers of Norwich cathedral priory, five from the muniments of Wix priory) throwing some light upon the later history of the Domesday holding in Suffolk and Essex of Theodoric, brother of Walter the deacon, and in particular explaining how it was that Edith, widow of Edward the Confessor and possibly daughter of **30.74i**

Walter, came to hold at Purleigh in Essex land which had belonged to Theodoric. Two of the charters relate to the church of St. Edmund of Hoxne; one of these is the foundation charter for the cell at Hoxne.]

Willoughby deeds. Edited by J. C. Holt. [Transcripts, Latin, of all the surviving docs. concerned with the purchase of land in Willoughby-on-the-Wolds by Ralph Bugge, merchant of Nottingham, together with other docs. belonging to the first half of the 13th century illustrating the descent of properties in Willoughby before the completion of Bugge's purchases *c.* 1240, and one 12th-century charter noted by W. H. Stevenson but not printed in his report on the mss. of Lord Middleton in 7.93. The docs. are of interest 'as illustrations of the acquisition of landed estate by a merchant' and because 'they demonstrate, within the bounds of a single village, a tenurial situation of astonishing complexity'.] **30.74*j***

A pre-Domesday Kentish assessment list. Edited by Robert S. Hoyt. [Transcript, Latin, of Lambeth Palace ms. 1212, p. 340. The closely argued introduction concludes that the list is neither an index to nor an epitome of Domesday Book but independent of Domesday and anterior to it: an administrative document the deficiencies of which may well illustrate one of the reasons leading to the decision to survey the whole of England in detail.] **30.74*k***

Blyborough charters. Edited by Kathleen Major. [Transcripts, Latin, of all the charters produced by the prior of Durham in support of the monks' claim to the church in Blyborough, 1214-15, and others relating to the same church and property.] **30.74*l***

Some Revesby charters of the soke of Bolingbroke. Edited by Dorothy M. Owen. [Transcripts, Latin, of 14 charters of between *c.* 1170 and 1198 relating to Stickney, some four miles from Revesby, in the wapentake and soke of Bolingbroke. Only seven of these occur in the 12th-century list of its charters which is the single entry for Revesby abbey in G. R. C. Davis's *Medieval cartularies of Great Britain.* The introduction outlines the post-Dissolution descent of the abbey's properties and docs., and considers the significance of the individual charters.] **30.74*m***

Whitley deeds of the twelfth century. By C. F. Slade. [Transcripts, Latin, of 13 deeds, some of them existing both as originals and as cartulary copies, interesting for local agrarian history and as the only sources of information for the creation by Reading abbey of a park at 'Cumba', its name later becoming Whitley.] **30.74*n***

Some charters relating to St. Peter's abbey, Gloucester. Edited by David Walker. [Transcripts, Latin, of 16 charters illustrating 'the process by which titles to lands and tenements were gradually made more explicit as the twelfth century advanced' and illustrating also 'something of the way in which disputes, and the formal agreements by which they were settled, came more and more into the purview of the king's justices'. The two latest docs. are dated to Nov. 1203.] **30.74*o***

A list of the published writings of Doris Mary Stenton. **30.74*p***

75 (37). Pipe roll 17 John, edited by R. A. Brown, and praes- **30.75**

85

tita roll 14–18 John, roll of summonses 1214, scutage roll 16 John, edited by J. C. Holt. 1964.

This vol. concludes the Society's work on the pipe rolls attributed to John's reign. Appended to Dr. Brown's introduction is a transcript of a further account for Yorkshire for half the year 17 John, evidently a later version of the account on the pipe roll 17 John, and a transcript of the statement on the sheriffdom of Norfolk and Suffolk from the K. R. Memoranda roll of 2 Hen. III. The docs. edited by Professor Holt make available 'for the first time ... some of the detailed organization behind early thirteenth century English armies'. His introduction includes a transcript of a fragment of a praestita roll of 14 John, 1212–13. The summonses were for the army taken to Poitou.

76 (38). The cartulary of Worcester cathedral priory (Register I). Edited by R. R. Darlington. 1968.

30.76

Transcript, Latin, with brief English summaries, of the cartulary compiled *c.* 1240, the text of the original doc. being preferred to that of the cartulary whenever it has been found.

The introduction (56 pp.) describes the kinds of docs. found in the cartulary, viz. royal charters (the only pre-Conquest doc. being the 'rather famous charter of King Edgar concerning the triple hundred of Oswaldslaw', thought by the editor to be 'too obviously framed in the interests of the monks to carry conviction'); charters of other laymen; charters relating to city properties; papal docs.; charters of the bishops of Worcester and other prelates (an excursus on the identity of the London church of St. Mary 'at the Strand' leads to the tentative conclusion that this is St. Mary le Strand and that it was known by this name 'much earlier than is generally supposed'); the priors of Worcester and their charters; and the archdeacons of the diocese. Appended is a transcript of the charter of King Stephen which, if genuine, belongs to 1136–9, the editor hesitating to accept the view that it is a forgery even though it shows several abnormalities, as in the regnal style and the seal.

77 (39). The great roll of the pipe for the second year of the reign of King Henry III, Michaelmas 1218. (Pipe roll 62). Edited by E. Pauline Ebden. 1972.

30.77

Transcript, Latin, with introduction.

78 (40). The charters of Norwich cathedral priory. Edited by Barbara Dodwell. Pt. 1. 1974.

30.78

Transcripts, Latin, of royal and episcopal grants to the cathedral priory and to the hospital of St. Paul; of royal grants pertaining to the bishopric; of archiepiscopal grants to the cathedral priory; of papal privileges to the cathedral priory and hospital, and of final concords, few of the docs. in these groups being earlier than 1100 or later than 1300, with *addenda*, 1298–1315. Docs. printed in other Pipe Roll Soc. vols., and royal *acta* of the reigns of Hen. III and Edw. I calendared elsewhere, are here given in English summary.

The introduction describes the growth of the archive, the security provided, the early arrangement of the muniments by sacrist and cellarer, the trend towards centralization in the early 14th century, the ensuing half-century of archival activity, and the compilation of registers and cartularies. The post-Dissolution history of the muniments is contd. into the preparation of this vol., when each of the original docs. here printed 'had to be located in a mass of over five thousand documents'. Nine surviving registers and an inventory are considered in detail as also is the scriptorium from the mid-12th century through to the late 13th.

79 (41). Liber memoralis Doris Mary Stenton, honorary secretary to the Pipe Roll Society 1923–1961. 1976.

30.79

A memoir of Lady Stenton (1894–1971) by C. F. Slade, including a summary history of the Pipe Roll Soc. from its formation in 1883 until her appointment as its secretary, followed by a list of her writings, 1962–72, continuing the list in **30.74**, with consolidated indexes (by Margaret Walker) to all the introductions to the pipe rolls and other financial records published by the Soc. for the reigns of Hen. II, Rich. I and John. Maitland's introduction to **30.14**, discussing how money was raised for Rich. I's ransom, is included in the consolidated indexes.

80 (42). The great roll of the pipe for the third year of the reign of King Henry III, Michaelmas 1219. (Pipe roll 63). 1976.

30.80

Text prepared by Jean Deas and Patricia M. Barnes, the introduction by B. E. Harris, the indexes by David Crook and B. E. Harris.

81 (43). The Beauchamp cartulary: charters, 1100–1268. Edited by Emma Mason. 1980.

30.81

Transcripts, Latin, with brief English summaries, of those docs. earlier than 1269 which relate to the Beauchamp and Mauduit estates, the lands of the Newburgh earls of Warwick, lands in Warwickshire acquired by the Beauchamps in the late-13th and early-14th centuries, and to fitz Geoffrey and Tosny lands acquired by the Beauchamps on marriage. The extent and history of these lands, and the offices held by the Beauchamp and Mauduit families, are treated in the introduction. Maps. Genealogical tables of Beauchamp of Elmley (to 1269), Mauduit of Hanslope, and Tosny of Flamstead.

82 (44). Roll of divers accounts for the early years of the reign of Henry III; account of escheats for the sixteenth, seventeenth and eighteenth years of the reign of Henry III; wardrobe receipt roll and fragments of household roll, 10 Henry III. Edited by Fred A. Cazel, Jr. 1982.

30.82

Transcripts, Latin, of (i) all the accounts on the five original rotulets of the *Rotulus de diversis compotis* (including the four accounts previously published, republished here 'to preserve the integrity of the record'), with the added sixth rotulet for the roll of the fortieth of 1232, the six together now classified as a Foreign roll, 'which does some violence to its uniqueness as an experiment of the Exchequer of the minority of Henry III'; (ii) escheators' accounts 'of exactly the same time as the Roll of the Fortieth, and like it separately enrolled', included here 'because they are of such great similarity to the *Rotulus de diversis compotis*'; (iii) the earliest extant wardrobe receipt roll; and (iv) the remaining fragments of the earliest household roll of the wardrobe. The make-up and matter of the rolls are minutely described, questions raised by their form and nature are considered, and their contribution to the history of Henry III's minority is indicated.

33. ROYAL HISTORICAL SOCIETY, CAMDEN THIRD SERIES

89. The chronicle of Walter of Guisborough, previously edited as the chronicle of Walter of Hemingford or Hemingburgh. Edited by Harry Rothwell. 1957.

Latin. From 1066 to 1315. The introduction describes and classifies the ten mss. in which the chronicle survives in whole or in part, the numerous other mss. in which considerable portions of the chronicle are preserved in an adapted form, and the transcripts whose originals are still extant. None is the original of the chronicle, or even an immediate copy of it. Elaborate textual analysis leads to the selection of one particular ms., now lost, as 'the source of all known manuscripts of the chronicle proper and of the adaptation made at Leicester [and preserved in Henry Knighton's chronicle]'. Though 'not the original, but a copy already corrupt', the lost ms. is advanced as 'the earliest recoverable text' and as 'almost if not quite ... as near to the original text ... as we can get with the manuscripts available'. Similarly elaborate investigation supports the attribution to 'Walter of Guisborough' as 'the only name that the manuscripts will justify'. And since Walter 'was remote from much he wrote of', and his information either not precise or not precisely reported by him, his usefulness to the historian depends upon when he wrote. The editor inclines to the view that the chronicle was not begun before 1300, that the bulk of it was written very quickly by Walter who in fact carried it on into 1305, and that the entries to 1312 and jottings to 1315 were the work of a continuator or continuators 'for whom ... it would be well to look in the direction of Durham'.

90. Camden miscellany. Vol. xxi. 1958.   **33.90**

The chronicle attributed to John of Wallingford. Edited by Richard Vaughan. 1958. [Transcript, Latin. Pre-Conquest history from Brutus to Cnut and hagiology evidently excerpted from a *legenda sanctorum*, the whole written after about 1220 and before 1258, the historical parts and the lives of the saints having 'scattered pieces of information not recorded elsewhere'. Doubtless a St. Albans production, and in some ways strikingly similar to Roger of Wendover's *Flores*, there are reasons enough for believing that Roger and the anonymous chronicler are wholly independent.]

A journal of events during the Gladstone ministry, 1868-1874, by John, first earl of Kimberley. Edited by Ethel Drus. 1958. [Transcript. Introductory outline and appraisal of Kimberley's opinions and career.]

91. The diurnal of Thomas Rugg, 1659–1661. Edited by **33.91**
William Sachse. 1961.

Transcript of about one-third of the journal, from May 1659 to Apr. 1661, seemingly written month by month, in content 'something of a hodge-podge', and in large measure a London chronicle. The introduction identifies and discusses its sources—personal observations; a wide assortment of newsbooks, pamphlets and broadsides; letters received by Rugg or his acquaintances, perhaps including newsletters; the coffee-house, and 'the conversational grist of his fellow Londoners'—and assesses its usefulness as 'a record of the moment'.

92. Liber Eliensis. Edited by E. O. Blake. 1962. **33.92**

Transcript, Latin, with some Old English, of the most complete of the early versions of the 12th-century cartulary/chronicle described in the foreword by Dorothy Whitelock as 'unique among post-Conquest monastic histories' in its extensive use of vernacular docs. and hence 'an important source for the history in pre-Conquest times of an area of England for which evidence is not plentiful'. The nature of those docs. (chief amongst them a version of the *Libellus quorundam insignium operum beati Æthelwoldi episcopi* translated from a vernacular source between 1109 and 1131) and the types of information they afford are considered in the foreword. A transcript of the prologue and first three chapters of the *Libellus* is appended to the main text.

Other appendices print extracts, Latin, from the Book of Miracles of Etheldreda; editorial comments on the litigation arising from the establishment of a bishopric at Ely, regarding the archdeacon's customs in the abbey's churches in Cambridgeshire, the chronology of the disputed ownership of the manor of Stetchworth, the monks' opposition to the king's claim to the possessions of the priory during a vacancy in the see, and the monks' claim to Bawdsey; editorial comments on Book II of the *Liber*, including a chronology of the abbots of Ely, notes on the docs. of the Anglo-Saxon period, notes on some Ely estates, and an extended reconsideration of the Ely land pleas, 1071–87. Appendix E reconstructs the activities of Bishop Nigel of Ely between 1139 and 1144, the account in Book III of the *Liber* being unacceptable 'as it stands'. Appendix F, a note on the Ely *passio* of St. Thomas Becket, claims that 'the present state of the evidence printed suggests that the *Passions* all go back to one by Edward Grim'.

The introduction (36 pp.) considers the mss. of the *Liber*, its sources, the relationship of the mss., the authorship and date, and the value of the *Liber*. Concludes: 'it is a sad epitaph on the industry and good intentions of the compiler that his history is most useful where his own work can be altogether undone ...'.

93. The household papers of Henry Percy, ninth earl of Nor- **33.93**
thumberland, 1564–1632. Edited by G. R. Batho. 1962.

Transcripts of (i) examples of accounting docs., (ii) declarations of account for the audit period 1585–7, (iii) selected general accounts, and (iv) inventories, the 9th earl's will and the 10th earl's account as administrator. In the appendices, lists of the summary accounts of the household, of servants, and of creditors, all for the period 1585-1632, and a pedigree of Percy.

The introduction (40 pp.) treats in some detail (i) the organization of the relatively small household, the duties of the chief officers and servants, and the earl's increasingly close supervision of its most economical management, (ii) the estates, spread over some eight counties in England and Wales, the nucleus being in Yorkshire, and the principal residence at Petworth, (iii) the profligate expenditure and financial stringency of his earlier years changed into moderate affluence in later life, (iv) the nature and extent of his borrowing, and (v) the household accounts themselves, including stage-by-stage attention to the processes by which they were produced.

94. The parliamentary diary of Sir Edward Knatchbull, 1722–   **33.94**
1730. Edited by A. N. Newman. 1963.

Transcript, together with the diary of Samuel Sandys for the parliamentary year 1722–3; extracts from letters in the Finch mss. reporting two debates in 1722; two accounts of the debate of 7 May 1728 in the Egmont papers; extracts from notes made by Thomas Tower during debates and proceedings in the Commons in 1729 and 1730; and a list of other printed sources for those days for which Knatchbull has an entry.

The introduction sketches Knatchbull's career and its significance as showing clearly 'the pattern by which many of the country gentlemen were adapting themselves to the change of dynasty'. For an ambitious, capable Parliamentarian there was no future in opposition; 'at the same time he was one of those men whom Walpole was endeavouring to attract to . . . the court party'. The Knatchbull diary shows the process at work. Its value as a source for procedure and proceedings, in a period when there is a paucity of such material, is assessed—and rated high.

34. SELDEN SOCIETY, PUBLICATIONS*

73. Lord Nottingham's chancery cases. Edited . . . by D. E. C. **34.73**
Yale. Vol. 1. 1957.

Transcript of a copy of his reports of cases prepared by Heneage Finch,
1st earl of Nottingham, when lord keeper and later lord chancellor, with
biographical sketch and a study of his contribution to English law, particularly in regard to the place of precedent in equity. In this vol. cases 1–
578 (Michaelmas 1673–Michaelmas 1676). Contd. in **34.**79 below, with
continuous pagination of cases.

74. Select cases in the court of king's bench. Edited by G. O. **34.74**
Sayles. Vol. iv: Edward II. 1957.

Transcripts, Latin, part French, with facing English translation, from
Coram Rege rolls 161–263 (1308–26). Contd. in **34.**76, 82, 88 below. For
previous vols. in the series see **34.**55, 57, 58.

The introduction (on the justices of the king's bench, 1307–40, its
jurisdiction, and king's bench bills) has appendices on the justices of the
king's bench and the common bench, 1327–40, the itineraries of the king's
bench, 1273–1340, and the evolution of the crown roll, as well as analyses
of rolls 251 (Hilary 1323) and 271 (Hilary 1328).

75. Select cases in the council of Henry VII. Edited by the **34.75**
late C. G. Bayne and completed by William Huse Dunham,
Jr. 1958.

English translation (in part contemporary) of the *Liber intrationum*, of
copies of entries (English) in the council register, and of cases from
numerous other sources.

The introduction ranges over the establishment of the council, its membership, jurisdiction and procedure, as well as the background to and
particulars of the Act of 1487 *pro camera stellata* which established a court
distinct from the Star Chamber, the term 'court of Star Chamber' being
'almost an anachronism when used to describe a court of law in Henry
VII's reign'.

76. Select cases in the court of king's bench. Vol. v: Edward **34.76**
III. 1958.

---

*Attention is drawn to A. K. R. Kiralfy and Gareth H. Jones, *General guide to the*
[*Selden*] *Society's publications. A detailed and indexed summary of the contents of the*
introductions, volumes 1–79. (1960).

Transcripts, Latin, part French, with facing English translation, from Coram Rege rolls 267–322 (1327–40).

The introduction (on the clerks, marshal and other officials, the king's attorney and king's serjeant, the close connexion between king's bench and chancery, and the absence of any rigid division between common law and equity) has, as appendices, an analysis of rolls 190–322 (Michaelmas 1307–Michaelmas 1340), lists of king's attorneys, 1290–1340, and of king's serjeants, 1278–1340, and transcripts (some French, others Latin) of docs. on royal justices, officials of the court, legal representatives, jurisdiction and process, and chancery and chancery jurisdiction.

77. **Royal writs in England from the Conquest to Glanvill.**   34.77
Studies in the early history of the common law. By R. C. Van Caenegem. 1959.

Transcripts, Latin, with English translation, of 200 royal writs of the 11th and 12th centuries.

The introduction (400 pp.) 'deals with the English royal writs as they led up to the classic writs of the common law' and is 'a study of diplomatic, of institutions and of law in England ... between 1066 and 1189'.

78. **Pension book of Clement's Inn. Edited by Sir Cecil Carr.**   34.78
1960.

Transcript, by Nellie Kerling, of the minutes of the governing body of the inn, Nov. 1714–Mar. 1750, with the 'Constitutions and Orders' compiled from two sources (includes extracts from Pension books of a period from 1620 to 1781), and a list of members, with their sureties, 1658–1883.

The introduction treats of the origin and early separation of the two kinds of legal inns (of court and of chancery), the administration and functioning of Clement's Inn, and the end of the inns of chancery.

79. **Lord Nottingham's chancery cases. Vol. 2. 1961.**   34.79

Cases 579–1170 (Michaelmas 1676–Michaelmas 1682), with appendix of speeches and notes, and tables of statutes, of cases, and of year books and abridgements.

The introduction, 'An essay on mortgages and trusts and allied topics in equity', sets out and evaluates Lord Nottingham's contribution to the development of equitable principles.

80. **Novae narrationes. Edited by the late Elsie Shanks. Com-**   34.80
pleted, with a legal introduction, by S. F. C. Milsom. 1963.

Transcripts, Anglo-Norman, with facing English translation, of the text as it appears in three mss. of differing types.

'*Narrationes* is a series of counts illustrating the forms for presenting in court typical cases of various sorts, right, dower, replevin, wardship, etc.'

81. **Year books of Edward II. Vol. xxv: 12 Edward II, part of**   34.81
Easter and Trinity, 1319. Edited by John P. Collas. 1964.

Transcripts, law-French and Latin, with facing English translation. See note to the first vol. of the series, **34.17**.

The introduction is concerned with 'the nature of the language in which the Year Books were written, and above all its interpretation'.

82. Select cases in the court of king's bench. Vol. vi: Edward III. 1965.   **34.**82

Transcripts, Latin, part French, with facing English translation, from Coram Rege rolls 323-465 (1341-77).

The introduction (on the journeys of the court, record evidence, the justices of the bench, the king's attorney and king's serjeant, the court records and the keeper of the rolls and writs, the criers, and the marshal) has, as appendices, an analysis of rolls 323-466 (Hilary 1341-Trinity 1377), lists of justices of the king's bench and common bench, of king's attorneys and keepers of writs, and of king's serjeants, all for the years 1341-1422, a list of king's serjeants promoted justices, 1290-1420, and a list of clerks of the king's bench, 1341-77.

83. Pleas before the king or his justices, 1198-1212. Edited by Doris Mary Stenton. Vol. iii: Rolls or fragments of rolls from the years 1199, 1201, and 1203-1206. 1967.   **34.**83

Transcripts, Latin, with English translations as necessary, of cases relating to the counties of Gloucester, Hereford and Worcester omitted from Assize roll 800 (Sept. 1199) printed in **62.**3, with Assize rolls 732 (Shropshire, 1203) and 1039 (pleas heard at York and elsewhere in the king's presence, 1204), and essoins omitted from *Curia Regis rolls*, vols. ii, iii and iv (1201-6) in **3.**38. Includes additions and corrections to vols. i and ii, **34.**67, 68, and a memoir of T. F. T. Plucknett by S. F. C. Milsom.

The introduction, concentrating 'on the evidence that can be wrung from the essoins rolls and the careers of those who came hopefully to the courts of justice looking for a means of livelihood from the law', is followed by three appendices: a survey of the judiciary, 1100-1215; careers of minor professional men—attorneys and essoiners—in the courts; and the markings in Assize rolls 1039 and 558.

84. Pleas before the king or his justices, 1198-1212. Vol. iv: Rolls or fragments of rolls from the years 1207-1212. 1967.   **34.**84

Continues the preceding, with essoins omitted from *Curia Regis rolls*, vol. v (1208) in **3.**38; pleas of the crown at York, 1208, from Assize roll 1039; pleas and assizes at Norwich, 1209, from Assize roll 558; attorneys received before the king in Trinity 1212, and essoins, 1207-12, from Curia Regis rolls 44, 45, 47, 49, 50, 55, 57, 62. Corrections to vol. iii, **34.**83 above. No introductory matter.

85. Year books of Edward II. Vol. xxvi (pt. 1): The eyre of London, 14 Edward II, A.D. 1321. Edited by the late Helen M. Cam. Pt. 1. 1968.   **34.**85

Transcript, part Latin, part French, of the preliminaries of the eyre and the pleas of the crown, with facing English translation. Contd. in the following, the text with continuous pagination.

The introduction (on the unique character of this eyre, its sources, political setting, course, personnel—justices, clerk, recorder, counsel—

and certain of its legal aspects, with notes on cases, on the religious foundations, on aliens, and on topography) has appendices analysing the mss. of the eyre, the chronology of the eyre, and docs. tracing the course of the suit between Sir John Dagworth and the city concerning the marshalsy of the eyre.

86. Year books of Edward II. Vol. xxvi (pt. 2): The eyre of London, 14 Edward II, A.D. 1321. Pt. 2. 1969.   **34.86**

Text completed. Summaries of cases (for both pts.) and a memoir of Helen M. Cam by S. F. C. Milsom. Index by C. W. Ringrose.

87. Early registers of writs. Edited by Elsa de Haas and G. D. G. Hall. 1970.   **34.87**

Transcripts, Latin, with facing English translation, of (i) the Irish register, in Cotton mss. Julius D. ii, (ii) the pre-Mertonian register, in Cambridge University Library, (iii) the Luffield register, in the same place, (iv) a Bodleian register, in Rawlinson ms. C292, and (v) a register of judicial writs, in BL Additional ms. 35179, the texts and translations of the first three and the last, and also the general introduction, by Miss de Haas, the text and translation of the fourth, as well as the indexes and commentary on these and other registers (beginning with the justiciar's writs of c. 1199) by G. D. G. Hall. The appendices contain lists of ms. *registra brevium* in Great Britain and the United States, of writs 'of course' and writs 'of grace', and transcripts, Latin, of two short registers in Corpus Christi College Cambridge ms. 297.

88. Select cases in the court of king's bench. Vol. vii: Richard II, Henry IV and Henry V. 1971.   **34.88**

Transcripts, Latin, with facing English translation, from Coram Rege rolls 467–643 (Michaelmas 1377–Hilary 1422).

The introduction (on the justices of the king's bench, the clerks, keepers of rolls and writs, criers, the marshal, the records, the journeys of the king's bench, the serjeants-at-law, and the *aula regis* or household court) has, among its appendices, analyses of the rolls and lists of the clerks.

89. Fleta. Vol. iii: Book III and book IV. Edited, with a translation, by H. G. Richardson and G. O. Sayles. 1972.   **34.89**

Latin, with facing English translation, continuing the text printed in **34.72**. The introduction, notes and indexes are to be in vol. i.

90. The roll and writ file of the Berkshire eyre of 1248. Edited by M. T. Clanchy. 1973.   **34.90**

Transcript, Latin, with English translation, of the plea roll and the more unusual writs; the writs which are repetitive have been shortened, in Latin, and not translated. In the appendices, Roger of Thirkleby's eyre circuit, 1246–9; a list of fines made at Reading, 1248; the chief bailiwicks in Berkshire in 1248; and a list of early sheriffs' precepts.

The introduction treats of the eyre and its records *temp.* Hen. III, and of eyres in Berkshire, 1219–84 (analysed in an appendix), franchises, the profits of justice, the jurisdiction of sheriff and bailiffs, and the execution of royal writs. The occurrence, in the writ file, of 75 jury panels is noted; they are used to describe in chronological order the stages in the life of a possessory assize jury from its first selection up to the day when it gave its verdict.

91. St. German's 'Doctor and student'. Edited by the late T. F. T. Plucknett and J. L. Barton. 1974.   34.91

First published 1523 and 1530. The text of the Second Dialogue here printed, conflating the two English versions, and the introduction, are the work of J. L. Barton; the First Dialogue, accommodating the two English and the Latin versions and a translation of those portions which exist only in the Latin, is the work of Professor Plucknett. Bibliography of editions.

92. Sir Matthew Hale's 'The prerogatives of the king'. Edited by D. E. C. Yale. 1976.   34.92

Hale's text in modern form and as far as possible free from error, its citations tacitly corrected. The introduction, concerned with *inter alia* Hale's historical method and treatment of the royal prerogative, has an appendix on his bequest of mss. to Lincoln's Inn.

93. The reports of Sir John Spelman. Edited by J. H. Baker. Vol. i. 1977.   34.93

The complete Yelverton text (BL, Hargrave ms. 388) of Spelman's legal notebook, rearranged from chronological to alphabetical sequence and collated with other texts when substantial discrepancies have been noted, the Latin and law-French with facing English translation.

The introduction discusses Spelman's career and writings, and includes a genealogical table of his descendants. A longer introduction, with transcripts, Latin, and facing English translation of an illustrative selection of records bearing on the principal achievements of the common law under Hen. VII and Hen. VIII, is in the following vol. Pagination of Spelman's text and the selected records is continuous.

94. The reports of Sir John Spelman. Vol. ii. 1978.   34.94

Ancillary to the preceding, and containing nothing from Spelman's own hand, this vol. surveys English law and the Renaissance, the courts, the practical working of the law, the intellectual life of the law, pleading and litigation as sources of the law, law reporting, the law of property, actions on the case for wrongs, the establishment of *assumpsit* for nonfeasance, and pleas of the crown. The appendix lists the judges and officers of the common law courts from late-15th century dates to the mid-16th century and occasionally later, with biographical apparatus.

95. Select cases from the ecclesiastical courts of the province of Canterbury, *c.* 1200–1301. Edited by Norma Adams and Charles Donahue Jr. 1981.   34.95

Full Latin text, with facing English translation, of fifteen cases of *c.* 1200 and of three rolls of court of Canterbury *acta*, Sept. 1270–Jan. 1272, during vacancy of the see, followed by the full Latin text of cases from the years 1267–72 and 1284–1301, the text interspersed with a summary in English, except that some repetitious or purely formal parts have occasionally been omitted and a few docs. from the longer cases of the 1292–4 vacancy have been calendared. A brief introduction to each case sets out its earlier and later history, the chronology of the docs. printed, and some indication of its significance. The selection has been made from 'cases in which the provincial jurisdiction of the see was invoked', and seeks 'to illustrate the different types of documents found in the records, the different types of cases and issues brought before the court, the practice of the provincial court (the Court of Canterbury) and also the practice of the various courts from which appeal was made to the Court of Canterbury'. Appended is a short calendar of 88 of the 90 docs. identified by the editors as 'relating to church court cases' from the last years of Hubert Walter (d. 1205), and of which the importance 'can hardly be exaggerated'.

The introduction (almost 100 pp.) narrates the history of the court of Canterbury from the time of Hubert Walter to 1300, with particular regard to the *sede vacante* jurisdiction claimed and to some extent exercised by the prior and chapter of Christ Church, and gives in some detail an account of the court's procedure, officials, and records. Similarly detailed consideration is then given to the law and the practice of the church courts of the southern province during the latter half of the 13th century. The last section illustrates the jurisdiction of the court of Canterbury by considering the subject-matter of the cases heard, and concludes with an account of what the selected docs. reveal of the relationship between the secular courts and the courts Christian.

96. The roll of the Shropshire eyre of 1256. Edited by Alan Harding. 1981.   **34.96**

Transcript, Latin, with English translation, common form slightly shortened.

The introduction sets out the course of the general eyre of 1252–8 (of which the Shropshire session was an integral part), gives biographical details of the justices, and discusses in some detail the crown and civil cases. The rest of the introduction is a discussion of the origins of trespass, tort and misdemeanour, illustrated by an appendix of cases from eleven other eyre rolls from 1235 to 1292. 'Trespass' meant at first the offence against the king's peace alleged in an appeal of felony, for which the accused was tried and punished even if the appellant was non-suited for failure to complete the appeal's rigid procedures. The king then ordered his justices to listen to informal complaints (*querelae*) of trespass, originally of the personal injuries—violent assault, unjust imprisonment, extortion—inflicted by his own officials. 'Plaints' of trespass, soon written down as bills, brought before the courts the whole mass of injuries between the felonies and the infringements of land-rights which were remedied by writ. Trespass itself quickly split into civil and criminal categories. As writs of trespass were provided to define and obtain damages for the various sorts of private wrong or *tort* (though they still needed to be labelled 'against the king's peace'), bills of trespass prosecuted at the king's suit only became the basis of indictments of a new level of crimes, below the felonies, later called 'misdemeanours'.

PART 3
ENGLISH LOCAL SOCIETIES

35. BEDFORDSHIRE HISTORICAL RECORD SOCIETY, PUBLICATIONS

37. English wills, 1498–1526, edited by A. F. Cirket. Diana Astry's recipe book, c. 1700, edited by Bette Stitt. 1957.   **35.37**

The wills are those in English in the first surviving register of wills proved in the court of the archdeacon of Bedford. Abstracts, a few of the earlier wills and some of the more interesting fully transcribed. Glossary. For the wills in Latin see **35.45** below.

The recipes—culinary, medicinal, for wines, cordials, preserves and pickles, etc.—were collected by Diana Orlebar *née* Astry. Includes her notes of menus, 1701–8, and a list of the chief recipe books in the county record office.

Continuous pagination. Separate indexes.

38. 1958.   **35.38**

A Bedford fragment and the burning of two Fraticelli at Avignon in 1354. By D. W. Whitfield. [Transcript, Latin, of an isolated folio giving the indictment of friars John de Castellione and Francis ab Arquata, with Friar John's profession of faith.]

John Lord Wenlock of Someries [*d.* 1471]. By J. S. Roskell.

The Tower of London letter-book of Sir Lewis Dyve, 1646–47. Edited by H. G. Tibbutt. [Transcripts of copies of letters from Dyve to Chas. I and John Ashburnham.]

Inventory of furniture at Houghton House, c. 1726–28. Edited by Evelyn Curtis. [The house, near Ampthill, belonged at the time to Thomas Bruce, 2nd earl of Ailesbury, then in exile.]

39. The taxation of 1297: a translation of the local rolls of assessment for Barford, Biggleswade and Flitt hundreds, and for Bedford, Dunstable, Leighton Buzzard and Luton. By A. T. Gaydon. 1959.   **35.39**

For a ninth on movables. The introduction treats of the circumstances of the ninth, its assessment and collection, the relation of stock and crops assessed to actual holdings, and the character of Bedfordshire farming. Glossary, analytical tables, and translation of the roll for a fifteenth from a moiety of Shillington, 1301.

40. Some Bedfordshire diaries. 1960.   **35.40**

John Harvey of Ickwell, 1688–9. Edited by Margaret Richards. [On the Grand tour.]

Edmond and Christian Williamson of Husborne Crawley, 1709–20. Edited by F. J. Manning. [Recording the births of his children by his second wife.]

Henry Taylor of Pulloxhill, 1750-72. Edited by Patricia Bell. [An account, by his brother George Chalkley Taylor.]

John Salusbury of Leighton Buzzard, 1757-9. Edited by Joyce Godber.

John Pedley of Great Barford, 1773-95. Edited by F. G. Emmison.

Elizabeth Brown of Ampthill, 1778-91. Edited by Joyce Godber. [Of Quaker interest.]

Edward Arpin of Felmersham, 1763-1831. Edited by C. D. Linnell. [Parish clerk and grave-digger.]

Catherine Young (later Maclear) of Bedford, 1832-5 and 1846. Edited by Isobel Thompson.

Sir John Burgoyne, Bart., of Sutton, 1854. Edited by P. Young.

Major J. H. Brooks and the Indian mutiny, 1857. Edited by Aileen M. Armstrong. [Text of a lecture given by Major Brooks in 1893.]

The Rev. G. D. Newbolt of Souldrop, 1856-95. Edited by Patricia Bell.

Some letters from Bedfordshire pioneers in Australia, 1842-86. Edited by Andrew Underwood. [Written by Charles Cartwright, John Feazey, Dr. George Witt, Joel Croxford, Priscilla Dodson.]

41. Bedfordshire coroners' rolls. Edited by R. F. Hunnisett.   **35·41**
1961.

Calendar of rolls, c. 1265-1317, in the P.R.O., and of Cambridge, Gonville and Caius College, roll 26, for 1378-80, with lists of the medieval coroners for Bedfordshire, Bedford, Dunstable, and the Bedfordshire liberties of the abbot of St. Albans and Eton College.

42. The letter books of Sir Samuel Luke, 1644-45. Edited by   **35·42**
H. G. Tibbutt. 1963. [HMC JP 4]

Calendar of 1615 items from the letter books kept while Luke was parliamentary governor of Newport Pagnell, followed by 261 scout reports.

43. The cartulary of Newnham priory. Edited by Joyce God-   **35·43**
ber. 1 vol. in 2, 1963-4.

Early 15th century, the docs. from 1166 to 1409. Transcript, Latin, except that seven late docs. and docs. printed previously in summary or in full are here summarized, and rents have been abbreviated. Pt. 1 (docs. 1-462) is preceded by a tribute to Frederick Joseph Manning, d. July 1962.

44. The Oakley hunt. Edited by Joyce Godber. 1965.   **35·44**

Docs. relating to private hunts, 1708-97, and to the Oakley hunt, 1795-1920, from several collections, calendared in varying degree. List of masters of the Oakley hunt, 1798-1915.

45. Bedfordshire wills, 1480-1519. Edited by Patricia Bell.   **35·45**
1966.

Abstracts, in English, of the Latin wills in the earliest surviving register of wills proved in the court of the archdeacon of Bedford, with full transcripts of four.

46. The Grey of Ruthin valor: the valor of the English lands **35.46** of Edmund Grey, earl of Kent, drawn up from the ministers' accounts of 1467-8. Edited ... by R. I. Jack. 1965.

Transcript, English, late 1468. Other valuations of the estate to 1524 are summarized in the introduction which analyses in some detail the income of the family, the gross value of the estate manor by manor, and the charges upon it. The estate lay in the counties of Bedford, Buckingham, Essex, Huntingdon, Leicester, Norfolk and Northampton.

47. The Marchioness Grey of Wrest Park. By Joyce Godber. **35.47** 1968.

A life, 1722-97, put together as a guide to more than 7,000 letters addressed to the Marchioness and her two daughters, and also to the copies of her own letters, all in the county record office, using the words of the letters wherever possible. Includes a transcript of the journal of his travels in England and Scotland kept by her husband, Philip Yorke, 1744-63.

48. Sessions of the peace for Bedfordshire, 1355-1359, 1363- **35.48** 1364. Edited by Elisabeth G. Kimball. 1969. [HMC JP 16]

Transcripts, Latin, of two peace rolls, with English summaries of all entries. The analytical introduction describes the rolls and treats of the commissions, the justices, the sessions of the peace, the offences on the rolls, and the punishment of offenders.

49. Miscellanea. 1970. **35.49**

Contracting arable lands in 1341. By Alan R. H. Baker. [The evidence of the published *nonarum inquisitiones* for Bedfordshire.]

Two monastic account rolls. Edited by G. D. Gilmore. [English translations of the cellarer's roll for Newnham, 1519-20, and the Harrold roll, 1401-2.]

The building accounts of Harrold Hall. Edited by John Weaver. [Transcript of the accounts of the builder, Francis Farrar, 1608-10.]

Minutes of the Bedfordshire committee for sequestrations, 1646-7. Edited by Patricia Bell. [Transcript.]

The exempt jurisdiction of Woburn. By Dorothy Owen. [Transcripts of six letters, 1711-16, arguing for and against exemption.]

Alderman Heaven, 1723-94. By G. D. Gilmore. [Parliamentary elections and control of the corporation of Bedford.]

Some documents relating to riots. Edited by Joyce Godber. [Incidents in the county occasioned by abuse of common rights at Blunham, probably in 1604, at Harrold in 1770, at Maulden in 1796; by the Militia Act, 1757; by distress, at Stotfold in 1830; by the poor law, at Ampthill in 1835.]

The Bedford election of 1830. By Carlos T. Flick.

Letters of Richard Dillingham [of Flitwick], convict. Edited by Harley W. Forster. [Transcripts. Sent from the hulks at Woolwich, 1831-2, and Van Diemen's Land, 1836-9.]

Leighton Buzzard and the railway. By P. S. Richards.

50. Samuel Whitbread's notebooks, 1810–11, 1813–14. Ed   35.50
ited by Alan F. Cirket. 1971.

Whitbread's notes of cases heard by him as magistrate when he was in residence at Southill. Analytical introduction.

51. Some early nonconformist church books. Edited by H. G.   35.51
Tibbutt. 1972.

Transcripts. Kensworth, 1675–94; Keysoe Brook End, 1658–77; Stevington, 1673–1721; Carlton, 1688–1703; Rothwell, c. 1692; Kimbolton, 1692–1711; Bedford/Southill, 1693–1723; Hail Weston/St. Neots, 1691–1724.

52. The inhabitants of Cardington in 1782. By David Baker.   35.52
1973.

A list 'of persons in each house on January 1st, 1782' transcribed and, for the purpose of the detailed analytical introduction, supplemented from other categories of demographic sources including overseers' accounts, wills, parish registers, tombstones, land tax docs., and material created in the course of the 1784 parliamentary election.

53. The railway age in Bedfordshire. By F. G. Cockman.   35.53
1974.

An account of 'the impact made by railways on Victorian society in Bedfordshire', 1846–90.

54. Elementary education in Bedford, 1868–1903, by D. W.   35.54
Bushby. Bedfordshire ecclesiastical census, 1851, edited by
D. W. Bushby. 1975.

55. The minutes of the first Independent church (now Bunyan   35.55
meeting) at Bedford, 1656–1766. Edited by H. G. Tibbutt.
1976.

Includes periodical lists of church members.

56. A study of Bedford prison, 1660–1877. By Eric Stockdale.   35.56
1977.

In the appendices: plans of Bedford in 1765 and 1841 and of the jail in 1849; site plan of Bunyan's jail; list of jailers, 1710–1885; deed of appointment of jailers, 1740; genealogical tables for the Richardson–Howard family, the Whitbread–Howard link, and Lord John Russell's family.

57. Worthington George Smith and other studies, presented   35.57
to Joyce Godber. 1978.

Bedfordshire chapelries: an essay in rural settlement history. By Dorothy Owen.
Bedfordshire heraldry: a conspectus. By F. W. Kuhlicke.
Middlemen in the Bedfordshire lace industry. By Anne Buck.
Joshua Symonds [1739–88], an eighteenth-century Bedford dissenting minister. By H. G. Tibbutt.
The 1830 riots in Bedfordshire—background and events. By A. F. Cirket.

A Bedfordshire clergyman of the reform era and his bishop. By Joan Varley. [Transcripts of letters to Bishop Kaye of Lincoln and of a few draft replies, 1830-38, concerning the Rev. Timothy Matthews (*d*. 1845), 'a law to himself'.]

Worthington George Smith. By James Dyer. [Antiquary, archaeologist, architect, botanist and illustrator, *d*. 1917.]

Aspects of Anglo-Indian Bedford. By Patricia Bell.

The 1919 peace riots in Luton. By John G. Dony.

58. Bedfordshire wills proved in the prerogative court of Canterbury, 1383-1548. Edited by Margaret McGregor. 1979.   35.58

Abstracts, English, with brief biographical notes. Glossary.

59. Miscellanea. 1980.   35.59

'Deprived of our former place': the internal politics of Bedford, 1660 to 1688. By Michael Mullet.

Sir John Kelyng, chief justice of the king's bench, 1665-1671. By Eric Stockdale.

The Bedfordshire county petitions of 1795. By Clive Emsley.

The Earl de Grey's account of the building of Wrest House. Edited by A. F. Cirket. [Transcript. The account, describing the house and contents, room by room, and the garden, is in the form of a letter to his daughter, Anne Florence, Countess Cowper, Apr. 1846.]

The memoirs of Jane and William Inskip. Edited by Yvonne Nicholls and Sylvia Woods. [Transcripts of reminiscences written in 1915 and 1924 by Mrs. Inskip *née* Street, of Harrowden Farm, and of the Bedfordshire parts of the memoirs written by her son in 1940.]

60. The Bedfordshire farm worker in the nineteenth century. By Nigel E. Agar. 1981.   35.60

A compendious collection of extracts from parliamentary Blue Books and from documentary material in the county record office, beginning with general views of the life of the farm worker in 19th-century Bedfordshire as a background for the following sections concerned with the poor law, the life of the labourer, migration and emigration, housing, access to land, education, and the Labourers' Union. Plates. In the preliminary matter, a tribute to Harold Owen White, secretary of the Society 1965-80.

36. BUCKINGHAMSHIRE RECORD SOCIETY

11. The first ledger book of High Wycombe. Transcribed and   **36.11**
edited by R. W. Greaves. 1956.

Somewhat shortened transcript of an unsystematic record of 'matters
thought needful to be remembered' begun in 1475, the entries running
from *c.*1300 to 1734, re-arranged in broadly chronological order, with
English translations of the Latin.

12. The cartulary of Missenden abbey. Pt. iii. Edited ... by   **36.12**
J. G. Jenkins. 1962. [HMC JP 1]

Transcripts, Latin, with English summaries. Continues and completes
36.2, 10. Includes final concords (many of which are not in **36.**4), papal
bulls, and records of legal actions. The area covered extends to the counties
of Bedford, Huntingdon, London, Middlesex, Oxford and Suffolk, as well
as Buckinghamshire. In the introduction, a brief history of the abbey, a
summary of revenues and outgoings from 25 Dec. 1528 to 24 June 1530,
and a list of abbots.

13. Ship money papers and Richard Grenville's note-book.   **36.13**
Edited by Carol G. Bonsey and J. G. Jenkins. 1965.

Transcripts of official papers, private notes, accounts, letters and warrants
among the papers of Sir Peter Temple in the Huntington Library, illustrating the administration of the ship money writ of 1635 in Buckinghamshire. The note-book (in the county record office), kept while Grenville was sheriff of Buckinghamshire, 1641–2, sets out 'the most approved
way of proportioning and dividing public taxes set upon the whole shire'.

14. Early taxation returns: taxation of personal property in   **36.14**
1332 and later. With introduction by A. C. Chibnall. 1966.

English summaries of assessment rolls for the fifteenth and tenth levied in
Buckinghamshire in 1332, the assessment rolls for Horton and Stone in
1336, the particulars of account for the county in 1332, 1336 and 1446/7,
the assessment roll for Emberton in 1512/13, the carucage of 1217, and
docs. of the twentieth levied in 1327. Glossary of surnames denoting
occupation, a personal characteristic, or place of abode.

The introduction explains the nature of the fifteenth and tenth. The
docs. relating to the 1332 levy are 'the earliest survivals of this particular
species of tax' and also (because of administrative changes made in 1334)
'the last representatives of fractional taxes on movables which give intimate details of the commodities concerned'. The administrative background, from the grant of the subsidy to the final accounting at the

exchequer, is described, as also are the commodities exempted from the tax, the changed system of assessment introduced in 1334, and the seemingly paradoxical result that 15th-century landowners, while objecting to the direct taxation of land, accepted 'a tax that, ostensibly levied on movables [had become in reality] little more than a disguised tax on land'.

15. Luffield priory charters. Edited ... by G. R. Elvey. Pt. i. 1968.   **36.15**

Transcripts, Latin, with brief English summaries, of the surviving originals, preserving the order and arrangement of the cartulary compiled c. 1470 and using the cartulary versions where the originals are unknown. Docs. (146 in number) not in the cartulary have been included. Contd. in **36.18** below. Both vols. published jointly with the Northamptonshire Record Soc. See **55.22**, 26 below.

16. The letter-books of Samuel Wilberforce, 1843–68. Transcribed and edited by R. K. Pugh with the assistance of J. F. A. Mason. 1970.   **36.16**

The text of 732 letters printed in full and in date order. Wilberforce's relations with the churches at Alverstoke, the 'Buckinghamshire Archaeological Society', and Bloxham school, are the subjects of appendices by Dr. Mason. Published jointly with the Oxfordshire Record Soc. See **58.47** below.

17. The certificate of musters for Buckinghamshire in 1522. Edited by A. C. Chibnall. 1973. [HMC JP 18]   **36.17**

Transcript, part English, part Latin, of a copy of the original return, the editor inclining to the view that it was made for Francis, 4th earl of Bedford. At the end of the copy are listed the chief justices of the common bench, 1399–1606, and of the king's bench, 1348–1607. The introduction considers the assessment of benefices, chantries, religious houses and colleges, private estates, and goods.

18. Luffield priory charters. Pt. ii. 1975.   **36.18**

Includes corrections to pt. i (**36.15** above), a general introduction supplementing the history of the priory in *VCH Bucks.* (i. 347) and *VCH Northants* (ii. 95), a topographical introduction contd. from pt. i, a list of priors, and genealogies of Wolverton, Fraxino, Baivel, de Westbury and Hareng, FitzNigel, de Horwode and de Morton, and de Billing.

19. The courts of the archdeaconry of Buckingham, 1483–1523. Edited ... by E. M. Elvey. 1975.   **36.19**

Transcripts, mainly Latin, of miscellaneous, even fragmentary, court records, including some 250 wills. The business of the courts, largely but not exclusively testamentary, is described in the introduction (21 pp.). Numerous features of the probate and registration of wills and the trial of actions arising from them are considered. Map.

20. The letters of Thomas Hayton, vicar of Long Crendon, **36.**20
Buckinghamshire, 1821–1887. Edited by Joyce Donald. 1979.
Collected from several archives, transcribed, and arranged in chronological order.

37. CUMBERLAND AND WESTMORLAND ANTIQUARIAN AND ARCHAEOLOGICAL SOCIETY, EXTRA SERIES

19. Antiquary on horseback. The first publication of the collections of the Rev. Thos. Machell, chaplain to King Charles II, towards a history of the barony of Kendal. Transcribed and edited by Jane M. Ewbank. 1963. **37.19**

> The journal and general notes, 1691-3, including numerous sketches, monumental inscriptions, coats of arms, and pedigrees (among them Midleton of Middleton Hall, Layburne of Cunswick and Witherslack Hall, Thornborrow or Thornborough of Selside, Philipson of Thwatterden and Calgarth, Fleming or le Fleming of Rydal, Benson of Elterwater and Ambleside).

20. The building of Hadrian's wall. By C. E. Stevens. 1966. **37.20**

21. An armorial for Westmorland and Lonsdale. By R. S. Boumphrey, C. Roy Hudleston, and J. Hughes, with a foreword by Roger Fulford. 1975. **37.21**

> Endeavours to include the armorial bearings used by every armigerous family and institution within the county and the hundred of Lonsdale (except those in the Shire Hall, Lancaster, and in the east window of Windermere church), with genealogical notes and descents of property.

22. Maryport, Cumbria: a Roman fort and its garrison. By Michael G. Jarrett. 1976. **37.22**

> Includes a report (with A. R. Birley) on the excavations of 1966, and descriptions by other contributors of the finds in that year.

23. Cumberland families and heraldry, with a supplement to *An armorial for Westmorland and Lonsdale*. By C. Roy Hudleston and R. S. Boumphrey. Illustrated by J. Hughes and others. 1978. **37.23**

38. CUMBERLAND AND WESTMORLAND ANTIQUARIAN AND ARCHAEOLOGICAL SOCIETY, RECORD or CHARTULARY SERIES

9. Naworth estate and household accounts, 1648–1660. **38.9**
Edited by C. Roy Hudleston. 1958.

See 41.168 below.

39. CUMBERLAND AND WESTMORLAND ANTIQUARIAN AND ARCHAEOLOGICAL SOCIETY, TRACT SERIES

15. Early Westmorland M.P.s, 1258-1327. By George   **39.**15
S. H. L. Washington. 1959.

> Biographical notices of 67 knights and burgesses 'compiled many years ago ... for the late Lord Wedgwood's *History of Parliament* ...', including 14 names additional to the *Official Return*, comprising the knights in the parliaments of Oct. 1258, Nov. 1294, May 1300 and Jan. 1301, besides one burgess in the parliament of Jan. 1307.

16. The monumental inscriptions of the church and church-   **39.**16
yard of St. James, Whitehaven, Cumberland. Edited by H. B.
Stout. 1963.

> Copied when the churchyard was in course of being taken over by the borough and the gravestones moved. Church built 1752-3. No inscriptions more recent than 1954.

17. The Westmorland protestation returns, 1641/2. Edited by   **39.**17
M. A. Faraday. 1971.

> Transcript. The introduction includes, in tabular form, estimates of the total population of the county, parish by parish, based on the returns, the hearth tax of 1671, and the census of 1801.

18. A short history of the manor and parish of Witherslack to   **39.**18
1850. By G. P. Jones. 1971.

19. Monumental inscriptions at Ulverston. By Robert and   **39.**19
Florence Dickinson. 1973.

40. DEVON AND CORNWALL RECORD SOCIETY, PUBLICATIONS, NEW SERIES

1. Devon monastic lands: calendar of particulars for grants, **40.25**
1536–1558. Edited ... by Joyce Youings. 1955.

Calendar of all surviving particulars relating to grants of former monastic property lying within the boundaries of 16th-century Devon made by the crown during the period, considerably amplifying the terms of relevant letters patent and illustrating the work of the court of augmentations. Appended is a *valor* compiled from ministers' and receivers' accounts for 1558-9 showing the income due to the crown from its Devon monastic lands, and a list of charges honoured by the crown on the revenues from Buckfast abbey estates.

The introduction outlines the setting up of the court, the responsibilities and practice of its officers in Devon, and the nature of the estates; it also describes (in rather more detail) the valors prepared, the proceedings of the auditors with regard to woods and advowsons, the rates of purchase, the duration of the process, the grants and grantees, and the general effect of the disposal of monastic lands on the pattern of landownership in the county. Other sources of information on the disposal of the Devon monastic lands are considered.

2. Exeter in the seventeenth century: tax and rate assessments, **40.26**
1602–1699. Edited by W. G. Hoskins. 1957.

Transcripts. For the subsidies of 1602 and 1629, the poll tax of 1660, the hearth tax of 1671, and the poor rate of 1699. Map.

3. The diocese of Exeter in 1821: Bishop Carey's replies to **40.27**
queries before visitation. Edited ... by Michael Cook. Vol. i: Cornwall. 1958.

Transcripts of the replies of the clergy, in alphabetical order of parishes, to questions addressed to them by the bishop before his primary visitation. Contd. in the following. Each vol. has a list of livings returned in 1808 as less in value than £50 a year.

4. The diocese of Exeter in 1821. Vol. ii: Devon. 1960. **40.28**

5. The cartulary of St. Michael's Mount. Edited ... by P. L. **40.29**
Hull. 1962.

Transcript, Latin, with English abstracts, of Hatfield ms. 315, the docs. ranging from *c.* 1070 to 1372. Appended are the undated charter of

Edward the Confessor, the grant of manors by Robert of Mortain, and a list of priors before 1266.

The introduction describes the foundation, early history and possessions of the priory, and comments on some of the corrodies, the priors and benefactors, and grants to the priory.

6. The Exeter assembly. The minutes of the assemblies of the United Brethen of Devon and Cornwall, 1691–1717, as transcribed by the Reverend Isaac Gilling. Edited ... by Allan Brockett assisted by Roger Thomas, with shorthand transcriptions by the late R. Travers Herford. 1963.   **40.30**

Includes biographical notices of the ministers.

7. The register of Edmund Lacy, bishop of Exeter, 1420–1455: *Registrum commune*. Edited by G. R. Dunstan. Vol. i. 1963.   **40.31**

Contd. in **40.34**, 37, 40, 42 below. All vols. issued jointly with the Canterbury and York Soc. See **14.60** above.

8. The cartulary of Canonsleigh abbey: a calendar. Edited ... by Vera C. M. London. 1965.   **40.32**

Early 14th-century original, with some later additions. Extents in the original have been omitted. Among the appendices a list of priors and abbesses.

The introduction outlines the history of the house, from its foundation apparently in 1160 as a priory of Augustinian canons, through its refoundation in 1284 as an abbey for Augustinian canonesses—'a not too cloistered retreat for the local ladies'—to its surrender in 1539, and comments upon the possessions of the house, the grants made to it, and its occasional financial difficulties. There are notes on the benefactors and on many features of the cartulary.

[9] Benjamin Donn, A map of the county of Devon, 1765. Reprinted in facsimile with an introduction by W. L. D. Ravenhill. 1965.   **40.33**

Scale one inch to the mile. Published jointly by the Society and the University of Exeter.

10. The register of Edmund Lacy ... *Registrum commune*. Vol. ii. 1966.   **40.34**

11. Devon inventories of the sixteenth and seventeenth centuries. Edited ... by Margaret Cash. 1966.   **40.35**

Probate inventories and valuations dated between 1531 and 1699, all but 11 of the 266 docs. later than 1590. Analytical introduction. Glossary.

12. Plymouth building accounts of the sixteenth and seventeenth centuries. Edited ... by Edwin Welch. 1967.   **40.36**

Transcripts. For the building of the Guildhall (receiver's accounts), 1564–

5; for the building of the Guildhall, 1606–7; and the Orphans' Aid accounts, 1614–20.

The introduction briefly considers the buildings, the regulations of the Orphans' Aid (the buildings survived until 1871), building methods, materials and prices, and the builders and their wages. Glossary. Maps.

13. The register of Edmund Lacy . . . *Registrum commune*. Vol. iii. 1968.   **40.37**

14. The Devonshire lay subsidy of 1332. Edited . . . by Audrey M. Erskine. 1969.   **40.38**

Transcript, the Latin translated, of the Devon roll of assessment for the fifteenth and tenth, being the last to contain taxpayers' names and the basis for the new system of assessment introduced in 1334.

The introduction, besides giving a detailed description and analysis of the ms., treats of lay subsidies before and after 1334, gives the sums assessed and actually raised in Devon between 1290 and 1334, shows that over this period Devon's contribution to the total levied from the country appreciably increased, and explains that the amounts described as raised in Devon 'were in practice reduced by the exemptions from taxation of the tin miners of the Stannaries'. Map of the hundreds.

15. Churchwardens' accounts of Ashburton, 1479–1580. Edited . . by Alison Hanham. 1970.   **40.39**

Transcript, the Latin translated, followed by several pages of memoranda, obits, agreements etc. The introduction surveys the range of the accounts ('exceptional in being so full and in furnishing a nearly unbroken record over the hundred years from 1479'), comments on the use of West Country words and forms, and on the quality of the Latin. Glossary.

16. The register of Edmund Lacy . . . *Registrum commune*. Vol. iv. 1971.   **40.40**

17. The caption of seisin of the duchy of Cornwall, 1337. Edited . . . by P. L. Hull. 1971.   **40.41**

Modified transcript, Latin or French, with translation and abstracts, omitting common form. Appended, the charter, Latin, of Reginald de Valletort to Saltash, *c.* 1230.

The introduction (60 pp.) considers the purpose and scope of the survey (a consequence of the creation of the first duke of Cornwall), the preceding assession roll of 1333, the feudal honours within the duchy, the tenants of the *antiqua maneria*, the boroughs, the hundreds, the worth of the stannary courts, the value of the coinage, the advowsons belonging to the duchy, the values of the constituent parts of the duchy revenues from Cornwall, the size and nature of the tenements, and the variety of sizes for the Cornish acre. Map.

18. The register of Edmund Lacy . . . Vol. v. 1972.   **40.42**

19. A calendar of Cornish glebe terriers, 1673–1735. Edited by Richard Potts. 1974.   **40.43**

Includes 'The parsonage house: a note on the architectural content of Cornish glebe terriers', by Veronica M. Chesher, and the orders for the making of such terriers in Gloucester diocese, 1679, and Lincoln diocese, 1706.

The introduction sets out the ecclesiastical jurisdictions in Cornwall and the contents of the terriers here calendared; the entire collection for the county comprises over 700 docs. and extends in date from 1601 to 1821. Glossary.

20. John Lydford's book. Edited ... by Dorothy M. Owen. **40.44**
1974. [HMC JP 22]

A memorandum book compiled at the instance of 'an important and successful member of the ecclesiastical establishment', a canon lawyer who became Bishop Wykeham's official at Winchester in 1377 after practising in the court of Canterbury; the introduction traces his career. Transcript, Latin, of 'all entries for which no similar material can be found readily available in print', almost all the other entries calendared.

21. A calendar of Early Chancery Proceedings relating to **40.45**
West Country shipping, 1388–1493. Edited ... by Dorothy
M. [*recte* A.] Gardiner. 1976.

Petitions (or bills) for redress of grievances and reparation for loss or injury, many of the 97 separate proceedings annotated by the compiler.

The introduction describes the form and language of the petitions, the early history of petitioning for justice, and the content and background of the petitions here selected, providing 'illustrations of the way the laws and customs of the sea and the measures taken by government to regulate maritime activities in a time of active warfare were carried out'.

22. Tudor Exeter: tax assessments, 1489–1595, including the **40.46**
military survey, 1522. Edited by Margery M. Rowe. 1977.

Assessments for the tenth of 1489, the military survey of 1522, and for the subsidies of 1524/5, 1544, 1557/8, 1577, 1586, and 1593/5, all in English translation and considered in the introduction. Appended is an abstract of appeals against assessment endorsed on the 1524 doc., and a note, by Hugh Peskett, on the starting dates of Exeter parish registers.

23. The Devon cloth industry in the eighteenth century: Sun **40.47**
Fire Office inventories of merchants' and manufacturers'
property, 1726–1770. Edited ... by Stanley D. Chapman.
1978.

Abstracts of a thousand or so insurance policies issued to principal textile manufacturers and merchants in Devon, with a list of earlier policies, presented as an important and hitherto little known source here utilised to add extensive detail to W. G. Hoskins's *Industry, trade and people in Exeter, 1688–1800*, 'identifying hundreds of families that were engaged in the trade and manufacture [of Devon serge], demonstrating the size and structure of the manufacturing units, and modifying the broad generalisations of Hoskins's outline'.

24. The accounts of the fabric of Exeter cathedral, 1279–1353.   **40.48**
Edited and translated . . . by Audrey M. Erskine. Pt. 1: 1279–
1326. 1981.

Calendar. The weekly lists of named tradesmen, with their wages, have
been extracted and arranged in tables following the calendar. The considerable quantity of fabric records, the form of the accounts, and the
general working of the fabric fund are described in the introduction. Pt.
2 is to contain the remainder of the text, a further introduction, and the
index to both pts.; pagination will be continuous.

25. The parliamentary survey of the duchy of Cornwall. Ed-   **40.49**
ited . . . by Norman J. G. Pounds. Pt. 1: Austell Prior – Saltash.
1982.

Calendar, the first entry of each type printed in full, from the text in the
Duchy office. The introduction summarizes the 'precise and workmanlike'
legislation of 1649 for the survey and describes the surveyors' procedure
(by questions to sworn juries), the instructions given them for the valuation and sale of crown lands, their proceedings in Devon and Cornwall,
the sales effected, and the eventual resumption of most of the lands by
their former owners. The differing origins of the lands which made up the
duchy are described. The variety of tenures and customs (freehold, lease-
hold, assessionable, copyhold) and the income derived from each category
of tenure in the duchy and crown manors of the south-west, are set out in
tables. Pt. 2 is to contain the manors from the Isles of Scilly to West
Antony in Cornwall, all the duchy's possessions in Devon, and the index.

41. SURTEES SOCIETY, PUBLICATIONS

166. The register of Thomas Langley, bishop of Durham, **41.166**
1406–1437. Edited by R. L. Storey. Vol. ii. 1957.

Folios 51–110, continuing the edition begun in **41.**164. Transcript, Latin,
shortened in part by the omission of recurrent passages and the calendaring of entries in common form. Contd. in **41.**169, 170, 177, 182 below.

The introduction, in **41.**164, makes the point that Langley, in spite of
his little previous concern with ecclesiastical affairs, 'was eminently qualified to be bishop of Durham', the see then requiring 'an administrator of
the first rank, not so much as spiritual ruler of the diocese but as lord of
the Bishopric'. Diocesan administration operated satisfactorily during his
long absences, but there was still much unavoidable business that had to
be discharged by correspondence, requiring the assistance of an organized
secretariat. The functioning of Langley's secretariat, of his chancellor and
registrars, is described.

167. The law books of the Crowley ironworks. Edited by **41.167**
M. W. Flinn. 1957.

Part transcript, part summary, of the codification of the regulations issued
for their ironworks in County Durham—'probably the largest in Europe
in their day'—by Sir Ambrose and John Crowley, arranged in three
groups, viz. the laws and their enforcement, the administration of the
factory (subdivided according to their bearing on administration, finance,
and accounting, duties of officers and clerks, the handling and processing
of iron, and the workmen), and welfare services and the finance of poor
relief. Glossary.

The introduction outlines the life of the founder, Ambrose, later Sir
Ambrose Crowley (*d.* 1713), and the development of his nail manufacturing business into a nationwide organization controlled in succession by
him, by his son John (*d.* 1728), and by John's widow Theodosia (*d.* 1782).
'The control of so highly integrated a concern by a single entrepreneur
called ... for leadership of unusual calibre'; it also required an uncommon
degree of devolution and the creation of peaceable and contented conditions for the workers. These conditions the laws were designed to preserve:
they are described and assessed, as also are the method of enforcement by
informers, the court for the punishment of offenders, the system of management by committees, the accessibility of the head of the firm to the
least of his workmen, the original system of time reckoning in ten-week
periods, and the complex industrial organization of the works.

Possessing 'the personal characteristics of the successful entrepreneur—
undying energy, remorseless insistence on thoroughness and honesty, and
a complete conviction of the correctness and validity of his own princi-

ples'—the Crowleys provide in their law books 'a picture of industrial organization in England nearly a century earlier than other comparable examples'. After Waterloo, and with the business no longer in Crowley hands, the regulations were anachronistic, the court became an empty ritual, and the formerly Tory workers became Chartists 'of the most militant type'.

168. Naworth estate and household accounts, 1648–1660. Edited by C. Roy Hudleston. 1958.   **41.168**

Closely similar to Lord William Howard's (see **41.**68), the accounts are primarily concerned with the Cumberland estates administered from Naworth, and with the expenses of the household there. The books were kept by the steward to Charles Howard, Lord William's great-grandson and later 1st earl of Carlisle (*d.* 1685); his life is briefly told in the introduction. Also issued by the Cumberland and Westmorland Antiquarian and Archaeological Soc. See **38.**9 above.

169. The register of Thomas Langley ... Vol. iii. 1959.   **41.169**

Folio 110 contd.–folio 174.

170. The register of Thomas Langley ... Vol. iv. 1961.   **41.170**

Folio 174 contd.–folio 236.

171. The diaries and correspondence of James Losh. Edited by Edward Hughes. Vol. i: Diary, 1811–1823. 1962.   **41.171**

Transcript, omitting reports on the weather and various 'bald entries', mainly of a social kind. A Cumbrian by birth, and a 'man of mark' in his adopted Tyneside, James Losh of The Grove, Jesmond, knew Coleridge and was a friend of Wordsworth and Southey. A dissenter, he yet became an active and successful practitioner on the northern circuit. And he was a 'quite omnivorous reader'. Contd. in **41.**174 below.

172. Clifford letters of the sixteenth century. Edited by A. G. Dickens. 1962.   **41.172**

Transcripts of 44 letters, presumed to have once been part of the family archives, 41 of them addressed to successive heads of the house of Clifford and almost all of them datable to the reign of Hen. VIII, illustrating noble and clerical life in the north on the eve of the Reformation and during its early stages. Genealogical table of Clifford. The family and their correspondents are considered at length in the introduction. Appended are extracts from a version of the account of her ancestors written by Anne Clifford, countess of Pembroke.

173. Durham recusants' estates, 1717–1778. Edited by C. Roy Hudleston. 1962.   **41.173**

Transcripts, slightly shortened, of registration certificates, in alphabetical order to Salvin (Bryan). Contd. in **41.**175 below.

174. The diaries and correspondence of James Losh. Vol. ii: **41.174**

Diary, 1824–1833; letters to Charles, 2nd earl Grey, and Henry Brougham. 1963.

175. Miscellanea. Vol. iii. 1965.   **41.175**

Durham recusants' estates, 1717–1778. Pt. 2. [Continues **41.**173 above, from Salvin (Edward) onwards, with six registrations, 1717–22, additional to pt. 1.]
Durham entries on the recusants' roll, 1636–7, extracted and annotated by Ann M. C. Forster.

176. Ancient petitions relating to Northumberland. Edited by   **41.176** C. M. Fraser. 1966.

Transcripts, Latin or French, with English summaries. Mainly of the 14th century, selected from the Special Collection in the P.R.O. and grouped into ten themes, each theme with its own introduction, viz. licences, emergency administration, miscarriage of justice, accountancy, administrative abuses, the rebellion of Sir Gilbert de Middleton, war service claims, war damage claims, customs and taxation, and trade.

177. The register of Thomas Langley ... Vol. v. 1966.   **41.177**

Folio 236 contd.–folio 294.

178. The correspondence of Sir James Clavering. Edited ...   **41.178** by H. T. Dickinson. 1967.

Transcripts of 214 letters to and from Sir James Clavering, of Lamesley and Greencroft, d. 1748, 'in many ways ... a typical member of the lesser gentry in County Durham in the first half of the eighteenth century', with genealogies of the Claverings of Axwell Park, of Chopwell, and of Greencroft.

179. Durham episcopal charters, 1071–1152. Edited by H. S.   **41.179** Offler. 1968.

New transcriptions, Latin, with brief English abstracts, of the 40 or so surviving episcopal *acta* of the period, each with a commentary. A few are published for the first time. Brought together, they can be used to criticize each other and 'be persuaded to yield fully what they have to tell about the management of the bishopric in Norman times'.

180. Selections from the disbursements book, 1691–1709, of   **41.180** Sir Thomas Haggerston, Bart. Edited by Ann M. C. Forster. 1969.

Illustrating the quiet, comfortable, ordered life of a Catholic country gentleman and his family at Haggerston in a period of comparative toleration.

181. The records of the company of shipwrights of Newcastle   **41.181** upon Tyne, 1622–1967. Edited by D. J. Rowe. Vol. 1. 1970.

Orders and rules 'almost in their entirety', 1622–1908; 'major resolutions and decisions', 1712–1967; selections from annual accounts, 1674–1967.

The history of the company is sketched in the introduction. Members (by apprenticeship, by patrimony, by presentation) and officers of the company are listed in **41.**184 below, which also contains examples of fines, 1717–1805, and the index. Pagination is continuous.

182. The register of Thomas Langley . . . Vol. vi. 1970.   **41.**182

Folio 294 contd.–folio 304, with *corrigenda* to earlier vols., and indexes.

183. Parliamentary surveys of the bishopric of Durham. Edited by D. A. Kirby. Vol. i. 1971.   **41.**183

c. 1647, with some of later date. Calendar for (in this vol.) the 'manors' of Auckland, Darlington, Evenwood, and Wolsingham, with a table of sales of bishopric lands, 1647–51.

The introduction, after describing how the surveys were commonly made, dismisses many of them as 'inaccurate approximations to the truth' and 'not worth the name'. Exceptionally, for reasons given, the Durham surveys for the most part are seen as 'probably an accurate account of the bishopric'. Basic to their appreciation is some understanding of the very varied physical, economic, and social framework in which they are set. Consideration is therefore given to the nature of the ground surveyed, the differences in soil structure, the effects of increased coal production on the agrarian economy, and the agricultural innovations peculiar to certain areas.

For the 'manors' of Chester le Street, Whickham, Gateshead, Houghton le Spring, Easington, and Bishop Middleham, and the re-survey of the collieries of Gateshead and Whickham see **41.**185 below.

184. The records of the company of shipwrights . . . Vol. 2. 1971.   **41.**184

185. Parliamentary surveys of the bishopric of Durham. Vol. ii. 1972.   **41.**185

186. York memorandum book B/Y. Edited by Joyce W. Percy. 1973.   **41.**186

Begun in 1371 and continued to 1596, with some items of earlier date. Similar in content to A/Y (see **41.**120, 125). Deeds, more numerous than in A/Y, are calendared; other entries if in English are transcribed, if in Latin translated.

187. The royal visitation of 1559: act book for the northern province. Transcribed and edited . . . by C. J. Kitching. 1975.   **41.**187

Latin, the lay presentments and text of recognizances calendared for the most part. Procedure of this and the earlier royal visitations of 1535 and 1547 is described and commented upon in the introduction. In the appendices are set out the details of the sessions (date, place, name of preacher, names of visitors), and tables of the offences in presentments concerning the laity and in presentments concerning church and clergy.

188. Lonsdale documents. Edited by Elizabeth Playne and G. **41.188**
de Boer. 1976.

Transcripts of letters, Jan. 1799–Mar. 1804, addressed by the Rev. John
Lonsdale (*d.* 1807) to the surveyor general or his deputy at the Land
Registry Office about a new lease of the reclaimed land known as Sunk
Island on the northern side of the lower part of the Humber estuary, and
of letters to his wife. Also, William Whitelock's survey and plan of Sunk
Island, 1797, and genealogical tables for Lonsdale and Gylby. The intro-
duction gives a brief account of the Lonsdale family and, at greater length,
sets out the points at issue regarding Sunk Island.

189. Commercial papers of Sir Christopher Lowther, 1611– **41.189**
1644. Edited by D. R. Hainsworth. 1977.

Transcribed in the main from letter-books and note-books, illustrating
the industrial development of Whitehaven and west Cumberland by the
Lowthers, 1632–44, especially in coal mining, salt and rope making, iron
smelting, and milling. Genealogical table of Lowther.

190. The meditations of Lady Elizabeth Delaval, written be- **41.190**
tween 1662 and 1671. Edited by Douglas G. Greene. 1978.

Transcript. Prayers and meditations. Lady Elizabeth, *née* Livingston, *d.*
1717.

191. Lowther family estate books, 1617–1675. Edited by C. **41.191**
B. Phillips. 1979.

Transcripts of two compact records of rents and receipts, with the evidence for the amounts due, and of major expenditure on land and the
family, the formal and repetitive matter mostly calendared. Appended are
the autobiography by Sir John Lowther (*d.* 1637); his statement of wealth,
1634; the 'Memorable observations and rememberances' of the house and
grounds at Lowther and of his own achievements and family affairs by a
later Sir John (*d.* 1675); a pedigree of the Lowther family in the 17th
century; and a map showing the growth of the estates.

192. York city chamberlains' account rolls, 1396–1500. Ed- **41.192**
ited by R. B. Dobson. 1980.

Transcripts, Latin, with a list of mayors and chamberlains for the period,
and a table of selected annual receipts and expenses.
 The introduction explains that the accounts—running from St. Blaise's
day, 15 Jan.—'follow the common form of late medieval charge and
discharge accounts in which the final entry is the sum of money owed to
or by the accountant' and emphasizes that 'the income recorded ... was
based on the total revenue due' and is not necessarily identical with the
cash actually paid in. It follows that 'any attempt to estimate the real
income of the late medieval city chamber from its annual account rolls
must accordingly be made with considerable caution'. Similar problems
of interpretation are shown to apply to expenditure.
 A descriptive consideration of the city's receipts and outgoings shows
that while real income tended to decline, the annual expenditure could be

held 'comparatively stable' apart from the short-term strains caused by exceptionally long parliaments, visits by magnates or the sovereign, and urgent repairs to walls and civic buildings.

Re-election of chamberlains was virtually unknown. Originally three, later four, their annual fee remained unchanged at 3s. 4d. each. During the late 15th century 'evidence for a widespread reluctance to serve becomes most plentiful'.

193. A seventeenth century flora of Cumbria: William Nicol- **41.193**
son's catalogue of plants, 1690. Edited by E. Jean Whittaker.
1981.

Transcript of the bishop's unpublished finding list, modelled on the work of John Ray and giving locations within the ancient kingdom of Northumbria. The introductory life is particularly concerned with Nicolson's botanical interest and achievement. His record of the flora of Great Salkeld is compared with the record made 250 years later by his successor as rector there, Canon G. A. K. Hervey.

20. The trade of Bristol in the eighteenth century. Edited by **42.20**
W. E. Minchinton. 1957.

Transcripts of docs. and of extracts from docs. selected to provide a statistical picture of the dimensions, range and content of the trade, and to illustrate commercial procedures and the conduct of a merchant's business.

The introduction includes a summary indication of the main sources and categories of unprinted material in England relating to Bristol's trade in the 18th century. Appended tables give the number of ships paying anchorage, the yield of Greenwich Hospital levy for Bristol seamen, the tonnage and crews of shipping in foreign and coastal trade, the number of ships entering and clearing the port, 1764-96, the number and tonnage of ships registered in 1788 and 1790-1800, and particulars of bankruptcies of Bristol merchants, 1711-93. Glossary.

21. Cartulary of St. Mark's hospital, Bristol. Edited by C. D. **42.21**
Ross. 1959.

Late 15th century, completed 1505. Calendar, with transcripts, Latin, of docs. concerned with the foundation and constitution of the hospital, as well as of all deeds earlier in date than 1200 and of docs. the meaning of which is not entirely clear. Also, notes on some mayors and bailiffs or reeves in the 13th century, and a summary of John Easterfield's ordinances for Forster's almshouse in so far as they concern St. Mark's.

22. Some manorial accounts of St. Augustine's abbey, Bristol, **42.22**
being the computa of the manors for 1491-2 and 1496-7 and other documents of the fifteenth and sixteenth centuries. Edited by Arthur Sabin. 1960.

Transcript, Latin, of the roll for 1491-2 with a note of the principal differences in that for 1496-7, and of extracts from numerous other docs. (temporalities, accounts, valors, the only known register of deeds of Bristol dean and chapter, Dean Chetwyn's survey made 1619-22, leases, and court rolls) grouped by manors. The introduction is written around the manor of Lygh, now Abbotsleigh. Appended are lists of stock mentioned on the manors, and of annuities granted out of the abbey, 1527-42.

23. Politics and the port of Bristol in the eighteenth century: **42.23**
the petitions of the Society of Merchant Venturers, 1698–
1803. Edited by W. E. Minchinton. 1963.

Transcripts, slightly abridged, of petitions, memorials, remonstrances, loyal addresses, and related papers, linked by a brief commentary, the whole constituting 'a record of the most articulate and considered means' used by the Society to express its opinion on commercial matters. Includes a list of honorary freemen of the Society, lists of Bristol pilots, haven masters and ballast masters, and a register of members continuing the list in **42.17**.

24. City chamberlains' accounts in the sixteenth and seven-   **42.24**
teenth centuries. Edited by D. M. Livock. 1966.

Transcripts of accounts for 1556–7 (showing the effect of the purchase of monastic estates on the income and expenditure of Bristol) and 1627–8 (showing the demands of the wars of Chas. I). Analytical introduction.

25. The inhabitants of Bristol in 1696. Edited by Elizabeth   **42.25**
Ralph and Mary E. Williams. 1968.

Transcripts of the assessments, parish by parish, made for the city and county of Bristol under an Act of 1694 commonly known as the Marriage Act, for taxing burials, births, marriages, bachelors, and childless widows, to help finance the wars against France.

26. Minute book of the Men's Meeting of the Society of   **42.26**
Friends in Bristol, 1667–1686. Edited by Russell Mortimer.
1971.

Transcript, supplemented from other Friends' records in the Bristol Archive Office, with biographical notes on persons mentioned. Contd. in **42.30** below.

27. The records of a church of Christ in Bristol, 1640–1687.   **42.27**
Edited by Roger Hayden. 1974.

Transcript of the history of Broadmead church begun by Edward Terrill, *d*. 1685, superseding editions by the Hanserd Knollys Soc. (see **22.2**) and in the Bunyan Library series, with an added account of 17th-century Bristol nonconformity, and biographical notes.

28. The ledger of John Smythe, 1538–1550. From the tran-   **42.28**
script made by John Angus, edited by Jean Vanes. 1975.
[HMC JP 19]

The book of accounts of a prosperous merchant, twice mayor of Bristol, with appendices, among them a genealogy of Smythe of Long Ashton, and a table of prices showing the effects of inflation. Glossary.

29. Bristol and its municipal government, 1820–1851. By   **42.29**
Graham Bush. 1976.

An examination of Bristol government in the years preceding and following the Municipal Corporations Act of 1835. Includes biographical notes on members of the corporation and town councillors.

30. Minute book of the Men's Meeting of the Society of   **42.30**
Friends in Bristol, 1686–1704. Edited by Russell Mortimer.
1977.

Transcript, with biographical notes on persons mentioned.

31. Documents illustrating the overseas trade of Bristol in the sixteenth century. Edited by Jean Vanes. 1979.   **42.31**

Selected from many sources, central as well as local, among them the records of Bordeaux notaries, and printed in full or calendared, so as to depict the trends of trade in general and trade with the northern and southern countries and with France. Glossary.

32. The great white book of Bristol. Edited by Elizabeth Ralph. 1979.   **42.32**

Transcript, calendared in part, of the third of the city's custumals (the others being the Little and the Great red books), some entries in Latin, and all of a miscellaneous nature, ranging in date from 1491 to 1598.

33. Calendar of the Bristol apprentice book, 1532–1565. Pt. ii: 1542–1552. Edited by Elizabeth Ralph and Nora M. Hardwick. 1980.   **42.33**

Apprenticeship enrolments, calendared in English. Continues **42.14**.

34. Accounts of the constables of Bristol castle in the thirteenth and early fourteenth centuries. Edited by Margaret Sharp. 1982.   **42.34**

For the years 1221–4, 1224–5, 1282–4, 1289–91, 1294–6, 1300–3, from the pipe rolls of the exchequer, the first three transcribed, Latin, the others calendared, together with a complementary account (also calendared) of the burgesses in respect of the farm of their town for one year, 1224–5.

The introduction, after indicating other accounts of value for an understanding of Bristol in this period, describes the influence of the castle in Bristol history, its use as a prison, the state prisoners and hostages it held, and sets out the little that is known about its garrison. Detailed consideration is given to the area covered by the accounts, known as the king's barton, comprising the hamlets of Mangotsfield, Stapleton, and Easton, and the forest or chase of Kingswood.

45. SOUTHAMPTON RECORDS SERIES

4. The brokage book of Southampton, 1443-1444. Edited ... **45.4**
by Olive Coleman. Vol. 1. 1960.

Transcript, Latin, of the daily record of traffic at the Bargate, 30 Sept.
1443-2 Mar. 1444, with the names of the carters (or horse drovers), the
nature of the goods carried, the names of the owners of the goods, the
destinations on outward journeys, and the tolls collected.

The introduction, which is not limited by the term of the transcribed
text, describes the functions of the Bargate broker, the variety of levies
(custom, brokage, pontage, and other dues), the rates levied, the classes of
persons exempted from payment, the overland distribution of goods from
Southampton, and (though less amply) the land traffic inwards. Contd.
with continuous pagination in **45.6** below.

5. The local port book of Southampton for 1439-40. Edited **45.5**
... by Henry S. Cobb. 1961.

Transcript, chiefly Latin, with facing translation for the first two folios
and for the audit page. The introduction treats of 'the history and incid-
ence of the tolls levied at the port and attempts to assess the value and
limitations of the port books as evidence of the sea-borne trade of Southampton'. List of 15th-century port books (water-bailiff's accounts) of
Southampton. Glossary.

6. The brokage book of Southampton, 1443-1444. Vol. 2. **45.6**
1961.

3 Mar.-29 Sept. 1444, with a list of Southampton brokage books of the
15th century and tables showing the overland distribution of woad and
wine in the 15th century. Glossary.

7. The local port book of Southampton for 1435-36. Edited **45.7**
... by Brian Foster. 1963.

Transcript, chiefly Anglo-Norman, with facing translation. Glossary.

8. The third book of remembrance of Southampton, 1514- **45.8**
1602. Edited by A. L. Merson. Vol. iii: 1573-1589. 1965.

Transcript, with introduction and 18 appendices concerned *inter alia* with
the town's officers, the earl of Leicester and the sweet wine grant, the
Pascall family of Essex and Southampton, chandlers' contracts, the dispute with the lord admiral in the 1580s, Southampton schoolmasters, the
innkeepers of the 'Dolphin' and 'Star', Richard Etuer, the Armada crisis,

Capt. James Parkinson, and the Sir Thomas White loans. Contd. in **45.22** below. For earlier vols. see **45.2**, 3.

[9] Southampton maps from Elizabethan times. By Edwin **45.9** Welch. 1964.

Notes on 24 maps (contained in separate portfolio), followed by chapters on the geography, population, municipal government, communications, port and trade, religion, and buildings. Also, a list of Acts of Parliament relating to Southampton (excluding those concerned with estates and personal matters) compiled by C. E. C. Burch. Published by the City of Southampton. Not uniform with the Records Series.

10. A selection from the Southampton corporation journals, **45.10** 1815–35, and borough councils minutes, 1835–47. Edited . . . by A. Temple Patterson. 1965.

Transcripts or summaries illustrative of the more important or unusual business, with added explanatory or amplifying matter, a list of the corporation's fifth of the port dues, 1815–47, a list of borough rates, 1836–47, and maps of the town in 1802 and 1844.

The introduction describes the government of the town in the years preceding and following the 1835 Municipal Reform Act.

11. A history of Southampton, 1700–1914. By A. Temple **45.11** Patterson. Vol. i: An oligarchy in decline, 1700–1835. 1966.

Contd. in **45.14**, 18 below.

12. A calendar of Southampton apprenticeship registers, **45.12** 1609–1740. Compiled by Arthur J. Willis and edited . . . by A. L. Merson. 1968.

From two ms. vols. in the city archives, the General Register and the Poor Child Register, both of them described and considered (along with many aspects of the apprenticeship system) in the introduction. Includes some settlement orders, 1616–20, in the Poor Child Register.

13. The admiralty court book of Southampton, 1566–1585. **45.13** Edited . . . by Edwin Welch. 1968.

Transcript, the formal entries in Latin. Introduction on jurisdiction and procedure. Includes a tentative list of boroughs possessing or claiming some kind of admiralty jurisdiction. Map. Glossary.

14. A history of Southampton, 1700–1914. Vol. ii: The begin- **45.14** nings of modern Southampton, 1836–1867. 1971.

15. The Southampton terrier of 1454. Edited by L. A. Bur- **45.15** gess, with an introduction by L. A. Burgess, P. D. A. Harvey and A. D. Saunders. 1976 [HMC JP 21]

Transcript, Latin, with facing translation, of a survey of the medieval town within its walls at the period of its greatest prosperity, the indications of earlier ownership of properties covering in some cases several generations. Appended is a description of the wards of the town *c.* 1488, and in the introduction are five plans of the wards from the late 13th century to the late 16th. Also appended is a transcript of the so-called muster book of 1544. Plan in end pocket.

16. Southampton notarial protest books, 1756–1810. Edited ... by Geoffrey Hampson. 1973. **45.16**

Transcript of four vols. containing ship protests (statements made by ship masters before a notary public 'protesting' that everything was done to bring a ship and cargo safely to destination) and entries relating to the 'protesting' and dishonouring of bills of exchange.

The introduction explains the technicalities and pleads for more attention to the history and functions of notaries in England.

17. The Beaulieu cartulary. Edited by S. F. Hockey, with an introduction by P. D. A. Harvey and S. F. Hockey. 1974. **45.17**

Transcript, Latin, with brief summaries by the editor, of the cartulary drawn up soon after 1250, continued into the 1320s and later, concerned with the property of the abbey in Berkshire, Hampshire and Cornwall. The ms., its history and compilation are described by Dr. Harvey, the descriptions of the abbey site, the estates and the charters themselves are by Dom Hockey. Plates. Maps.

18. A history of Southampton, 1700–1914. Vol. iii: Setbacks and recoveries, 1868–1914. 1975. **45.18**

19. The cartulary of God's House, Southampton. Edited by J. M. Kaye. Vol. 1. 1976. **45.19**

Transcript, Latin, with brief summaries by the editor, of the 14th-century cartulary. The introduction outlines the early history of the hospital from its foundation in the 1190s, and gives some account of the buildings on the site. Contd. in the following. Pagination is continuous.

20. The cartulary of God's House, Southampton. Vol. 2. 1976. **45.20**

Appendices: (i) a chronological list of God's House rentals prior to 1603, and (ii) notes on the history and devolution of Southampton tenements within the walls owned by the hospital or in which it had some interest. Maps.

21. The Southampton mayor's book of 1606–1608. Edited by W. J. Connor. 1978. **45.21**

Transcript of the earliest surviving minute book of the town, recording the deliberations of the assembly at its regular meetings. The introduction treats of the condition of the town in 1600, its administrative boundaries and wards, the assembly and courts, its officers and servants, financial administration, poor relief, and the office of town clerk under John Friar.

22. The third book of remembrance of Southampton, 1514– **45.22**

1602. Vol. iv: 1590–1602. Edited by T. B. James. Transcribed by A. L. Merson. 1979.

23. The minute book of the French church at Southampton, **45.23** 1702–1939. Edited ... by Edwin Welch. 1979.

Transcript, French, 1702–1833, then, after a break of 23 years, the text continues in English and is calendared in this edition. In the appendix, a selection of letters relating to the church. The introduction describes its history and archives.

24. The cartulary of the priory of St. Denys, near Southamp- **45.24** ton. Edited by E. O. Blake. Vol. 1. 1981.

Compiled between 1343 and, probably, 1349. Transcripts, Latin, of all docs. issued before the end of the 12th century and others of particular interest; common form deeds and leases of the 13th and 14th centuries presented as Latin abstracts with standard clauses in abbreviated form represented by a code; every entry with brief English summary and notes.

The introduction lists the priors, describes the ms., and treats at some length the history and endowment of the priory and its possessions in the town and suburbs of Southampton. Plates, maps, diagrams. Contd. in the following. Pagination is continuous.

25. The cartulary of the priory of St. Denys, near Southamp- **45.25** ton. Vol. 2. 1981.

The cartulary contd., with appendices on royal charters not in the cartulary, sources used for the dating of 13th-century docs., a detailed list of plates and maps, and a microfiche supplement (in end pocket) giving topographical notes on the priory's possessions and listing the benefactors.

47. KENT ARCHAEOLOGICAL SOCIETY, KENT RECORDS*

17. A seventeenth century miscellany. 1960.   **47.20**

Court rolls of the manor of Chilham, 1645–56. Edited by F. W. Jessup. [Transcript.]

The Tufton sequestration papers, 1644–7. Edited by Felix Hull. [Transcripts of orders, certificates, petitions, etc., with schedules of stock etc. taken during sequestration, and rent accounts etc. relating to estates in Kent and Sussex owned by John Tufton, 2nd earl of Thanet.]

A book of church notes by John Philipot, Somerset herald. Edited by C. R. Councer. [For Kent, made 1613–42. Transcript, reproducing many of the original sketches, the shields blazoned and missing tinctures indicated by the editor.]

An account book of the Committee of Kent for 1647–1648. Edited by Alan Everitt. [Transcript of 'an analytical summary of the year's transactions, arranged by subject, not by date', reflecting 'the genesis of the movement to overthrow the Committee, which culminated in the rebellion of 1648 and the Second Civil War'.]

The Compton census of 1676: the dioceses of Canterbury and Rochester. Edited by C. W. Chalklin. [Providing, for nearly nine-tenths of the parishes in Kent, the numbers of Anglicans, Roman Catholics and protestant dissenters, with a map showing the distribution of non-conformity in the county, and a calculation of the population of the county as at least 150,000.]

18. Documents illustrative of medieval Kentish society.   **47.21**
General editor F. R. Du Boulay. 1964.

A list of the archbishop of Canterbury's tenants by knight-service in the reign of Henry II. Edited by H. M. Colvin. [Transcript, Latin, with translation and commentary, of a list compiled soon after the death of Archbishop Thomas in 1170, and a comparison with the *Domesday monachorum* of 1093/6.]

The pipe roll account of the see of Canterbury [during vacancy] 9 December 1292 to 4 February 1295. Edited by F. R. H. Du Boulay. [English abstract.]

The Kent lay subsidy of 1334/5. Edited by H. A. Hanley and C. W. Chalklin. [An edition of the fifteenth and tenth, containing (exception-

---

ally for 1334) more than 11,000 names and assessments. The introduction considers the background of the subsidy and its usefulness as
a source for the distribution of population and the distribution of
wealth. Map, largely conjectural, of hundredal boundaries. Index.]

The earliest Canterbury freemen's rolls, 1298–1363. Edited by Sylvia B.
Thrupp with the assistance of Harold B. Johnson. [Names of 892 newly
admitted freemen. See the 'reconsideration' in 47.24 below.]

Some ancient indictments in the king's bench referring to Kent, 1450–
1452. [Translated and calendared] by R. Virgoe.

Calendar of the demesne leases made by Archbishop Warham, 1503–32,
excerpted from Dean and Chapter of Canterbury mss. register T, by
F. R. H. Du Boulay.

19. A calendar of the white and black books of the Cinque ports, 1432–1955. Prepared and edited by Felix Hull. 1966. [HMC JP 5]

47.22

Minutes of meetings of the ports (the 'brodhull, 'brotherhood', 'guest-
ling'). Index to personal names by Mrs. J. Elliot.

20. Timber and brick building in Kent: a selection from the J. Fremlyn Streatfeild collection. By Kenneth Gravett. 1971.

47.23

Plates and figures, including all those drawings in the collection which
relate to timber and brick constructions, with a list of the omitted drawings. J. Fremlyn Streatfeild d. 1886.

21. A Kentish miscellany. Edited by F. Hull. 1979.

47.24

Canterbury's earliest rolls of freemen admissions, 1297–1363: a reconsideration. By A. F. Butcher. [Sets out to provide 'an accurate description
of the rolls of freemen admissions, to correct the more substantial errors
of transcription, and to re-evaluate the evidence they contain for the
economic and social history of Canterbury'.]

A rental of the manor of East Malling, 1410. Edited by C. L. Sinclair
Williams. [English translation, with indexes of persons and places, and
notes on some of the place-names.]

Memoranda from the Queenborough statute book. Edited by Felix Hull.
[Miscellaneous entries, 1452–1556, occurring on fly-leaves and in
vacant spaces, including bye-laws and names of burgesses, translated
or transcribed, with a list of mayors and an index of persons named.]

The view and state of the commandery of Swingfield and its appurtances
in 1529. Edited by L. R. A. Grove and S. E. Rigold. [Transcript of a
searching inquiry into physical conditions made by two officials of Sir
William Weston, the last prior in England, so as to conclude a period of
abuse and misappropriation by Sir John Rawson.]

A sixteenth-century ms. of precedents of indictments. Edited by R. E. A.
Poole. [Translation, the text in part reconstructed, of a collection of
some 40 forms of indictment seemingly made by or for the use of the
clerk of the peace for Kent. Index of persons named.]

22. Lost glass from Kent churches: a collection of records from the sixteenth to the twentieth century. By C. R. Councer. 1980.

47.25

Arranged alphabetically by parish. 'The churches dealt with are those where only a little ancient glass has survived *in situ*, or where there is none at all. This leaves something like 58 churches for which records—sometimes copious, sometimes no more than a line or two—of lost glass exist'. A list of those of the 58 which have been published, wholly or in part, is given in the introduction; for the remainder, reference is made to the projected Kent vol. of *Corpus vitriarum medii aevi*. The chief concern of the introduction is to acknowledge the previous recorders of painted glass in the county, from the 17th-century heralds to Charles Winston (*d.* 1864).

48. LANCASHIRE AND CHESHIRE RECORD SOCIETY, OTHERWISE THE RECORD SOCIETY FOR THE PUBLICATION OF ORIGINAL DOCUMENTS RELATING TO LANCASHIRE AND CHESHIRE

107. An index to the wills and administrations formerly pre- **48.**107
served in the probate registry at Chester, for the years 1821–
1825 both inclusive. Edited by Robert Dickinson. 1961.

Continues the index begun in **48.**2, the wills and administrations in three alphabetical lists (Lancashire, Cheshire, and Welsh) with comprehensive indexes of places and trades. Contd. in **48.**113, 118, 120 below.

108. The registers of estates of Lancashire papists, 1717– **48.**108
1788. Edited by R. Sharpe France. Vol. ii: 1717. 1960.

Continues **48.**98, which contains abstracts of Register rolls, I, II and part of III. This vol. abstracts the remainder of roll III and the whole of roll IV. Contd. in **48.**117 below.

109. A Lancashire miscellany. Edited by R. Sharpe France. **48.**109
Indexed by Mrs. M. Fielden. 1965.

The founding of Bretherton school, 1655. [Transcript of the account written by Jane Rose of Bretherton, wife of James Fletcher, her third husband, describing the endowment and building of the school, later benefactions, and naming the householders who most strongly opposed the setting up of the school.]

Lancashire parsonages, 1662–1825. [Descriptions from terriers.]

The statutes and ordinances of Warrington, 1617. [Transcript, with an inventory of weights, measures and branding irons owned by the town in 1622.]

The order book of Ormskirk, 1613–1721. [Transcripts of the orders for the good government of the town and manor.]

The will, inventory and accounts of Robert Walthew of Pemberton [d. 1676]. Edited by J. J. Bagley. [Transcript of will, inventory of goods, inventory of debts due to the deceased, and the executor's account, with pedigree and, in the introduction, some account of the Walthew family and of Robert's management of his farm and estate.]

110. The great diurnal of Nicholas Blundell of Little Crosby, **48.**110
Lancashire. Transcribed and annotated by Frank Tyrer, edited ... by J. J. Bagley. Vol. i: 1702–1711. [1968.]

Transcript, beginning 27 July 1702, ending 31 Dec. 1711, an entry for every day, recounting his activities about the house, in farm and garden, his business, pastimes, troubles of tenants and labourers, the comings and goings of family and friends, their ailments and the treatments prescribed, etc. etc., and at the end of every month a succinct description of the weather. Genealogical tables of Blundell of Crosby, Butler of Ireland, and Langdale of Holme. Also transcripts of numerous accounts of expenses, among them one for making a parlour at Crosby Hall, Dec. 1706. Contd. in **48.**112, 114 below.

111. Chester customs accounts, 1301–1566. Edited by K. P.   **48.**111
Wilson. 1969.

Contains (i) a tabulated list, year by year, of the palatinate customs returns of the port of Chester from 7 Feb. 1301 to Mich. 1554 (when the last surviving account ends) for the three customable commodities, wine, iron and hides, giving name of ship and port of origin; (ii) transcript of an answer to a royal exchequer enquiry into concealment of customs at Chester, 22 Apr. 1532; (iii) a list, as in (i), of customs accounts for Chester and Liverpool, from the port books extending from Mich. 1565 to Mich. 1566, covering overseas shipments only; (iv) Chester local customs accounts, calendared, for the years 1404–5, 1467–8 and 1525–6; rates of local customs *c*. 1400 and *temp*. Hen. VIII; and (vi) a table showing port of origin of all ships entering the port of Chester, 1422–1566. Glossary.

The introduction stresses, as the key factor in the customs organization of Chester, its independence from direct royal control until palatinate privileges were ended in the mid-16th century.

112. The great diurnal of Nicholas Blundell ... Vol. ii: 1712–   **48.**112
1719. [1970.]

Continues the daily entries to 31 Dec. 1719, as in **48.**110 above, and shows the impact of the 1715 Jacobite rebellion on a recusant family, their flight first to London and then to Flanders, to Dunkirk, Gravelines, Bruges, Ghent (where two sisters and his mother entered the house of the English Benedictines) and elsewhere, meeting and recording the names of almost one hundred religious and almost twice as many lay men and women, most of them Catholic exiles. Also, accounts of expenses and other docs. illustrating some of the consequences of the family's Catholicism. Map of Little Crosby, 1702, and another showing Blundell's travels in Flanders, 8 Mar. 1716–5 Aug. 1717.

113. Index to wills and administrations formerly ... in ...   **48.**113
Chester, 1826–1830. Edited by Robert Dickinson. 1972.

114. The great diurnal of Nicholas Blundell ... Vol. iii: 1720–   **48.**114
1728. [1972.]

The daily entries contd. to the abrupt conclusion of the journal on 4 Apr. 1728, with the inventory of the writer's goods and chattels at his death, 21 Apr. 1737, his account of expenses on his journey to Flanders, May–Oct. 1723, various other accounts, and letters written by him concerning likely suitors for his daughters.

115. Marriage bonds for the deaneries of Lonsdale, Kendal, **48.**115 Furness, Copeland and Amounderness in the archdeaconry of Richmond, now preserved at Preston. Pt. vii: 1746–1755. Edited by Robert Dickinson. 1975.

Continues the edition of abstracts begun in **48.**74.

116. Letters and accounts of William Brereton [*d.* 1536] of **48.**116 Malpas. Edited by E. W. Ives. 1976.

Letters and analogous docs., 1524–34, transcribed; business docs. (vouchers, bonds, patents, letters), 1508–35, calendared; ministers' (i.e. bailiffs') accounts for certain Savage family property held by Brereton, 1528–30, and for his own estates, 1530–4, transcribed or summarized; accounts of John Norbury, his receiver-general, 1530–2, transcribed, with summary for 1532–3; a summary of the clear value of properties, fees and annuities for the year 1534–5 transcribed; extracts, transcribed, from the rental of his Shropshire estates, 1531; and a transcript of the schedule of his outstanding debts, 1545, attached to the will of his widow.

In the introduction, a description of accounting procedures, and a list of crown offices and grants held by Brereton, with accompanying considerations of office-holding, the profitability of royal grants *temp.* Hen. VIII, the traffic in crown offices, the political power exercised by Brereton in Cheshire and the March, and the faction struggles of the 1530s. Also, and derived from the accounts, an insight into estate management: tithes, grain, pasture for sheep, cattle and horses, the management of deer, his pack of hounds, manorial rights, and wages paid. Concludes with a tentative assessment of Brereton's wealth.

117. The registers of estates of Lancashire papists, 1717– **48.**117 1788. Vol. iii: 1717, with list of persons registered, 1718–1785. 1977.

Abstracts of rolls V and VI, completing the initial registration to the end of 1717. The list of persons registering estates serves as an index to the remaining rolls of the series.

118. Index to wills and administrations formerly ... in ... **48.**118 Chester, 1831–1833. Edited by Robert Dickinson and Florence Dickinson. Prefaced by a history of the Society and guide to publications vols. 1–117, 1878–1977, by Brian E. Harris. 1978.

119. Northwich hundred poll tax, 1660, and hearth tax, 1664. **48.**119 Edited by G. O. Lawton. 1979.

Transcripts, with analytical introduction, tables, and map of the hundred showing parish and township boundaries.

120. Index to wills and administrations formerly ... in ... **48.**120 Chester, 1834–1837. Edited by Florence Dickinson. 1980.

121. Proceedings of the Lancashire justices of the peace at **48.**121 the sheriff's table during assizes week, 1578–1694. Edited by B. W. Quintrell. 1981.

Transcript, drawing together 'the table's surviving records from its earliest days until the end of the first extant order book in 1694, amplified where possible from related sources'. Chief among the related sources are the record compiled by William Farington, household steward to the 4th earl of Derby and himself a magistrate, of the earliest known meetings in 1578 and 1586, and the notebook of Oswald Mosley of Ancoats in which he entered details of magistrates' proceedings between 1616 and 1625.

The use by magistrates of the sheriff's table for formal business meetings during assizes—'almost certainly unique to Lancashire'—and the opportunity thereby given to circuit judges, and through them the Privy Council, 'to press home ... the exhortations contained in assize court addresses and in Conciliar correspondence' receives detailed consideration in the introduction. The range of business is described, as also are the table's relations with the Council and assize judges, with the duchy, and with the quarter sessions and the lieutenancy.

51. CHETHAM SOCIETY, REMAINS HISTORICAL AND LITERARY CONNECTED WITH THE PALATINE COUNTIES OF LANCASTER AND CHESTER, THIRD SERIES

7. The church in Chester, 1300-1540. By Douglas Jones. 1957.   **51.7**

Includes biographical notices of the clergy of the city and of the prioresses of St. Mary's.

8. A schoolmaster's notebook; being an account of a nineteenth-century experiment in social welfare, by David Winstanley of Manchester, schoolmaster. Edited by Edith and Thomas Kelly. 1957.   **51.8**

Transcript, re-arranged, of a record kept by David Winstanley, 1810-71, agent for the property of Sir Benjamin Heywood in Miles Platting, Manchester, and principal executor of the welfare schemes devised by Heywood for his tenants. Subjects dealt with include the day school, the Sunday school, the mechanics' institution, estate management, housing, social reform, and emigration. Appended reports on the condition of the working classes in east Manchester in 1834, in Miles Platting in 1837, and of the handloom weavers in Miles Platting in 1835. Map of Miles Platting, showing the Heywood estate.

9. The early history of the Davenports of Davenport. By T. P. Highet. 1960.   **51.9**

Ends with John de Davenport, fl. 1426. Appended to the chapter on serjeants of the peace are transcripts, Latin, of a robber roll of 1333 and attachments 1352, puture rolls of the 14th and early 16th centuries, a kelk roll of 1406-7, and selected Davenport charters to 1398, some in French. Maps.

10. The agricultural history of Cheshire, 1750-1850. By C. Stella Davies. 1960.   **51.10**

Chapters on land tenure and conditions of tenancy, enclosure, the farming community, and agrarian economy, with appended tables and docs. including, from the Dorfold mss., surveys and rentals, 1773-99, extracts from minute books, 1803-21, and correspondence relating to the sale of the Wilbraham estate, 1745-8. Maps of Witton, 1721, Cheshire, 1804, and Snelson tithe map, 1848.

11. The social institutions of Lancashire: a study of the chang-   **51.11**
ing patterns of aspirations in Lancashire, 1480–1660. By
W. K. Jordan. 1962.

Maintains that Lancashire, 'poor, isolated, and backward in 1480, . . . had
drawn level with the realm' before the period was out, of very great
importance in this accomplishment being 'the fact that Lancashire was
one of the favourite regions in the whole of the realm for the flow of the
restless and evangelical charitable wealth of London'.

12. The family economy of the working classes in the cotton   **51.12**
industry, 1784–1833. By Frances Collier. Edited by R. S.
Fitton. 1965.

Concerned in the main with McConnel and Kennedy's mill at Manchester, 1795 and 1810–19, Burrs mill at Bury, 1801–2, and the Quarry
Bank community at Styal, with numerous tables of wages in the cotton
industry, prices of food, family budgets, etc. Memoir of Miss Collier
(1889–1962) by T. S. Ashton.

13. Some aspects of education in Cheshire in the eighteenth   **51.13**
century. By Derek Robson. 1966.

Chapters on the S.P.C.K. and its influence, the grammar schools, private
teachers and academies, the pupils, school finance, and school founders
and trustees, with appended lists of the schools, the schoolmasters in
grammar and parish schools, Cheshire boys at Oxford and Cambridge,
and extracts from wills of Cheshire schoolmasters. Map showing the
location of schools.

14. The autobiography of William Stout of Lancaster, 1665–   **51.14**
1752. Edited by J. D. Marshall. 1967.

Transcript, copiously annotated, with excerpts from the Public Records
relating to Stout's shipping ventures, by R. Craig and M. M. Schofield;
a list of distraints upon him (a Quaker) for non-payment of tithes, by
W. G. Howson; his account with the Backbarrow Iron Company, 1713–
29, by W. H. Chaloner; and an investigation into his places of work and
residence, by K. H. Docton. Pedigree of Stout of Bolton Holmes and
Hatlex, with details of the families of Butler of Kirkland and Butler
Rowley, compiled by R. Sharpe France and J. D. Marshall. Maps.

15. Liverpool registry of merchant ships. By Robert Craig   **51.15**
and Rupert Jarvis. 1967.

Introduction, giving an outline history of English statutory ship registry,
followed by transcripts, in parts abbreviated and re-arranged, of the
registration particulars contained in the first register book, Sept. 1786–
Dec. 1789, of the port of Liverpool, at that time 'unique among English
ports in that . . . it had no dependent members', and possessing 'the largest
and best preserved collection of such register books in all British registry
. . .'. The particulars include the physical details of each vessel, the names,
occupations and places of residence of owners, the names of masters, dates
of previous and subsequent registrations, and whether lost, sold, captured,

broken up or condemned. Appended tables, some being annual summaries to 1805, set out *inter alia* the number and tonnage of vessels built and registered at Liverpool or in the Mersey, the number and tonnage of Liverpool vessels taken prize, and the names of owners and investors.

16. The diary of Richard Kay, 1716–51, of Baldingstone, near Bury, a Lancashire doctor. Extracts edited with a joint introduction and notes by W. Brockbank and F. Kenworthy. 1968.   **51.16**

Comprising between one third and one half of the diary, 1737–50, the extracts illustrate general medical training and practice and the life and worship of Lancashire nonconformity. Kay trained at Guy's and attended the protestant dissenting chapel in Silver Street, Bury. Table showing the relationships between the Kay families of Sheephay and Baldingstone, compiled by W. J. Smith.

17. The last days of the Lancashire monasteries and the Pilgrimage of Grace. By Christopher Haigh. 1969.   **51.17**

Includes lists of Lancashire religious before the suppression, and of the recipients and lessees of monastic lands. Map showing the location of the religious houses in 1536.

18. An edition of the cartulary of Burscough priory. Transcribed, edited and introduced by A. N. Webb. 1970.   **51.18**

Transcript, Latin, of the late 14th-century cartulary, with English abstracts, additional charters, and a list of priors. Pedigrees of Scarisbrick and Lathom. The foundation and territorial expansion of the priory, its management of its estates, and the extent of its ecclesiastical property, are treated in the introduction. Map.

19. Elizabethan recusancy in Cheshire. By K. R. Wark. 1971.   **51.19**

Part narrative, part analysis of the chief extant evidence. Includes biographical notices of recusants or probable recusants, and of recusant priests, and notes on the family background and religious loyalties of gentlemen suspected of popery *c.* 1583. Map.

20. The Lancashire textile industry in the sixteenth century. By Norman Lowe. 1972.   **51.20**

The woollen and linen industries; the sources of raw material; trade and markets; government regulation and control. Includes six inventories, 1570–98, representative of different groups of workers in the industry. Glossary. Also a brief commemorative notice of Professor E. F. Jacob, president of the Society, *d.* 7 Oct. 1971.

21. The early records of the Bankes family at Winstanley. Edited by Joyce Bankes and Eric Kerridge. 1973.   **51.21**

The memoranda book of James Bankes, 1542–1617, and his probate inventory, with farm accounts, 1667–78, and rentals, 1668(?)–77. Map of Bankes land in 1770.

22. Provision for the relief of the poor in Manchester, 1754– **51.22**
1826. By G. B. Hindle. 1975.

Statutory provision (the Poor House, Workhouse, and abuses), voluntary
provision (the Strangers' Friend Society, the Soup Charity, and relief by
committee and public subscription), and provision by bequest. Appendices on the Irish poor and additional voluntary provision, 1815-25.

23. Victoria Park, Manchester: a nineteenth century suburb **51.23**
in its social and administrative context. By Maurice Spiers.
1976.

'A factual account of the internal administration of the Park and its
relations with local government' from the formation of the Victoria Park
Company in 1836 (later the Victoria Park Trust) to the final absorption of
the Park by Manchester corporation in 1954. Includes sketches of the
social history of the area, with plans and numerous plates, and a list of
prominent residents of the Park, their addresses and years of residence.

24. The encouragement of the fine arts in Lancashire, 1760– **51.24**
1860. By C. P. Darcy. 1976.

A study of the 'new men' of fortune by whose patronage, exercised singly
or in groups, art and artists were encouraged, public and private collections formed, and exhibitions organized. Treats also of the preferences
shown, and of the nature and quality of the works collected. Briefly
touched on are the formation and activities of academies, art unions,
literary and philosophical societies, architectural societies, public and
private museums, and the Manchester School of Design.

25. The Lancashire gentry and the great rebellion, 1640–60. **51.25**
By B. G. Blackwood. 1978.

The longer-term consequences (gain/loss, rise/decline) are considered to
c. 1700.

26. Methodist secessions. The origins of Free Methodism in **51.26**
three Lancashire towns: Manchester, Rochdale, Liverpool. By
D. A. Gowland. 1979.

27. Elizabethan Manchester. By T. S. Willan. 1980. **51.27**

A study of the manor and township, the place of agriculture and industry
and trade in the town economy, wealth and family, house and home.
Omitted, for reasons given in the preface, are the administration of the
town and its religious life. Appended are a rental of the manor, 1599-
1600, and a list of probate inventories, 1570-1602, in the county record
office at Preston. Map of the ancient parish and of the town c. 1650.

28. The financial administration of the lordship and county of **51.28**
Chester, 1272–1377. By P. H. W. Booth. 1981.

A study of one aspect of the government of an English county unusual in
being a 'landed estate' as well as a 'local government unit', subject to the
'royal lordship' of the earl of Chester (in this period either the king or his

eldest son), and its organs of administration distinct from those of the rest of England. Includes a detailed consideration of the financial records of the county, disentangling their archival origins and explaining the working of the administrative structure which produced them. The methods of account and audit employed in the Chester exchequer are described. Specially valuable to the study are the virtually complete series of records for the lordship of Macclesfield, yielding 'an overall view of the manor's financial history for the best part of two centuries (1182–1376)'. Taxation and the search for revenue is the theme of the final chapter. Set out in appended tables are (i) a list of the chief accountants—justiciars and chamberlains—of Cheshire, 1270–1374, (ii) revenues from Macclesfield and other parts of the county, and (iii) a summary of the *valor* of the late Black Prince's lands, 1376.

29. The industrial archaeology of north-west England. By Owen Ashmore. 1982.   51.29

A gazetteer of sites of industrial and archaeological interest in the old counties of Cheshire and Lancashire excluding Furness and Cartmell, an area comprising the new counties of Cheshire, Lancashire, Greater Manchester and Merseyside. Maps. Many illustrations.

52. LINCOLN RECORD SOCIETY, PUBLICATIONS

51. The *Registrum antiquissimum* of the cathedral church of **52.51**
Lincoln. Vol. viii. Edited by Kathleen Major. 1958.

Items 2185–2389, continuing the edition begun with **52**.27 and including, as in preceding vols., many charters additional to those in the original register. Transcripts, Latin, with English summaries and notes, the text as far as possible reproducing the docs. 'letter for letter, with all the marks of accentuation'. This vol., the first of three designed to contain charters of cathedral property in the city of Lincoln, comprises the parishes of St. John in Newport, St. Swithin, St. Edmund, St. George, St. Cuthbert, St. Michael on the Mount, St. Peter Stanthaket, St. Martin in Dernstall, and All Saints Hungate. Docs. connected with chantries other than those administered by the common fund are omitted. The appendix, on the mayors and bailiffs in the 13th century, supplements and reconsiders the list in J. W. F. Hill, *Medieval Lincoln*. Corrections and additions to earlier vols. Contd. in **52**.62, 67, 68 below.

52. The rolls and register of Bishop Oliver Sutton, 1280– **52.52**
1299. Edited by Rosalind M. T. Hill. Vol. iv: Memoranda,
May 19, 1292–May 18, 1294. 1958.

Continues the edition begun with **52**.39, calendaring the formal entries and transcribing, Latin, with English summaries, those which have particular interest. Contd. in **52**.60, 64, 69 below.

53. The state of the ex-religious and former chantry priests in **52.53**
the diocese of Lincoln, 1547–1574, from returns in the exchequer. Edited by G. A. J. Hodgett. 1959.

Calendar, with full Latin texts of specially interesting entries, of pensions paid or assigned to ex-religious resident in the diocese, then comprising the counties of Lincoln, Leicester, Huntingdon, Bedford, Buckingham, and much of Hertfordshire.

54. The records of the commissioners of sewers in the parts of **52.54**
Holland, 1547–1603. Vol. i. Edited by A. Mary Kirkus. 1959.

Transcripts. The introduction surveys the work already done on commissions of sewers; describes the physical conditions that led to the setting up of the courts of sewers and the early methods of containing flooding; considers the history and constitution of the courts, and, for the reign of Eliz. I, the commissions, the officers, the working of the courts, and the connection between the courts and central government. Also, biographical notes on commissioners known to have acted in south Lincolnshire, 1544–1603, and whose activities are not fully recorded in Dugdale. Glossary. Contd. in **52.63** below.

55. The building accounts of Tattershall castle, 1434–1472. **52.55**
Edited by W. Douglas Simpson. 1960.

Transcript, Latin, by Lucy Drucker, from five account rolls, with English translation and commentary by the editor. The introduction notes the affinity of Lord Cromwell's tower-house with similar contemporary castles in France and more particularly with the brick-built castles of the Teutonic Order in Old Prussia, and argues that its master-mason was in fact the brickmaker Bawdwin Docheman (Baldwin the German). Plans.

56. Records of some sessions of the peace in Lincolnshire, **52.56**
1381–1396. Edited by Elisabeth G. Kimball. Vol. ii: The parts of Lindsey. 1962.

Continues **52.49**. Transcript, Latin, of the Lincolnshire peace roll, with brief English abstracts and a table of sessions of the peace in Lindsey, 1381–8, 1395–6.

57. The register of Bishop Philip Repingdon, 1405–1419. Ed- **52.57**
ited by Margaret Archer. Vol. 1: Memoranda, 1405–1411. 1963.

Transcript, Latin, except that all but the first of a recurring form of entry are calendared. The introduction summarizes the 'clear picture of diocesan administration and the state of religious life in the see of Lincoln' given by the Memoranda. Contd. in the following (pagination is continuous) and **52.74**.

58. The register of Bishop Philip Repingdon, 1405–1419. Vol. **52.58**
2: Memoranda, 1411–1414. 1963.

59. Letters and papers of the Cholmeleys from Wainfleet, **52.59**
1813–1853. Collected and edited by Guy Hargreaves Cholmeley. 1964.

Transcripts of letters etc. (part of an accumulation extending to 1874) collected from various descendants of the Rev. Robert Cholmeley, with pedigrees of Cholmeley, Waldo, Adye and Miller.

60. The rolls and register of Bishop Oliver Sutton, 1280– **52.60**
1299. Vol. v: Memoranda, May 19, 1294–May 18, 1296. 1965.

61. An episcopal court book for the diocese of Lincoln, 1514– **52.61**
1520. Edited by Margaret Bowker. 1967.

Transcript, Latin, an occasional entry in English, of proceedings in Bishop Atwater's court of audience held *coram episcopo* or before an official deputed by him, with the bishop's itinerary from 3 Nov. 1514 to his death.

62. The *Registrum antiquissimum* ... Vol. ix. Edited by Kathleen Major, with a memoir of Sir Frank Merry Stenton. 1968.

Items 2390–2666, being charters relating to property in the parishes of St. Peter at Arches, St. Peter at Pleas, St. Stephen in Midhergate or in Newland, St. John in Wigford, Holy Trinity in Wigford, St. Botolph, All Saints in the Bail, St. Clement in the Bail, St. Paul in the Bail, St. Nicholas in Newport, and in the fields of Lincoln. Also, corrections and additions to earlier vols., and an appendix on the archdeacons of Stow (concerned particularly with those called William) in the years 1214–40.

63. The records of the commissioners of sewers in the parts of Holland, 1547–1603. Vol. ii. Edited by A. E. B. Owen. 1968.   **52.63**

Selected verdicts, some fully transcribed, others described or printed only in part, with extracts from accounts showing what actually was done to repair banks and drains, 1565–76.

64. The rolls and register of Bishop Oliver Sutton, 1280–1299. Vol. vi: Memoranda, May 19, 1297–September 12, 1299. 1969.   **52.64**

65. Records of some sessions of the peace in the city of Lincoln, 1351–1354, and the borough of Stamford, 1351. Edited by Elisabeth G. Kimball. 1971.   **52.65**

Transcripts, Latin, of a peace roll for Lincoln (showing in unusual detail the work of an efficient justice, William de Skipwith) and of a single membrane from a gaol delivery roll containing the peace commission for Stamford and the record of two sessions held under this commission. The roll is analysed in the introduction.

66. Letters from John Wallace to Madam Whichcot, edited by C. M. Lloyd, and some correspondence of John Fardell, deputy registrar, 1802–1805, edited by Mary E. Finch. 1973.   **52.66**

Whichcot of Harpswell letters, 1721 or 1722 to 1727, chosen for the picture they give of household life and the information they contain about politics and other county affairs. The Fardell correspondence illustrates the actual functioning of one particular ecclesiastical office and some long-established characteristics of office-holding in the church.

67. The *Registrum antiquissimum* ... Vol. x. Edited by Kathleen Major. 1973.   **52.67**

Items 2667–2980, relating to property in the parishes of St. Peter in Eastgate, St. Margaret in Pottergate, St. Rumbold, St. Mary Magdalene, St. Augustine, St. Andrew on the Hill, St. Edward in Wigford, and of uncertain parish. Corrections and additions to earlier vols.

68. The *Registrum antiquissimum* ... Facsimiles of charters in vols. viii, ix and x. 4to, 1973.   **52.68**

69. The rolls and register of Bishop Oliver Sutton, 1280–1299. Vol. vii: Ordinations, May 19, 1290–September 19, 1299. 1975.   **52.69**

The ordination lists for the first ten years of Sutton's episcopate, in common with the rest of his register, have not survived. The substance of letters connected with the lists is given in English.

70. Letters and papers concerning the establishment of the Trent, Ancholme and Grimsby Railway, 1860–1862. Edited by Frank Henthorn. 1975.   52.70

Transcripts. Includes statements of expenses connected with the Private Bill and subsequent Act, and of the lawyers' charges. Short-lived, and never really independent (it was vested in the Manchester, Sheffield & Lincolnshire Railway in 1882) the T.A.G.R. was successful: through its means the ironstone of the district yielded a good profit. The history of the line is recounted in the introduction. Maps, plans, plates.

71. The records of the commissioners of sewers in the parts of Holland, 1547–1603. Vol. iii. Edited by A. E. B. Owen. 1977.   52.71

Verdicts, 1577 onwards, some abbreviated to a varying extent, one entirely omitted, with some of the laws transcribed by the editor of vol. i, a set of dikereeves' accounts, an illustration of the work of the surveyor, and, in the introduction, some account of these officials. Additions and corrections to earlier vols.

72. Lincolnshire returns of the census of religious worship, 1851. Edited by R. A. Ambler. 1979.   52.72

Transcript, with an extensive introductory analysis concerned, for example, with the accuracy and reliability of the census, attendance patterns, church and chapel accommodation, the Anglican clergy, nonconformity and dissent in all forms, education, social conditions, and worship.

73. The minute-books of the Spalding Gentlemen's Society, 1712–1755. Selected and introduced by Dorothy M. Owen, with the help of S. W. Woodward. 4to, 1981.   52.73

Facsimile reproduction of the minutes for 1732. The introduction sets out to convey the type of information contained in the minutes for other years.

74. The register of Bishop Philip Repingdon, 1405–19. Vol. iii: Memoranda, 1414–1419. 1982.   52.74

Text reduced by about one-third; many docs. omitted, and others summarized. These changes are explained in the preface.

54. NORFOLK RECORD SOCIETY

A register (one of several) into which the bishop's secretary, Anthony Harison (1563-1638), copied or reconstructed evidences relating to the temporal possessions of the see of Norwich and other docs. created in the course of its administration, spiritual as well as temporal, some in Latin. This pt. begins in 1603 and ends with a list of the clergy of the diocese in 1605, showing their dates of institution, their degrees, and the names of their curates if they were double-beneficed. Pt. 2 below, of equally miscellaneous content, ends in 1613; it includes notes on the docs. and the index. Pagination is continuous.

33. The *Registrum vagum* of Anthony Harison. Pt. 2. 1964.   **54.33**

34. Index of wills proved in the consistory court of Norwich,   **54.34** 1687-1750, and now preserved in the Norfolk and Norwich Record Office. Compiled by Thomas F. Barton and the late Miss M. A. Farrow. 1965.

35. A cartulary of Creake abbey. With an introduction by   **54.35** A. L. Bedingfeld. 1966.

English translation 'based on the work of Mr. K. C. Newton', of 242 deeds, more than half of them undated, the latest dated 1477, assumed to be but part of a larger compilation. The introduction sketches the history of the abbey from its inception *c.* 1206, with lists of priors and abbots, and briefly surveys the sequence of its buildings and furnishings.

36. Minutes of the Norwich court of mayoralty, 1632-1635.   **54.36** Edited ... by William L. Sachse. 1967.

Continues **54.15**, various abbreviations and codes being used to compress the transcription. Indexed by A. L. Bedingfeld. Includes five plates of weavers' marks and orders for the infected and the poor.

37. Mary Hardy's diary. With an introduction by B. Cozens-   **54.37** Hardy. 1968.

Transcript, 28 Nov. 1773-21 Mar. 1809, an entry for every day unless the writer was ill, each entry beginning with the weather. The diarist's husband in 1781 bought land at Letheringsett, a home since that date of the Cozens-Hardy family. Outline pedigrees of Raven, Hardy and Cozens. Indexed by A. L. Bedingfeld.

38. Index of wills proved in the consistory court of Norwich,   **54.38** 1751-1818, ... Compiled by the late Thomas F. Barton, the late Miss M. A. Farrow and A. L. Bedingfeld, with a foreword by Miss Jean Kennedy. 1969.

39. Great Yarmouth assembly minutes, 1538-1545, [edited   **54.39** by] P. Rutledge. The Norwich accounts for the customs on strangers' goods and merchandise, 1582-1610, [edited by] D. L. Richwood. 1970.

Great Yarmouth minutes transcribed, leases in general calendared, from the First Book of Entries (also known as the Great Black Book), with minutes of the period entered in other books and all the material in the *Liber ordinum*. The government of the town and its financial organization are briefly described in the introduction.

Norwich accounts transcribed in full, with an introduction outlining the early history of the stranger community.

40. The Norwich census of the poor, 1570. [Edited by] John **54.40**
F. Pound. 1971.

Transcript. The introduction revises and supersedes the editor's earlier analysis of the census in the *University of Birmingham Historical Journal* (1962).

41. The early communar and pitancer rolls of Norwich cath- **54.41**
edral priory, with an account of the building of the cloister. By
F. C. Fernie and A. B. Whittingham. 1972.

Transcript, Latin, of the first 18 rolls, 1282-1330. Pt. 1 of the introduction considers their nature, contents and significance, and also the distinction between communar and pitancer; pt. 2, by A. B. Whittingham, on the cloisters, seeks 'to provide a more accurate interpretation of their complex history than has previously been possible' and, incidentally, to further the understanding of medieval building works in general. Plans of close and cloisters. Glossary.

42. Faden's map of Norfolk [1797]. 1973. **54.42**

Black and white reproduction. Six sheets, with an introductory pamphlet by J. C. Barringer describing and evaluating the map, all in slip case.

43. The letter book of John Parkhurst, bishop of Norwich, **54.43**
compiled during the years 1571-5. Edited by R. A. Houl-
brooke. [1975.]

Transcript (omitting two items) of the book of copies of correspondence and other papers, dated for the most part between 1567 and 1575, with letters from John Jewel of the 1550s, the few Latin items in English translation. In the introduction, an account of Parkhurst's career and his administration of his diocese.

44. Crime in East Anglia in the fourteenth century: Norfolk **54.44**
gaol delivery rolls, 1307-1316. [Edited by] Barbara Hanawalt.
1976.

Calendar, with analytical introduction. Glossary.

45. Norfolk lieutenancy journal, 1660-1676. Edited by **54.45**
Richard Minta Dunn. 1977.

Transcript of the journal kept during the lieutenancy of Lord Townshend and the preceding one-year lieutenancy of the earl of Southampton, intro-duced by an account of the functions of the lieutenancy, its personnel, machinery, and procedures. Biographical appendix.

46. The papers of Nathaniel Bacon of Stiffkey. [Edited by] A. **54.46**
Hassell Smith, Gillian M. Baker and R. W. Kenny. Vol. i:
1556–1577. [1979.]

Aims to reconstitute the dispersed Stiffkey archive and whenever possible
to print the entire ms. or a calendar entry. The introduction includes an
account of the dispersal of the archive and gives the known location of its
principal groups. Pedigree of Bacon.

47. Index of wills proved in the consistory court of Norwich, **54.47**
1819–1857, and now preserved in the Norfolk Record Office.
Compiled by Claire Frostick, with a foreword by Jean Kennedy. 1980 [1982].

55. NORTHAMPTONSHIRE RECORD SOCIETY, PUBLICATIONS

20. Carte nativorum: a Peterborough abbey cartulary of the   **55.**20
fourteenth century. Edited by C. N. L. Brooke and M. M.
Postan. 1960.

Transcripts, Latin, with ample English abstracts, of two groups of charters in Peterborough Dean and Chapter ms. 39, the 'charters of villeins' and 'charters from the ancient registers of the precentor'. With few exceptions, both groups arise out of the administration of the abbot's manors, and this leads Professor Brooke, in his part of the introduction, to deduce that the ms. was made by or for Brother John of Achurch, monk warden of the abbot's manors, in or shortly after the later 1340s. The *carte nativorum* proper, their historical context and significance, and the fresh views they open up of medieval agrarian history, are discussed by Professor Postan in the second part of the introduction. In the appendices, lists of Peterborough abbots, 1155–1361, and of stewards, c. 1177–1330, and a glossary of field-name elements.

21. John Isham, mercer and merchant adventurer: two   **55.**21
account books of a London merchant in the reign of Elizabeth
I. Edited ... by G. D. Ramsay. 1962.

Transcripts, 'adapted to the reasonable requirements of economy', of personal ledgers which also comprise entries arising from the business of his firm, begun 1 Jan. 1559 and discontinued early in 1566. Also, the probate inventory, 1558, of Gregory Isham, John's brother. The origins of the Isham firm, and its export/import business, are set out in the introduction (100 pp.).

22. Luffield priory charters. Edited ... by G. R. Elvey. Pt. i.   **55.**22
1968.

Contd. in **55.**26 below. Both vols. published jointly with the Buckinghamshire Record Soc. See **36.**15, 18 above.

23. The royal forests of Northamptonshire: a study in their   **55.**23
economy, 1558–1714. By Philip A. J. Pettit. 1968.

Geographically limited to the three royal forests—Rockingham, Whittlewood, Salcey—and the parks associated with them, relatively remote from naval dockyard and iron furnace, yet each having a different history, social as well as economic. Includes numerous statistical tables for wood sales, composition fees for disafforestation, population changes, and so on, with a case study of Brigstock as a forest village. Maps. Select glossary.

24. The letters of Daniel Eaton to the third earl of Cardigan, 1725–1732. Edited by John Wake and Deborah Champion Webster. 1971.   **55.24**

Transcripts of letters from his land steward to George Brudenell, earl of Cardigan, keeping his master informed about the estate and household at Deene and Deenthorpe. The introduction by Joan Wake treats of the two main characters, the estates, manor courts, woodland, park, home farm, the workmen and labourers employed, building work, the accounts and finance, and fox-hunting. The language of the letters, their vocabulary, spelling, grammar, idiom and style are commented upon by the co-editor in a separate introduction. The appendices include agreements for alterations to the house, subsequently named Little Deene, 1725 and 1727, the bye-laws of Great Weldon in 1728, Daniel Eaton's will, 1742, and a note on the postal aspect of the letters by G. F. Oxley. Map. Glossary.

25. Northamptonshire militia lists, 1777. Edited by Victor A. Hatley. 1973.   **55.25**

Transcripts. Nearer to being complete for all the county than any for other years, the lists for 1777 omit the soke of Peterborough (otherwise known as Nassaburgh hundred). The system is described, and the lists are analysed statistically in the introduction. Glossary.

26. Luffield priory charters. Pt. ii. 1975.   **55.26**

27. Northamptonshire lieutenancy papers and other documents, 1580–1614. Edited by Jeremy Goring and Joan Wake. 1975.   **55.27**

The text (98 letters etc. relating to musters and militia affairs) established and supplied with editorial matter by Miss Wake, revised by Dr. Goring with five additional docs. and the introduction. He argues that the main text, which includes the Queen's commission of lieutenancy to Sir Christopher Hatton, cannot be Hatton's own 'lieutenancy book'. Instead, Dr. Goring surmises that most of the papers passed from Sir Richard Knightley to Sir William Tate and were brought together by Tate's younger brother Francis, 'an avid collector of manuscripts'. Hatton's lieutenancy is closely examined. Glossary.

28. The cartularies and registers of Peterborough abbey. By Janet D. Martin. (Dean and Chapter of Peterborough, Anthony Mellows Memorial Trust. Vol. i.) 1978.   **55.28**

A catalogue, describing in elaborate detail twelve cartularies (including a vol. of rentals and surveys) and seven abbots' registers, and reconstructing another cartulary (now destroyed) and parts of a lost register. The particulars given include the location of each ms., its description, contents, authorship, and former owners, together with principal bibliographical references and an indication of the extent to which it has been used by scholars, especially in the 17th and 18th centuries. The introduction sketches the history of the abbey, the making of its records, their dispersal at the dissolution, and the later spasmodic revivals of interest in them.

29. Calendar of the correspondence of Philip Doddridge, **55.29**
D.D., 1702–1751. By Geoffrey F. Nuttall. 1979. [HMC JP 26]

Letters, totalling 1814 in all, the earliest dated 28 Mar. 1720, and the
number of correspondents about 350. Appendices on donors of books to
the Northampton Academy, the Northamptonshire Book Society, Northamptonshire subscribers to *The Family Expositor*, the Northamptonshire earthquake on 30 Sept. 1750, and Doddridge's itinerary from Northampton to Falmouth in 1751.

30. The puritans in the diocese of Peterborough, 1558–1610. **55.30**
By W. J. Sheils. 1979.

31. The red earl: the papers of the fifth Earl Spencer, 1835– **55.31**
1910. Edited by Peter Gordon. Vol. i: 1835–1885. 1981.

Transcripts, in chronological order, from Spencer's correspondence, annotated and with an account of his life and work to the fall of the government in 1885. A description of the papers (part of the 'several thousand
items' at Althorp, arranged but as yet uncatalogued) is to be in vol. ii.

57. THOROTON SOCIETY, RECORD SERIES*

18. Poll-books of Nottingham and Nottinghamshire, 1710. **57.18**
With a political introduction by Myrtle J. Read and a bio-
graphical index by Violet W. Walker. 1958.
Texts of the earliest ms. poll-books known to be in Nottingham.

19. Lenton priory estate accounts, 1296 to 1298. Edited by **57.19**
F. B. Stitt. 1959.
Transcript, Latin, of detailed accounts, 31 Dec. 1296–Michaelmas 1298,
while the estates were being administered by the crown. The introduction
describes the modest, scattered nature of the estates and the diversity of
management. Analytical tables.

20. Lists of the clergy of north Nottinghamshire. Edited by **57.20**
K. S. S. Train. 1961.
The majority of the parishes considered were in the ancient rural deanery
of Retford, part of the archdeaconry of Nottingham. Excluded are all
parishes forming part of the peculiar of Southwell or not comprised within
Southwell diocese. Biographical notes. For central Nottinghamshire see
57.15.

21. A Nottinghamshire miscellany. 1962. **57.21**
Edited by J. H. Hodson:
An agreement [between John Willoughby of Wollaton and John Hippis,
   marbler, of Lincoln] for the construction of a tomb in Wollaton church,
   1515.
The Wollaton estate and the civil war, 1643–1647. [Transcripts of items
   in the estate accounts which record disbursements arising from the
   war.]
The building and alteration of the second Thoresby House, 1767–1804.
   [Transcripts of docs. summarizing costs of building and of later improvements.]
Edited by Violet W. Walker:
The confiscation of firearms in Nottingham in Charles Harvey's mayoralty, 1689–1690. [Transcripts of docs. illustrating the town's efforts to
   recover the muskets distributed for fear of a Jacobite rising and later

* General index to the Transactions of the Thoroton Society of Nottinghamshire,
vols. i–lxxx, 1897–1976, and the Thoroton Society Record Series, vols. i–xxxi.
Compiled by Laurence Craik. 1977.

seized by order of the earl of Kingston, action seen by the town as an affront to its loyalty.]

The will of the Rev. John Whitlock, 1700. [One time vicar of St. Mary's, Nottingham.]

Thomas Finningley, of West Stockwith, and the *Lady Ann*, 1760. [Letters of marque.]

Nottingham election expenses, 1779. [Transcript of expenses, mostly payments to innkeepers, at the unopposed election of Robert Smith, later Lord Carrington of Upton in the Irish peerage.]

Edited by P. A. Kennedy:

Verses on the puritan settlement in America, 1631. [Text of satirical doggerel written on the back of a will.]

Nottinghamshire settlers in the Cape of Good Hope, 1820. [Transcripts of letters and reports to the emigration committee from Thomas Calton, surgeon, of North Collingham, leader of the expedition, from the time he left Liverpool to his death in South Africa shortly after his arrival there.]

Nottinghamshire register of motor cars and motor cycles, 1903. [Giving in tabular form the name and postal address of the owner, the description or type of car, the type and colour of the car body, the weight unladen, and whether the car was for private use, trade, or public conveyance.]

22. Nottinghamshire household inventories. Edited by P. A. Kennedy. 1963.   57.22

Transcripts, compressed in part, of 118 inventories from the probate records of the peculiar court of Southwell, 1512–68. Glossary.

23. The Sherwood forest book. Edited by Helen E. Boulton. 1965.   57.23

Transcript, mostly Latin, part French, of the earliest extant forest book relating to Sherwood, assigned to the late 14th, early 15th century. Copies of statutes and ordinances, perambulations, inquisitions, examples of writs, chapters of regard, extents and rentals, and extracts from the forest eyres. Fourteen further books, all derived directly or indirectly from a common source, are described in the introduction. Maps.

24. Nottinghamshire miscellany, no. 4. 1967.   57.24

Willoughby letters of the first half of the sixteenth century. Edited by Mary A. Welch. [Transcripts, mostly of letters to Sir Edward Willoughby, *d.* 1540, and Sir John, *d.* Jan. 1549.]

The account books of Gertrude Savile, 1736–58. Edited by Marjorie Penn. [Receipts and expenses for 1736 (London and Rufford) and 1739 (London and Farnsfield); expenses only, Sept. 1746–Mar. 1747 (Bath), and Jan.–Mar. 1758 (London), selected from an abundantly detailed series. Pedigree of Savile.]

25. Calendar of Nottinghamshire coroners' inquests, 1485–1558. Edited by R. F. Hunnisett. 1969.   57.25

In the introduction, brief accounts of coroners' duties and of the surviving records, with lists of county coroners and of borough and franchisal coroners for the period covered. Select glossary.

26. Luddism in Nottinghamshire. By Malcolm I. Thomis. 1972.　　57.26

Docs. selected in the main from the letters of the town clerk of Nottingham, George Coldham, and the lord lieutenant of the county, the duke of Newcastle, supplemented by letters from two London police officers, from local industrialists and magistrates, and from random individuals, illustrating contemporary attempts to understand and explain the events of 1811–16.

27. The cartulary of Blyth priory. Edited by R. T. Timson. [Pt. 1.] 1973. [HMC JP 17]　　57.27

Transcript, Latin, with English summaries and annotations, the entries beginning in the late 11th century and continuing into the early 15th. In this pt. the first 329 docs. in the main cartulary. Contd. in the following. Pagination is continuous.

The introduction (more than 100 pp.) includes genealogies for the families of de Builli and Eu, Lisoriis and de Tilly, de Cressy, de Styrrup, de Meinil, Cossard, and Parole (or Winchester); lists of early priors and vicars; sections on relations with Rouen, with other religious houses, with parish churches, with the archbishops of York, on priory lands and revenues, the vill of Blyth, the honour of Tickhill. Maps.

28. The cartulary of Blyth priory. [Pt. 2.] 1973. [HMC JP 17]　　57.28

Docs. 330–529 of the main cartulary, with the additional docs. in other folios of the cartulary, docs. (calendared) relating to Blyth or its more important grantors in Dodsworth mss., and texts (with summaries) from the lost Saunderson roll. Indexes.

29. Rufford charters. Edited by C. J. Holdsworth. Vol. 1. 1972.　　57.29

Transcripts, Latin, with English summaries, the original texts (where they have survived) being preferred to the cartulary copies. Docs. which have no special features and appear to be in common form, have been calendared. In this pt. the first 179 docs. Contd. in 57.30, 32, 34 below. Pagination is continuous.

The introduction (more than 100 pp.) includes lists of abbots, c. 1146–1536, and seals; notes on families mentioned, and their seals; and a genealogy for Sutton of Sutton-on-Trent.

30. Rufford charters. Vol. 2. 1974.　　57.30

Docs. 180–799. Maps of Park Leys grange and the boundaries of Rufford.

31. Letters of John Holles, 1587–1637. Edited by P. R. Seddon. Vol. i. 1975.　　57.31

Letters by the 1st earl of Clare, from copies made by his eldest son, arranged in chronological sequence. Letters printed in HMC *Portland*, ix (see 7.48) have been summarized. In this pt. letters 1–260 (16 June 1617).

The introduction traces in some detail the growth of the Holles estates and in more than 70 pp. describes and analyses Holles' career.

32. Rufford charters. Vol. 3. 1980.   57.32

Docs. 800–1004. Additions and corrections.

33. The diary of Abigail Gawthern of Nottingham, 1751– 57.33
1810. Edited by Adrian Henstock. 1980.

Modernized transcript of a 'retrospective chronicle of personal, family, and local events set down in more-or-less chronological order year by year ... between 1808 and 1813 ... from entries in her "pocketbooks" for the relevant years' by Mrs. Gawthern *née* Frost, *d.* 1821. Genealogies for the families of Secker and Frost, Brough, and Gawthern.

34. Rufford charters. Vol. 4: Index. 1981.   57.34

58. OXFORDSHIRE RECORD SOCIETY

[38] Articles of enquiry addressed to the clergy of the diocese **58.38** of Oxford at the primary visitation of Dr. Thomas Secker, 1738. Transcribed and edited by H. A. Lloyd Jukes. 1957.

Replies by the clergy to the articles addressed to them.

[39] Some Oxfordshire wills proved in the prerogative court **58.39** of Canterbury, 1393–1510. Edited by J. R. H. Weaver and A. Beardwood. 1958.

The English wills transcribed, the Latin wills translated and condensed. Topics treated in the brief introduction are (i) the distinction between originals and registered copies, (ii) the prerogative exercise of testamentary jurisdiction by the archbishop of Canterbury, (iii) the two series of prerogative registers, one of wills proved *coram domino*, the other of wills proved before the commissary-general, (iv) the possession of *bona notabilia* in more than one diocese, 'a wholly fictious qualification for the intervention of prerogative authority', and (v) the distinction between 'last will' and 'testament'.

[40] Index to wills proved in the peculiar court of Banbury, **58.40** 1542–1858, edited by J. S. W. Gibson. Custumal (1391) and bye-laws (1386–1540) of the manor of Islip, edited by Barbara F. Harvey. 1959.

The Banbury index—published jointly with the Banbury Historical Soc. (see **88.**1 below)—includes a reprint of the notes on testamentary procedure in B. G. Bouwens, *Wills and their whereabouts.* The jurisdiction comprised the Oxfordshire parishes of Horley and Hornton, the parish of Banbury (then partly in Oxfordshire, partly in Northamptonshire), Cropredy (partly in Warwickshire, partly in Oxfordshire), and the parish of Kings Sutton, Northamptonshire. Wills proved in the manorial court of Sibford are included. Map. Separate index of trades.

The custumal and bye-laws relate to the abbot of Westminster's lands in Oxfordshire and principally to his manor of Islip. Transcribed, Latin, with facing English translation.

[41] Henley borough records: assembly books i–iv, 1395–1543. **58.41** Transcribed and edited by P. M. Briers. 1960.

Latin—'never more than dog-Latin'—giving way to English.

[42] The papers of Captain Henry Stevens, waggon-master- **58.42**

general to King Charles I. Transcribed and edited by Margaret Toynbee. 1962.

Annotated transcripts of his official papers, 1 Nov. 1643-20 Dec. 1644. Appended is a letter to Richard Stevens (Stephens), Henry's father, from William Lord Knollys about some nominations for boroughs for the Addled Parliament of 1614, and biographical notes on the less well known (sometimes obscure) Royalist officers.

The introduction sets out the little that is known of Stevens and his family, and briefly considers the King's transport service and the demands made upon it by the carriage of arms and ammunition, provisions, and the sick and wounded.

[43] The Royalist ordnance papers, 1642–1646. Transcribed and edited by Ian Roy. Pt. 1. 1964.   **58.43**

Transcripts of selected docs., arranged chronologically. In this vol. receipts, 30 Dec. 1642-12 June 1646, issues and inventories, 7 Jan. 1642-10 May 1643. In the appendices, a guide to the different kinds of cannon used, their calibre, weight and weight of shot, and a glossary of measures and technical terms.

The introduction (50 pp.) describes the eve-of-war state of the iron and gunpowder industries; the efforts of both sides to secure control of the Ordnance Office; the command and organization of the King's train of artillery; the establishment of the Office at Oxford, its financing and development through the war, and the changes in its personnel; the Royalists' efforts to augment the supplies of arms and munitions by foreign import as well as home manufacture (much of it locally improvised); the distribution of supplies to the King's field forces and garrisons; and the effect of arms supply—and the shortages which arose—on Royalist performance in the field. Contd. in **58.49** below. Pagination is continuous.

44. Household and farm inventories in Oxfordshire, 1550–1590. Edited by M. A. Havinden. 1965. [HMC JP 10]   **58.44**

Transcript (by M. A. Havinden, D. G. Vaisey and Miss J. E. Sayers) of all the known surviving inventories up to and including the year 1590 amongst the records of the Oxford consistory and archdeaconry courts and the peculiar courts of Banbury, Cropredy, Thame and Dorchester.

[45] Index of persons in Oxfordshire deeds acquired by the Bodleian Library, 1878–1963. By W. O. Hassall. 1966.   **58.45**

Published jointly with the Bodleian. Excludes deeds relating to the city of Oxford, the Goring charters printed in **58.13**, 14, and deeds placed on revocable deposit in the library in considerable numbers since 1945. Other limitations are stated in the preface.

[46] Oxfordshire hundred rolls of 1279. 1: The hundred of Bampton, edited by E. Stone. 2: The borough of Witney, edited by Patricia Hyde. [1969.]   **58.46**

In the first, a full translation of the first membrane followed by a 'drastically simplified' translation of the remainder. The introduction takes issue with Kosminsky on the question of negligent omissions from the roll, and with Ballard and Miss Levett on the relationship between money rent and labour services. In the second, a full transcript, Latin, with English translation. Separate indexes.

47. **The letter-books of Samuel Wilberforce, 1843–68. Tran-**   **58.47**
scribed and edited by R. K. Pugh with the assistance of J. F.
A. Mason. 1970.
Published jointly with the Buckinghamshire Record Soc. See **36.**16 above.

48. **Agricultural trade unionism in Oxfordshire, 1872–81. Ed-**   **58.48**
ited by Pamela Horn. 1974.
Transcripts of (i) the minute book of the Oxford district of the National
Agricultural Labourers' Union, 1872–9; (ii) the minute book of the Hors-
path branch of the same union, 1873–4; (iii) the rules of the Oxfordshire
and Adjoining Counties Association of Agriculturalists, 1872; (iv) correspondence between George Wallis and Hugh Hamersley, 1873–4, and (v)
extracts from incumbents' answers to the bishop of Oxford's visitation
questions for the archdeaconry of Oxford, 1875, 1878, 1881. These docs.
the introduction 'seeks to place ... in a wider context by surveying the
history of agricultural combination in the county during the two decades
after 1872'.

49. **The Royalist ordnance papers, 1642–1646. Pt. 2. 1975.**   **58.49**
Issues and inventories, 11 May 1643–15 Mar. 1645; correspondence and
miscellaneous docs., 17 Nov. 1642–24 May 1644; the train of artillery, 29
Jan.–6 Feb. 1645; notes (some 90 pp.) placing the docs. in historical
context and relating them to the other (unprinted) Ordnance papers.

50. **Manorial records of Cuxham, Oxfordshire, circa 1200–**   **58.50**
1359. Edited by P. D. A. Harvey. 1976. [HMC JP 23]
Transcripts, Latin, of charters, *c.* 1200–1361; terriers and lists of tenants,
1227–1448; subsidiary records of account, 1272–1355; account rolls,
1276–1359; records of the manorial court, 1279–1358, and tax assessments, 1295–1328. All the records of Cuxham's internal administration
before 1360 excluded from this edition are listed in appendix I, and the
persons named in the unpublished docs. are listed in appendix VII. Other
appendices are devoted to domestic and farm buildings, amounts of seed
sown per acre, types of corn sown and acreage sown with each crop, annual
crop yields per quarter sown, and numbers of stock on demesne. Word-
list and glossary, the word-list showing one way in which editors of texts
might contribute to building up a corpus of information on medieval
usage, in vocabulary and in syntax, that is based on actual mss. rather than
on editorial reconstructions.
  The introduction (some 70 pp.) treats of demesne farming and the
development of manorial accounting, shows how an account was drawn
up, describes the form and development of final accounts and subsidiary
records, and outlines the development of manorial surveys and court rolls.

51. **Village education in nineteenth-century Oxfordshire: the**   **58.51**

Whitchurch school log book, 1868–93, and other documents. Edited by Pamela Horn. 1979.

Transcript of the record of school activities required to be kept regularly in accordance with the Revised Code of 1862 by elementary schools open to public inspection and thus eligible for Government grant, with extracts from the school accounts of income and expenditure, and the returns made by Whitchurch in answer to various inquiries concerning its schools. The introduction gives a general history of elementary education in the county to the beginning of the 20th century. Includes lists of Whitchurch rectors, 1806–1914, principal inhabitants connected with the school, principal teachers to 1915, and of Oxfordshire school log books.

52. Bishop Fell and nonconformity: visitation documents from the Oxford diocese, 1682–83. Edited by Mary Clapinson. 1980. **58.52**

Transcripts of letters to the bishop from Oxfordshire incumbents reporting the numbers of nonconformists in their parishes; the bishop's queries after his visitation of 1682 addressed to the archdeacon of Oxford and the archdeacon's replies; and the archdeacon's list of dissenters. Also, the return of conventicles in Oxford diocese, 1669, with which the introductory account of nonconformity begins.

60. OXFORD HISTORICAL SOCIETY, NEW SERIES

12. The history of St. John's College, Oxford, 1598–1860. By W. C. Costin. 1958.

60.12

A 'history of the College springing out of the documents in its possession', with corrections to the early history in **60.**1.

13. The building accounts of the Radcliffe Camera. By S. G. Gillam. 1958.

60.13

Transcript of the 'Building Book', the record of 'all the work done on, and expenses incurred in, the Library from 1737 to 1759' and including 'estimates for work to be done, sometimes from more than one contractor, and in one instance, comparative figures for work done at Christ Church', together with extracts from the trustees' minute books and a history of the library to 1866. Indexed by W. A. Pantin, who was also responsible for the 67 pp. of illustrative plates, for the descriptive list of architectural drawings connected with the designing and building of the Camera, and for the appendix of stray entries of payments found in the minute books and accounts.

14. Survey of Oxford. By the late H. E. Salter. Vol. i. Edited by W. A. Pantin. 1960.

60.14

Aims to present Dr. Salter's ms. 'just as he left it'. This vol. covers the north-east and south-east quarters or wards of the city, giving the traceable history of each street and tenement from the 12th to the 18th or 19th century, together with sketch maps identifying the tenements. Reprints the memoir of Dr. Salter published (with a list of his chief publications since 1933) by the British Academy in its *Proceedings*. Contd. in **60.**20 below.

15. Oxford council acts, 1752–1801. By M[ary] G. Hobson, with a foreword by P. S. Spokes. 1962.

60.15

The fifth vol. of the edition, all vols. with prefatory summaries by Miss Hobson. Appendices give the form of oaths to be taken by the mayor, recorder, aldermen and other city officials; extracts from chamberlains' accounts; and the 'Proposals for the disengaging and beautifying the University and City of Oxford' by the Rev. E. Tatham (1773). For earlier vols. see **59.**87, 95 and **60.**2, 10.

16. Oxford studies presented to Daniel Callus. 1964.

60.16

Foreword by R. W. Southern.

60.16*a*

Northerners and southerners in the organization of the University to **60.16b** 1509. By A. B. Emden. [Concerned to show 'the deep imprint' made upon the organization and life of the University 'by the persistence of this regional animosity throughout the medieval period and later'. Argues, from an examination of the provenance of the successive pairs of proctors, that the river Nene rather than the Trent was the recognized boundary between north and south, and that the fact of regional animosity needs to be considered in every sort of quarrel and controversy among the secular clerks of pre-Reformation Oxford. Appended is a list of proctors, showing their provenance, with an account of the earliest known compilations of this kind, and a similarly differentiated list of university officers in 1454.]

The halls and schools of medieval Oxford: an attempt at reconstruction. **60.16c** By W. A. Pantin. [Brings together 'a good deal of information' on 'the essentially domestic, scattered, buildings in which . . . the vast majority of masters and scholars lived' and constructs a 'fairly convincing conjectural picture of academic home life'. Examines some 15 examples of academic halls, reconstructs their ground plans, and puts forward 'a generalized picture of what an academic hall in medieval Oxford was like and how it was lived in and used'. Similarly considered, but more briefly, are the schools, numbering about 54 for the whole University.]

Foreign Dominican students and professors at the Oxford Blackfriars. By **60.16d** W. A. Hinnebusch. [Sketches the development of the Order's elaborate scholastic organization throughout its many European provinces, with St. Jacques (Paris) at its apex, the incorporation of its general houses of study into the universities, the regulations for the sending of friars to the *studium* of the province or circle of provinces, the qualifications and obligations of the students so sent, the courses of study, the movement of students and teachers between *studia*, the privileges and dispensations granted to students and teachers, the disturbances caused by the required presence of these externs, the economic problem created by them, and the discrimination against them in the allocation of cells. Oxford priory, already functioning as a *studium generale*, was directed to admit foreign friars in 1248; the remainder of the essay is concerned with the disturbances that ensued (particularly grave in the last quarter of the 14th century and exacerbated by the attempt of Ireland to become a separate province), culminating in royal intervention when both Rich. II and Hen. IV ordered the prior of Blackfriars to expel those foreign friars who, because of the privileges renewed to all externs by the reforming master general of the Order, Raymond of Capua, did not observe the customs of the priory. Appended lists of foreign Dominicans at the Oxford Blackfriars name some 28 who were assigned for the basic theological courses, 1273–1494, and some 41 to read for degrees, *c.* 1313–1518, the last a lesser figure than that advanced by Emden.]

The curriculum of the faculty of canon law at Oxford in the first half of **60.16e** the fourteenth century. By L. Boyle. [Sets out to discover 'with what success one can trace a student's course from the statutes at any given period' within the chosen half-century, the enquiry being conducted under the following heads: (i) the licence to lecture, (ii) the course for the doctorate, (iii) quasi-ordinary teaching, (iv) extraordinary teaching,

(v) ordinary teaching, (vi) the licence to incept, (vii) inception, (viii) regency. Surmises that this long course of study 'produced a competent body of professional canonists' and notes the fact that 'all too few seem to have made an academic mark, even in their own country'.]

Oxford grammar masters in the middle ages. By R. W. Hunt. [An account **60.**16*f* of the writings of Richard of Hambury (*d.* 1293 or 1294), Adam Shidyard or Nidzard (probably *d. c.* 1308), John of Cornwall (possibly the John Brian who fl. *c.* 1350 and was 'the first teacher to replace French by English as the language of instruction'), and John Leland (teaching well before 1400, *d.* 1433). Includes numerous extracts, Latin, from their treatises and enumerates the authorities quoted. Concludes that these writings, which formed part of the curriculum of the Oxford grammar schools, demonstrate that by the end of the 14th century the standard of attainment 'had miserably declined'.]

Walter Burley [or de Burley, *c.* 1275-1344]. By C. Martin. [An account of **60.**16*g* his life, incorporating the information that can be put together about the chronology of his writings, with a brief introductory outline of the scope of his literary activity and of the modern research devoted to it. The life divides into three periods: his career at Oxford until *c.* 1306, his subsequent stay at Paris until 1326-7, and his activity in England and Europe, from 1327 to 1344, as an established master deputed for the prosecution of royal business.]

Roger Swyneshed, O.S.B., logician, natural philosopher, and theologian. **60.**16*h* By James A. Weisheipl. [Seeks to disengage one 14th-century schoolman from the obscurity and confusion of an amalgam of at least four others (among them Richard, author of the *Liber calculationum*) and one mythical character recently created. Identifies and considers Roger's logical treatises and his *De motis naturalibus*, with an analytical table of the latter.]

Wyclif's *Postilla* on the Old Testament and his *principium*. By B. Smalley. **60.**16*i* [Argues that the *Postilla* originated in a course of lectures begun by Wyclif before he incepted in 1372 or 1373 and identifies one of them as his *principium* or first (inaugural) lecture when he continued the course. Considers his technique as a postillator, his theological discussions, and his views as a moralist. Concludes with a close study of his *principium*, stressing the virtuosity of its construction and the conservatism of its thought: 'a backward-looking piece, a manifesto of the philosopher and of the sententiary bachelor', his ideas on reform as yet 'inchoate'. Nevertheless, the *Postilla*, covering the whole Bible and delivered by a secular doctor, marked the end of an era: 'Grosseteste walked again'. Appended are two passages, Latin, from the *Postilla* echoing Wyclif's controversy with the Oxford Carmelite John Kenningham on 'the coextension of time', and a third passage on the same, not known to have occurred in the controversy.]

Medieval aftermath: Oxford logic and logicians of the seventeenth cen- **60.**16*j* tury. By I. Thomas. [Begins with John Argall—'he threw overboard all logic elaborated between the twelfth and sixteenth centuries'—and outlines how it was that the older logical methods gave way to increased concern with rhetoric. Considers Argall's list of approved authors (among them John Seton and his commentator Peter Carter; Richard

Stanyhurst; and John Case); Edward Brerewood and his editor Thomas Sixesmith; Smiglecius, whose *Logica* was printed at Oxford in 1634 and in 1638; Robert Sanderson and his *Logicae artis compendium* (1615), often reprinted and one of the main Oxford textbooks of the century; Richard Crakanthorp's *Logicae libri quinque*; John Wallis; John Newton; and finally Henry Aldrich and his *Artis logicae compendium*. The list of books taken to Queen's by Henry Fleming in 1678 and subsequently augmented by purchases provokes the comment 'when he had read them all he would understand virtually no logic'.]

A bibliography of the published writing of Daniel Callus [from 1917 to 1963].   **60.**16*k*

17. **Summary catalogue of manuscripts in the Bodleian Li-**   **60.**17
brary relating to the city, county and university of Oxford.
Accessions from 1916 to 1962. By P. S. Spokes. 1964.

With brief notes (in the preface by R. W. Hunt) on the more important individual collectors: F. J. Morrell, F. P. Morrell, Percy Manning, Falconer Madan, W. J. Oldfield, H. E. Salter, and Henry Minn.

18. **The early rolls of Merton College, Oxford, with an appen-**   **60.**18
dix of thirteenth-century Oxford charters. Edited by J. R. L.
Highfield. 1964.

Transcripts, Latin, of (i) a contemporary copy, 1276-7, of the will of the founder, Walter de Merton, bishop of Rochester; (ii) the accounts, inventories, issues and receipts etc., and consolidated accounts, possibly the 'earliest surviving accounts of the executors of an English bishop', which with the accompanying charters, 'make it possible in large measure to see how the chancellor of Henry III and Edward I made his money and spent or invested it' and show in a remarkable way the clients' side of the day to day running of the royal administration and of the lay and ecclesiastical courts through which the executors did their business'; (iii) all the 13th-century rolls in the muniment room, 40 in all, showing how the college rose and flourished between 1277 and the end of the century, grouped as to wardens' rolls, sub-wardens' rolls, bursars' rolls, and rolls of other officers. Appended are the statutes of 1270 (with cross-references to the later 13th-century sets); 73 charters and other docs. associated with the site of the college or with other sites acquired in Oxford south of the High Street, contributing towards a picture of the site and its development before 1300, and yielding much incidental information about the mayors, bailiffs, and citizens of the city, with four original letters of Ela, countess of Warwick, a benefactress of the college, and one 14th-century doc., the earliest table of the founder's kin. Also plates of some of the seals.

The introduction, by intention less than a definitive biography yet more than merely a framework for the printed docs., is concerned firstly with the founder himself, his family, his training and career, his acquisition of property, his benefactions and their object, and the execution of his will, and secondly with his college in Oxford, its building, constitution, and personnel.

19. **The letter book of Robert Joseph, monk-scholar of Eves-**   **60.**19

164

ham and Gloucester College, Oxford, 1530–3. Edited by Hugh Aveling and W. A. Pantin. 1967.

Transcripts, Latin, with English summaries, of about 170 letters and some verses, written by a single private individual with an eye to their preservation, and copied by him into his letter-book, forming a collection seemingly unparalleled for its time. Appendices, by W. A. Pantin, print specimens of graces for degrees supplicated for by Robert Joseph and some of his contemporaries, illustrating the academic practice of the period; book lists of Edward Burton, M.A., of Mar. 1529, and William Wodrofe, of *c.* 1530; what seems to be a complete list of the monk-students resident at Gloucester College in 1537, viz. an agreement between the prior and monk-students on the one part and the superior bedels of theology, law, and arts on the other, concerning the annual payment of certain fees to the bedels; and the will, in English, of Robert Wyllis, vicar of Cropthorne, 1569, 'most probably to be identified with Robert Joseph'. A further appendix, by Hugh Aveling, is a biographical index of persons named in the letters.

20. Survey of Oxford. By the late H. E. Salter. Vol. ii. Edited by W. A. Pantin and W. T. Mitchell. 1969.　　　　　　　　　　**60.20**

Contains the survey of the south-west and north-west wards, and of North Oxford (i.e. the area immediately north of the Northgate, consisting mainly of Broad Street and St. Giles), together with the relevant maps and the indexes (general, of corporate landlords, and of tenements) to both vols.

21. Woodforde at Oxford, 1759–1776. Edited by W. N. Hargreaves-Mawdsley. 1969.　　　　　　　　　　**60.21**

Apart from some accounts kept by the Rev. James, extracts from which are given, and his three short visits, 'as a mere spectator of the academic scene' in 1777, 1779 and 1793, this edition transcribes 'every single entry written while Woodforde was at Oxford, not only when he was in residence but when he paid visits during the period from 1763 to 1773, being then a country curate', with added linking passages for his periods of absence.

The introduction summarizes the account of Oxford life, and more particularly of New College, given by 'a dull man', content to record the world he saw, and 'by reason of his very mediocrity representative of his class and age'.

22. The register of congregation, 1448–1463. Edited by W. A. Pantin and W. T. Mitchell, with an epilogue by Graham Pollard. 1972.　　　　　　　　　　**60.22**

Transcribed, Latin, and edited by W. T. Mitchell, who also made the indexes of names and subjects. The introduction, by W. A. Pantin, describes the register and its contents: lists of those taking degrees (altogether lacking for the years 1448–9, 1451–2, 1458–63 and, for the most part, for 1453–4) and graces and decisions of various kinds (particular graces, for individuals; general or common graces, for whole classes of persons; common university business, including the appointment of officials). The subject-matter of the business transacted and the graces granted is considered at length, as also is the place of congregation in the medieval university of Oxford (distinguishing between the 'congregatio magna', now called convocation, the 'congregatio minor', now called congregation, and the 'congregatio nigra'). Also dealt with is the general question why some kinds of record have survived while others have not. The statutory requirements for degrees in the five faculties (arts, theology, civil law, canon law, and medicine) are set out in detail, and a glossary, contributed by J. M. Fletcher, explains the technical words and phrases used in the register. Transcripts Latin, with English abstracts, of a dozen letters issued or received by the university and copied by John Manningham, three of them from or in the name of Hen. VI, asking for graces, are appended.

The 'epilogue' of the title-page consists of two appendices, one assembling 'what little is known about the [medieval] archives which have not survived: what they were; when they started; who compiled them; where they were kept; and how they were lost'. The other describes the physical features of the register: its paper, collation, procedure of the scribes, the original arrangement, the dates and causes of the present defects.

23. Registrum annalium collegii Mertonensis, 1521–1567. Edited by John M. Fletcher. 1974.

60.23

Transcript, Latin, completing the edition of the first vol. of the register begun in **59.76**, where a description of the vol. will be found. Contd. in the following.

24. Registrum annalium collegii Mertonensis, 1567–1603. Edited by John M. Fletcher. 1976.

60.24

Transcript, Latin, of pp. 1–202 of the second vol. of the register. The identity of its compilers may be inferred from the observation that changes in the handwriting coincide approximately with changes in the holders of the sub-wardenship.

The introduction considers the quality of the Fellows and the impact on contemporary society made by them in various ways, and notices the hints of how a predominantly graduate college was to be transformed into a college with an undergraduate majority. Ranking sixth in wealth (with St. John's) in 1592, and without in any way neglecting the requirements for a lively and continuous academic life, the college maintained a constant programme of repair and structural alteration, including the transformation of Postmasters Hall, the re-building of Alban Hall, and the rapid development of the library in both structure and contents, newly-elected probationary Fellows being required to contribute to a library fund. Index of books as well as a general index.

25. A bibliography of printed works relating to the city of Oxford. By E. H. Cordeaux and D. H. Merry. 1976.

60.25

26. Epistolae academicae, 1508–1596. Edited by W. T. Mitchell. 1980.

60.26

Dedicated to the memory of W. A. Pantin. Transcript, Latin, of 222 letters composed by successive registrars and copied into letter-book FF in accordance with statutory requirements. Summing up their value, the editor writes: 'all this means that as sources of information the letters are of very limited worth . . . Their more immediate value lies in the evidence they provide of the mental world of their writers and recipients, and especially of the standard reached in rhetoric by graduates in arts at this time.'

27. Registrum cancellarii, 1498–1506. Edited by W. T. Mitchell. 1980.   **60.27**

Calendar, in English, with more than 100 pp. of selected extracts fully transcribed, Latin. The introduction, after describing the disordered state of the ms. as now bound and the apparent loss of certain gatherings ('the only years for which practically complete records survive are 1501 to 1504 inclusive'), presents a chronological table of the contents and explains or describes numerous aspects of the court's administration, jurisdiction and procedure.

28. A bibliography of printed works relating to Oxfordshire (excluding the university and city of Oxford). By E. H. Cordeaux and D. H. Merry. Supplemenatary volume. 1981.   **60.28**

Cumulates the *addenda* in **60.11** with the further *addenda* and *corrigenda* printed in the *Bodleian Library Record* for Feb. 1958 and Apr. 1960, and includes all relevant items found subsequently, the limiting date in general being 1980.

61. SOMERSET RECORD SOCIETY

65. Somerset assize orders, 1629–1640. Edited by Thomas G. Barnes. 1959.   **61.66**

Transcripts, from the earliest of the surviving Western circuit order books, the single Latin doc. printed in translation. In the appendices, a doc. of 2 July 1586 among the Burghley papers, outlining assize procedure; also three charges to judges before going on circuit, four directions in law, given by the judges to justices of the peace, and one other doc. 'extraordinary by any definition', indicating the 'representative nature of the gathering at assizes and its importance as a source of intelligence for the government'. For subsequent order books see **61.72** below.

The introduction is briefly concerned with assize procedure, jurisdiction, its place in local government, the judges, counsel and clerk. The excision from this order book of certain Somerset cases is tentatively attributed to William Prynne.

66. The medieval customs of the manors of Taunton and Bradford on Tone. Edited by T. J. Hunt. 1962.   **61.67**

Transcript, Latin, with English translation, of the 16th-century copy of the 13th-century custumal of the bishop of Winchester's manor of Taunton and of the lesser 13th-century custumal of Bradford on Tone.

The introduction deals with knights' fees and lands of free tenants, manorial organization, labour services, financial dues, occasional and irregular money payments, payments for licences, the aid, and details of the peasants' way of life. The inclusion of Rimpton in the Taunton custumal is considered.

67. Sales of wards in Somerset, 1603–1641. Edited by M. J. Hawkins. 1965.   **61.68**

English abstracts of basic docs. (inquisition *post mortem*, extent, and schedule, supplemented where necessary from other records) relating to over 200 sales. In the introduction a description of the system, and tables to illustrate the average price of wards, average time allowed for payment, and so on.

68. The Hylle cartulary. Edited by Robert W. Dunning. 1968.   **61.69**

An English version (the formal entries calendared, all other entries translated in full) of the fair copy made c. 1416 and added to between 1416 and 1423. Compiled by Robert Hylle, and one of the comparatively few cartularies concerned with secular estates—in this instance scattered through Devon and Somerset—the cartulary has several docs. bearing on the history of Burtle priory (transcribed, Latin, in an appendix). Additional charters from Spaxton, Hylle's main house, are listed in appendix III. In the introduction, an account of the Fichet family.

69. The letters of Sir Francis Hastings, 1574–1609. Edited by Claire Cross. 1969. 61.70

Transcripts, in the main from the rough drafts kept by Hastings and now in the Henry E. Huntington library, supplemented by letters in other collections, preceded by a summary life of Hastings and table of family connexions.

70. Bridgwater borough archives. [Vol.] v: 1468–1485. Edited by R. W. Dunning and T. D. Tremlett from transcripts originally made by T. B. Dilks. 1971. 61.71

Continues the series begun in **61.48**. Transcripts, mainly Latin, of a wide range of docs. Bonds and quitclaims, after the first, have been calendared.

71. Somerset assize orders, 1640–1659. Edited by J. S. Cockburn. 1971. 61.72

Transcribed from the second and third of the Western circuit assize order books, with additional docs. related to the assizes of 1642 and the memorandum book of Robert Hunt, sheriff for a double term, 1654–6. The introduction includes lists of Western circuit judges, 1640–60, associate clerks, 1602–73, and of attorneys at Somerset assizes, 1649–60.

72. Wells cathedral chapter act book, 1666–83. Edited by Derrick Sherwin Bailey. 1973. [HMC JP 20] 61.73

The Latin entries (formal, and most of the minutes) calendared, the English entries transcribed. The introduction, with appended docs., begins with the chapter before 1660 and then surveys the post-Reformation chapter, its meetings and records, the residentiaries, the residence and remuneration of canons, the lease of Ashbury rectory, the vicars choral and their stipends, and the library.

73. Medieval deeds of Bath and district. 1974 [1975]. 61.74

Pt. 1: Deeds of St. John's hospital, calendared by B. R. Kemp from an 18th-century copy of a transcript made in the late 17th century for Toby Rustat, yeoman of the robes to Chas. II, with full Latin texts as well as calendar entries for additional acts of bishops Reginald and Savaric, *c.* 1180–*c.* 1205. Outline history of the hospital from its foundation.

Pt. 2: Deeds from the Walker-Heneage mss., edited, by D. M. M. Shorrocks. In all, 369 deeds, copy deeds, legal instruments and other memoranda, the earliest, 53 in number, dated between *c.* 1160 and 1290, transcribed Latin verbatim, the remainder calendared. These docs. passed in 1530 to William Button when he bought from John, Lord Hussey, and Sir William Hussey the manors and other property to which they relate in Somerset and Wiltshire. Genealogies for Forde, Malreward and Husee.

74. The diary of John Harington, M.P. 1646–53, with notes for his charges. Edited by Margaret F. Stieg. 1977. 61.75

Transcripts. The charges were to grand juries at quarter sessions.

75. The Somersetshire quarterly meeting of the Society of **61.76**
Friends, 1668–1699. Edited by Stephen C. Morland. 1978.

A 'transcription or amplification of drafts made at or soon after the day of
the meeting', with relevant extracts from minutes of monthly meetings.
In the introduction, extracts from a paper written in 1659, belonging to
Street meeting, describing the beginnings of Quakerism in Somerset, and
a compendium of Quaker principles and instances (cited from the minutes)
of failure to observe them. Miscellaneous docs. Biographical notes.

76. Somerset maps: Day and Masters, 1782; Greenwood, **61.77**
1822. Introduction by J. B. Harley and R. W. Dunning. 1981.

Facsimile reproductions, the first in nine sheets, the second on six sheets,
with introductory pamphlet on the map-makers, the methods they employed (geodetic survey and triangulation, topographical survey, drafting
and engraving, and decorative embellishment), and the contribution made
by the maps to the landscape history of the county. Some of the changes
which had occurred in the course of the forty years separating the two
maps are described in detailed studies of the Somerset coalfield, the
Levels, the area between Bridgwater and the mouth of the Parrett, south
Somerset, and Exmoor. All in slip-case.

62. STAFFORDSHIRE RECORD SOCIETY, COLLECTIONS FOR A HISTORY OF STAFFORDSHIRE, FOURTH SERIES

1. The committee at Stafford, 1642–1645: the order book of   **62.72**
the Staffordshire county committee. Edited ... by D. H. Pennington and I. A. Roots. 1957.

   Transcript. The appendices include extracts from accounts kept by the
   treasurer of the committee and by military commanders, accounts by the
   constables of Pelsall and Shareshill, an account for ammunition, two items
   from Sir William Brereton's letter book, biographical notes on members
   of the committee, and a map showing Staffordshire garrisons in 1644. The
   introduction (72 pp.) treats of the work of the committee and of the civil
   war in the county. Published simultaneously by the Society and Manchester University Press.

2. 1958.   **62.73**

   Index to previous volumes,
   The gentry of Staffordshire, 1662–1663. Transcribed by Ruth M. Kidson.
   [A list, compiled possibly by Col. Edward Vernon, second son of Sir
   Edward Vernon of Sudbury, showing places of residence, age, value of
   estates, personal ability, alliance by marriage, etc. Notes.]
   Active parliamentarians during the civil wars: list compiled in 1662.
   Transcribed by Ruth M. Kidson. [Compiled from returns for Stafford-
   shire made by the constables, arranged for the most part in alphabetical
   order of constablewick.]
   List of Staffordshire recusants, 1657. Transcribed by Michael Greenslade. [From quarter sessions records.]

3. 1960.   **62.74**
   Index to previous volumes.
   The registrations of dissenting chapels and meeting houses in Staffordshire, 1689–1852, extracted from the return in the General Register
   Office made under the Protestant Dissenters Act of 1852, by Barbara
   Donaldson. [From the returns by the dioceses of Lichfield and Worcester, the clerk of the peace for the county, and the clerks of the peace for
   the boroughs of Newcastle under Lyme, Tamworth, and Walsall. Index
   of persons and places by J. S. Moore.]

4. The cartulary of Tutbury priory. Edited ... by Avrom   **62.75**
Saltman. 1962. [HMC JP 2]

   Transcript, Latin, of the cartulary compiled between 1452 and 1458, with

English summaries and notes. The introduction treats of the foundation, endowment, and possessions of the priory in Staffordshire, Derbyshire, Leicestershire and other counties, the relations of the priory with its patrons and other religious houses, and its internal management. Noticed is the absence of all docs. relating to the mother house and the elimination of all traces of alien influence or domination. List of priors from before 1138 to 1538.

5. Probate inventories of Lichfield and district, 1568–1680.   62.76
Edited by D. G. Vaisey. 1969.

Transcripts, somewhat shortened, of inventories associated with wills proved, and letters of administration granted, in the peculiar courts of the dean or the dean and chapter of Lichfield, their jurisdiction embracing the cathedral close and city of Lichfield with its immediate neighbourhood. Analytical introduction. Glossary.

6. Essays in Staffordshire history presented to S. A. H. Burne.   62.77
Edited by M. W. Greenslade. 1970.

S. A. H. Burne: a biographical note. By J. S. Horne.

Some Staffordshire poll tax returns. By L. Margaret Midgley. [Includes a summary of the returns for 1377, and 'notes' (more specifically additions and corrections) on poll tax docs. and subsidies in **62.9**, 12, 19.]

Church lighting in Staffordshire since the Reformation. By Robert Sherlock. [Includes a gazetteer (mainly for Anglican buildings) of surviving and formerly existing chandeliers, coronae, candle fittings, pre-1914 electrical fittings and oil lamps, and the electrical fittings at Brewood (1964) and Tettenhall (1955). Plates.]

Staffordshire quarter sessions: archives and procedure in the earlier 17th century. By S. C. Newton. [Counters the 'myth' that 'enormous numbers of archives have been lost, particularly during the Civil War' and argues that 'there was a radical change, amounting almost to a revolution in record keeping' during this period.]

Shugborough: the end of a village. By F. B. Stitt. [Includes a plan based on a map of c. 1800.]

Steam-engine Bache, 1670–1712. By John S. Roper. [A contribution towards the identification of the 'Mr. Back of Wolverhampton' with whom Newcomen and Calley bargained to draw water in March 1712.]

The struggle for the Lichfield interest, 1747–68. By Ann J. Kettle. [Electoral history of the borough.]

Sir Edward Littleton's fox-hunting diary, 1774–89. By M. W. Farr. [Transcript, including the introduction added to the diary in 1847 by Sir Edward's heir, the first Lord Hatherton.]

William Moreton of Willenhall. By Norman W. Tildesley. [Curate at Willenhall for 45 years, d. July 1834.]

Joshua Drewry and the first Stafford newspapers. By D. A. Johnson. [Founder of the *Staffordshire Advertiser and ... Gazette*, d. 13 June 1841.]

The pledge of patriotism: Staffordshire and the voluntary contribution, 1798. By D. G. Vaisey.

Stebbing Shaw [d. 1802] and the *History of Staffordshire*. By M. W.

Greenslade and G. C. Baugh. [Includes a critical assessment of the *History*.]
A bibliography of the writings of S. A. H. Burne. By Beryl Daniels.

7. **Bishop Geoffrey Blythe's visitations, *c.* 1515-1525. Edited by Peter Heath. 1973.** 62.78

Transcript, Latin. Chiefly a record of visitations of religious houses in the diocese of Coventry and Lichfield. In the appendices, lists of houses and inmates extracted from the record of the *sede vacante* visitation in 1496, and of exempt orders and royal free chapels; transcripts, Latin, of docs. concerning the visitation of Lichfield dean and chapter in 1513, and of a letter close containing injunctions to Lilleshall abbey regarding its debts; notes on alleged abuses at Shrewsbury abbey; provision for a resigned prior of Repton and a resigned prioress of Brewood, and letters from the prioress of Henwood and the abbess of Polesworth at the dissolution.
The introduction (56 pp.) describes the visitation procedure and the nature of the evidence, considers the state of the religious, and sets out such information as can be gained about the secular clergy and lay matters.

8. **A list of families in the archdeaconry of Stafford, 1532-3. Edited by Ann J. Kettle. 1976.** 62.79

Transcript of a list of some 51,000 names (originally nearer 55,000 in its undamaged state) arranged in family groups within parish and town divisions, including some of the secular clergy and inmates of some of the religious houses. The explanation of the purpose of the list, 'put forward with some hesitation' after other possibilities have been considered and rejected, is that it is 'a list of families entitled to prayers or other benefits in return for a contribution towards the fabric fund of the cathedral'.

9. **Roman Catholicism in Elizabethan and Jacobean Staffordshire: documents from the Bagot papers. Edited by Anthony G. Petti. 1979.** 62.80

Annotated transcripts (preliminaries and routine endorsements omitted) of 117 items originally part of the private papers of the Bagots of Blithfield, spanning the years 1568-*c.* 1620 but more particularly the period 1579-96, illustrating how the central government handled recusancy in the counties and how Catholic communities fared at local level.

10. **Visitations of the archdeaconry of Stafford, 1829-1841. Edited by David Robinson. 1980. [HMC JP 25]** 62.81

The replies, in alphabetical order of parishes, and in summary form, to Archdeacon George Hodson's inspection of the churches within his jurisdiction in 1829-30, conflated with the results of later visits. The articles of inquiry, 86 in all, embrace the name and nature of the benefice, the size and condition of the church with its chancel, steeple and churchyard, the number and frequency of services held, the incumbent and curate (if any), the parsonage, the income, the day and Sunday schools, the dissenters, the population, and the parish clerk. Appended is a table to illustrate the range of expenditure undertaken by churchwardens in parishes of different sizes. Also, examples of Hodson's orders and of the response to them, and part of his correspondence with the earl of Lichfield's agent respecting the church and churchyard at Alrewas. Analytical introduction. Map.

63. SURREY RECORD SOCIETY

12. Chertsey abbey cartularies. Vol. ii. 2 pts., 1958–63.   **63.12**

Pt. 1, 'being extracts from the second portion of the cartulary in the Public Record Office', the deeds translated and calendared, all rubrics 'translated in full and with the utmost literalness', a few early deeds transcribed, Latin. Introduction and notes by C. A. F. Meekings.
Pt. 2, 'being extracts from British Museum Lansdowne ms. 435 and the Clifford cartulary, together with index to vol. ii', the calendar and introduction by Patricia M. Barnes, the index by Miss E. D. Mercer. Additions and corrections to both pts. Memoir of Sir Hilary Jenkinson.
See the preface to the present work.

24. Guildford borough records, 1514–1546. Edited ... by Enid M. Dance. 1958.   **63.25**

An edition of the earliest surviving minute book of the borough courts, supplemented from two other books, the formal Latin entries summarized, all other entries transcribed and/or translated. The courts (guild merchant, court leet, three weeks' court, and fair court) are treated in the introduction.

25. Wimbledon vestry minutes, 1736, 1743–1788: a calendar ... by F. M. Cowe. 1964.   **63.26**

The first surviving vestry minute book, with additional material. In the appendices: lists of vestrymen and overseers of the poor; a selective list of Wimbledon parish records in the Surrey Record Office; an examination as to settlement, 1744; transcripts of overseers' accounts, 1750–1 and 1780–1, an account for the education of workhouse children, 1767, an attorney's account for professional services to the overseers, 1775, and the workhouse account, 1775–6; the poor rate assessment and collection book, 1780, and lists of Wimbledon freeholders, 1762 and 1788.

26. Fitznells cartulary: a calendar ... by C. A. F. Meekings and Philip Shearman. 1968.   **63.27**

A calendar of those portions which are in Latin, with some Latin entries translated in full, and a transcript of the portions in English. Fitznells in Ewell, 'a complex of property held from many lords, ... given unity by the members of one family who built it up ... between about 1220 and 1310'. Extensive genealogical, tenurial and topographical introduction, with maps. Appendix of additional docs. selected from the Cuddington deeds in the P.R.O.

27. Mitcham settlement examinations, 1784–1814. Edited   **63.28**
... by Blanche Berryman. 1973.

Calendar of three books of examinations. In the introduction, a brief account of the process of examination and removal in general and as exemplified in the Mitcham records. Witnessing justices are listed in the appendix.

28. Kingston upon Thames register of apprentices, 1563–   **63.29**
1713. Edited ... by Anne Daly. 1974.

Calendar of apprenticeship indentures. In the appendix, transcripts of the corporation's ordinances for the four trading companies (mercers, woollen drapers, butchers and cordwainers), 1580, 1608 and 1635.

29. Ashley House, Walton-on-Thames, building accounts,   **63.30**
1602–1607. Edited ... by Michael E. Blackman. 1977.

Transcript. In the introduction, a brief history of the site and House (later Park), and a consideration of the accounts under numerous heads as, for example, brickwork, tilework, stonework, ironwork, timber, carpentry, glazing, and carriage. Glossary.

30. Deposition book of Richard Wyatt, J.P. 1767–1776. Edited ... by Elizabeth Silverthorne. 1978.   **63.31**

Calendar, in chronological order, of over 300 statements (examinations, informations and depositions) made before a Surrey justice acting alone, or with a colleague, out of sessions. Includes a table of fees payable to a justice's clerk.

31. The 1235 Surrey eyre. Edited ... by the late C. A. F.   **63.32**
Meekings and prepared for press by David Crook. Vol. i: Introduction. 1979.

Embraces the administration of civil and criminal justice in the second quarter of the 13th century. Appended are a bibliography of the common pleas eyre, listing all the eyre rolls in print for the period 1194–1293, and nearly 200 pp. of biographical details of the more important Surrey persons concerned in the eyre, the eyre justices, and the sheriffs and deputy-sheriffs of 1229–35.

56. The lay subsidy rolls for the county of Sussex, 1524-25. **64.58**
Transcribed and edited by Julian Cornwall. [1957.]
The introduction briefly details the need for the subsidy, the resulting
Act, its provisions, and the procedure followed. Also considered, as the
key question, is how far, if at all, an assessment indicates a man's wealth.

57. Custumals of the Sussex manors of the archbishop of **64.59**
Canterbury. Edited by B. C. Redwood and A. E. Wilson. 1958.
A 'literal but readable translation', slightly compressed, of the custumal
of c. 1285 existing only in a 15th-century or possibly early 16th-century
copy, with an abbreviated transcript of a South Malling rental of 1305-6
and a transcript of a late 16th-century copy—one of three—of a customary
of the same manor claiming to be of c. 1330.

58. The acts of the dean and chapter of the cathedral church **64.60**
of Chichester, 1545-1642. Edited by W. D. Peckham. [1960.]
Calendar.

59. The chartulary of Boxgrove priory. Translated and edited **64.61**
by Lindsay Fleming. 1960.
Abbots of Lessay, 1155-1225, and priors of Boxgrove, 1167-1350, mentioned in the cartulary, are listed in the introduction. Genealogical tables
of St. John, Albini (d'Aubigny) and Fitzalan. Also, in translation, a custumal or rental having an inserted heading with the date 1253.

60. Custumals of the manors of Laughton, Willingdon and **64.62**
Goring. Translated and edited by A. E. Wilson. [1962.]
All for estates in lay hands, viz. Willingdon, 1292 and 1296, Laughton,
1292 (with summaries for 1325 and 1338 in the appendix), and of the
Tregoz lands associated with Goring made in 1321. The introduction,
besides treating of manorial officials and some of the customary dues and
services, has sketch maps of the three estates.

61. A catalogue of Sussex estate and tithe award maps. Com- **64.63**
piled by Francis W. Steer. 1962.
Private estate maps from the early 17th century to 1884 (those later than
1850 being included for special reasons as, for example, to illustrate late
urban development), surveys of the Sussex (Goodwood) estates of the
Duke of Richmond, and tithe award maps prepared for each parish in
accordance with the Tithe Act of 1836. In the introduction, notes on the

land surveyors and cartographers, and on the quality of their work. See also **64.**68 below.

62. Minute book of the common council of the city of Chichester, 1783–1826. Edited by Francis W. Steer. 1963.   **64.**64

The first two entries given in full, most of the remainder summarized. List of mayors and bailiffs.

63. The book of Bartholomew Bolney. Edited by Marie Clough. 1964.   **64.**65

A translation, with some of the original Latin, of the record (compiled *c.* 1460) of a small, secular estate acquired piece-meal by an up-and-coming member of the administrative middle-class, illustrating the complexities of 15th-century landownership and land-market operations.

64. Rye shipping records, 1566–1590. Edited by Richard F. Dell. [1966.]   **64.**66

Transcripts of docs. selected to show the building, financing and voyages of Rye vessels, the customs system, the hazards of Tudor sea-faring, the passenger service, the fisheries, inventories and victualling, the mariners, and the ships owned by the town. Also, a chronological table of shipping movements at Rye, 1566–90, giving ship's name, home port, tonnage, name of master, destination or previous port, and summary of cargo, the details assembled from Exchequer Port Books and maltod books. Tables of surviving records of customs collection at Rye, 1566–90, of entries and clearances in the maltod books, 1580–1614, and of numbers of boats and men from Rye going on the Yarmouth voyage or engaged in local fisheries, 1565–96. Glossary.

65. The cellarers' rolls of Battle abbey, 1275–1513. Edited by Eleanor Searle and Barbara Ross. 1967.   **64.**67

In English translation, with accounts in tabular form for twenty years between 1385 and 1413, lists of cellarers' creditors, and the corn and stock account for 1405–6. The cellarer's function and performance at Battle are dealt with in the introduction. List of cellarers, 1275–1527. Glossary.

66. A catalogue of Sussex maps. Edited by Francis W. Steer. 1968.   **64.**68

Principally concerned with maps relating to the western division of the county. Comprises private estate maps, West Sussex inclosure award maps, deposited plans relating to West Sussex (with introduction), miscellaneous maps, 1620–1888, printed maps (a representative selection) for county and towns, and three maps of England and Wales (those of Mercator, Bell, and Horsley). Published jointly by the Society and the West Sussex County Council.

67. Two estate surveys of the Fitzalan earls of Arundel. Edited by Marie Clough. 1969.   **64.**69

Sets out to provide 'a guide to the contents of the three [late medieval] Fitzalan surveys, and secondly, a translation which is reasonably accurate but avoids as far as possible the use of archaic or obscure technical terms'. The first survey, datable to 1301, is possibly a copy of the second (the two are conflated here); the third was compiled between 1439 and 1464 from several much older docs. So different are the surveys in the ground covered and the methods used that 'it is practically impossible to identify any particular holding in both surveys or to make valid comparisons between them'. Maps. Select place-name glossary with grid references.

68. The journal of Giles Moore. Edited by Ruth Bird. 1971. **64.70**

Rector of Horsted Keynes, d. 1679. His 'day book', begun in 1655 and continued into the year of his death, in two parts. Of pt. 1 only the first seven pages have been transcribed for this edition, the following 230 pages, concerned largely with tithe in considerable detail, have been summarized into a single page. Pt. 2, transcribed and printed in full, lists his receipts and disbursements from 1655, with a 'wealth of detailed information about life in a Sussex village' and shows 'the obligations of a parish priest of that period to, and his relations with, the authorities in both Church and State, from the personal rather than the official point of view'. Genealogy of Moore (More). Glossary.

69. The town books of Lewes, 1702–1837. Edited by Verena **64.71**
Smith. [1973.]

Transcript. Contd. in the following. For the earlier town book see **64.48**.

70. The town books of Lewes, 1837–1901. Edited by Verena **64.72**
Smith. [1976.]

71. Accounts of the Roberts family of Boarzell, Sussex, **64.73**
c. 1568–1582. Edited by Robert Tittler. [1979.]

Transcript of the first two books of farm and household accounts. The introduction traces the earlier history of the family, identifies the writer of the accounts as Margaret (Margery) *née* Pigott, widow of Sir Walter Hendley and 'an experienced survivor of three marriages', and gives a summary of agricultural and industrial activity on the estate. Glossary.

72. Printed maps of Sussex, 1575–1900. By David Kingsley, **64.74**
with an introduction by Helen Wallis. 1982.

A descriptive catalogue, and as complete as possible, 'including any map which is described as a map of Sussex or in which the detail outside the county boundary is only shown incidentally', with notes on the map-makers and their methods and on the printing processes employed. Numerous reproductions. Appendices are devoted to manuscript maps, maps of the Sussex coast, maps of south-east England, perspective views, road books, Ordnance Survey maps, maps of part of the county, untraced and unidentified maps, Norden's known work on English county maps (updating and expanding an earlier account by R. A. Skelton), the dating of maps, railways in Sussex (including lines authorized but not built), county carto-bibliographies published 1900–1977, and works cited. Dr. Wallis's introduction surveys the art and craft of map-making in England.

65. DUGDALE SOCIETY, PUBLICATIONS

23. Correspondence of the Reverend Joseph Greene, parson, **65.23**
schoolmaster and antiquary, 1717–1790. Edited by Levi Fox.
1965. [HMC JP 8].

Transcripts of letters (i) to his brother Richard, apothecary first at Shrewsbury, then at Lichfield, founder of the Lichfield museum, 1733–89, and
(ii) to James West of Alscot, Preston-on-Stour, and King Street, Covent
Garden, London, 1749–64, with miscellanea by and about Greene, and a
biographical sketch by the editor.

24. The Stoneleigh leger book. Edited by R. H. Hilton. 1960. **65.24**

Transcript, Latin (substantially as left by Dr. Nellie Neilson) of the book
written c. 1392, containing (i) charters and other evidences within a short
and inaccurate chronicle of English history, (ii) a summary statement of
the court procedure and customs of Stoneleigh manor, (iii) a rental and
survey of the lands and tenants of Stoneleigh manor when the book was
compiled, beginning with a survey of the lands held by Kenilworth priory
and ending with a perambulation of the bounds of the manor, (iv) a short
history, incomplete, of the outstanding acts of successive abbots. Many
later additions to the main text.

The analytical introduction includes a description and evaluation of a
considerable body of further evidence for the history of the medieval
estate. Map.

25. The records of King Edward's school, Birmingham. Vol. **65.25**
v. Edited by Philip B. Chatwin. 1963.

Continues **65.**4, 7, 12, 20. Orders of the governors, 1764–98; school
accounts, 1764–97. Contd. in **65.**30 below.

26. Ministers' accounts of the collegiate church of St. Mary, **65.26**
Warwick, 1432–85. Transcribed and edited by Dorothy
Styles, with a memoir of Philip Boughton Chatwin by Philip
Styles. 1969.

Annotated transcripts, Latin, of six rolls of accounts, all copies of the
audited accounts of the farmers, bailiffs, and rent collectors of St. Mary's
estates, with additions in the introduction and notes from a seventh roll,
that of the canon treasurer, for the year 1410–11 (transcribed in **65.**31
below). The introduction summarizes the administration and fortunes of
the foundation until its surrender in 1544.

27. Ecclesiastical terriers of Warwickshire parishes. Tran- **65.27**

scribed and edited by D. M. Barratt. Vol. ii: Parishes Lo to
W. With a memoir of Sir William Stratford Dugdale, Bt., by
Levi Fox. 1971.

Continues **65.**22. The introduction to this vol. is concerned only with the
clergy's answers to the visitation articles of 1585; these answers are printed
with the terriers. In the appendices, a missing membrane of the terrier of
Cherington of 1585, a calendar of the returns of values of livings in
Warwick and Kineton deaneries worth less than £50 a year in 1707, a
table showing the values of livings in the area covered by the terriers in
1535, 1586, 1665 and 1707, and a list of all the Warwickshire parishes and
chapelries in the ancient diocese of Worcester showing what terriers (and
answers to the articles of 1585) have survived. Glossary.

28. Warwickshire printers' notices, 1799–1866. Edited by   **65.**28
Paul Morgan. 1970.

Annotated summaries of the notices required by the Act of 12 July 1799
(39 Geo. III, cap. 79) to be delivered to the clerk of the peace by persons
having any printing press or type for printing. A qualified list of unregis-
tered printers, also annotated, is given in the appendix. Succinct introduction to a class of historical record previously unremarked in this guide.

29. Warwickshire apprentices and their masters, 1710–1760.   **65.**29
Edited by K. J. Smith, with an introduction by N. J. Williams.
1975.

Abstracts of the entries relating to Warwickshire in the Apprenticeship
Registers in the P.R.O.

30. The records of King Edward's school, Birmingham. Vol.   **65.**30
vi: A supplementary miscellany. Edited by John Izon. 1974.

Copies and abstracts from 17th-century suits in the courts of chancery
and exchequer, and in the Commonwealth court of the committee of
indemnity, in the P.R.O., ranging in date from 1604 to 1709. They include
leases and transactions between the school governors and their tenants, as
well as full details of building, re-building and improvements, between
1565 and 1664. Also lists of alumni of the school identified in Oxford and
Cambridge and Inns of Court registers, and abstracts of all leases made
by the school between 1610 and 1651.

31. Miscellany I. Edited by Robert Bearman. 1977.   **65.**31

Woad accounts for the manor of Chesterton, 1638–1641. Edited by B. M.
   Baggs. [Transcripts. The method of cultivation is summarized in the
   introduction.]
The *Status maneriorum* of John Catesby, 1385 and 1386. Edited by Jean
   Birrell. [Transcripts, Latin, of manorial valors.]
Nicholas Eyffeler of Warwick, glazier: executors' accounts and other
   documents concerning the foundation of his almshouse charity, 1592–
   1621. Edited by M. W. Farr. [Transcripts of his probate inventory, the
   executors' account written in about 1597-8, the particulars of account
   for building the almshouse in 1597, the executors' subsidiary account

of about 1598, and a schedule of the fixtures in 1621. In the introduction a brief statement of his life and work.]

Diary of Robert Beake, mayor of Coventry, 1655–1656. Edited by Levi Fox. [Transcript, from (?)11 Nov. 1655 to 8 May 1656. A draper, and afterwards master of the Drapers' Company, Beake was M.P. for Coventry in 1654, 1659 and 1660.]

A financial account of St. Mary's, Warwick, Michaelmas 1410–Michaelmas 1411. Edited by Dorothy Styles. [Transcript, Latin, of the canon treasurer's account used in 65.26 above.]

'The genealogie, life and death of the right honourable Robert lorde Brooke ...'. Edited by Philip Styles. [Transcript, the original by Thomas Spencer, vicar of Budbrooke, a Warwick corporation benefice, from 24 Apr. 1635 until his death in 1667.]

Indexes to the several contributions.

32. The Langley cartulary. Edited by Peter R. Coss. 4to, 1980.   **65.32**

Made for William Langley of Knowlton, Kent, c. 1477–8, and concerned with the estates of the west midland Langleys of whom his mother, Isabel de la Pole, was the last surviving representative. Calendar, except that 12th-century docs. and docs. not in common form have been transcribed. Genealogy of Langley, with a history of the family and its estates.

68. WILTSHIRE RECORD SOCIETY

(UNTIL JUNE 1967 THE RECORDS BRANCH OF THE
WILTSHIRE ARCHAEOLOGICAL AND NATURAL HISTORY SOCIETY)

14. Accounts and surveys of the Wiltshire lands of Adam de   **68.**14
Stratton. Edited by M. W. Farr. 1959.

Transcripts, Latin, of extents of the manors of Sevenhampton, Stratton,
Upton and Blewbury, with other lands, 1271–7; ministers' accounts for
Sevenhampton and Stratton, 1269–75, and for Sevenhampton alone,
1275–88; the reeve's draft account for Sevenhampton, 1275–9; a view of
account for Stratton and Sevenhampton, 1278–9; and particulars of
account for building a barn in Sevenhampton, 1280.

The introduction briefly describes the development of the estates, the
seizure of them after Adam de Stratton's disgrace, the first royal keepers
and farmers, the history of the Wiltshire estates to the 1950s, and the
system of accounting. Glossary.

15. Tradesmen in early-Stuart Wiltshire. A miscellany. Ed-   **68.**15
ited by N. J. Williams. 1960.

English abstracts of fines before the royal clerk of the market, 1607;
recognizances to keep the law against selling meat in Lent, 1620; informations laid before the barons of the exchequer, *temp.* Jas. I; and a list of
licensed retailers of tobacco, 1637.

16. Crown pleas of the Wiltshire eyre, 1249. Edited by C. A.   **68.**16
F. Meekings. 1961.

English version of the crown pleas roll. The introduction treats briefly of
the evolution and crown pleas jurisdiction of the eyre; the importance of
the eyre in securing the profits of crown pleas for the king and as an
integral part of the fabric of judicial administration; the eyre visitations
leading to the visitation of 1246–9; the Wiltshire eyre of 1249; the form
and history of the Wiltshire crown pleas roll; the articles of the eyre, the
system of attachment and bail, the trial jury, criminal presentments,
indictments and appeals; court orders and judgments; the fiscal sessions
held towards the end of the eyre, and the issues of the eyre. Introduction
and appendices have their own persons and places index. For civil pleas
see **68.**26 below.

17. Wiltshire apprentices and their masters, 1710–1760. Ed-   **68.**17
ited by Christabel Dale, with an introduction by N. J.
Williams. 1961.

All the entries relating to Wiltshire abstracted in alphabetical order of surnames from the first thirteen surviving county registers of the Board of Inland Revenue, recording the payment of duties on apprenticeship indentures. Indexes of masters, of occupations and descriptions, and of places.

18. Hemingby's register. Edited by Helena M. Chew. 1963.   **68.18**

The earliest chapter act book of Salisbury cathedral, 1329–49, partly in full transcript, Latin, partly in English abstracts, with an extensive appendix of biographical notes on all the prebendaries and many of the 'ministri' mentioned.

The introduction considers in some detail the chapter, its personnel and recruitment, the vicars-choral and choisters, and, as the most important source of the *communa*, the system of leasing or farming to the dignitaries and residentiaries the churches appropriated to the chapter.

19. Documents illustrating the Wiltshire textile trades in the   **68.19** eighteenth century. Edited by Julia de L. Mann. 1964.

Transcripts of 713 items from the business letters of John Usher and John Jeffries, 1726–42, clothiers at Trowbridge, the papers of George Wansey, 1730–61, clothier at Warminster, and the letters of Henry Hindley, 1762–75, of Mere, Hamburg merchant dealing in linen, mainly ticking. The introduction includes a note on rates of exchange for the trade with Lisbon, Hamburg and Holland.

20. The diary of Thomas Naish. Edited by Doreen Slatter.   **68.20** 1965.

Transcript of the record, 1669–1728, kept 'with tantalizing brevity' and concerned mainly with ecclesiastical politics in Salisbury, where Naish was some-time vicar of St. Edmund's and sub-dean of the cathedral.

21. The rolls of Highworth hundred, 1275–1287. Edited by   **68.21** Brenda Farr. Pt. 1: Introduction; text, 1275–81. 1966.

Transcript, Latin. Map. Concluded in the following, with glossary and indexes. Pagination is continuous. The hundred, commonly known as 'Worth', was appurtenant to the manor of Sevenhampton.

22. The rolls of Highworth hundred ... Pt. 2: Text, 1281–7.   **68.22** 1968.

23. The Earl of Hertford's lieutenancy papers, 1603–1612.   **68.23** Edited by W. P. D. Murphy. 1969.

Transcripts of letters and other items in two entry-books kept by Edward Seymour as lord lieutenant of Somerset, Wiltshire and Bristol. This is the first vol. published under the imprint of the Wiltshire Record Society.

24. Court rolls of the Wiltshire manors of Adam de Stratton.   **68.24** Edited by Ralph B. Pugh. 1970.

Transcripts, Latin, of the surviving manor court rolls of Sevenhampton, 1275–88, and Stratton St. Margaret, 1277–88, and of the portmoot rolls of Highworth, 1275–88, completing, except for the deeds, the published text of the muniments of Adam de Stratton. Glossary. Detailed analytical introduction contributing to the adequate treatise on manor court procedure desired by the editor.

25. Abstracts of Wiltshire inclosure awards and agreements. **68.**25 Edited by R. E. Sandell. 1971.

For the period 1732–1867, with one earlier, for Hannington 1632, and one later, for Seagry and Christian Malford 1883. Includes a list of such awards and agreements in the Wiltshire Record Office, and a select list of principal allottees, showing the acreages allotted. Map.

26. Civil pleas of the Wiltshire eyre, 1249. Edited by M. T. **68.**26 Clanchy. 1971.

English version. The introduction describes the Wiltshire eyre, its rolls, the method of enrolling essoins and pleas, records of civil pleas in general, the basic pattern of lawsuit, fiction and omission in the record, the forms of action, the status of litigants, and ways of reaching agreement. For crown pleas see **68.**16 above.

27. Wiltshire returns to the bishop's visitation queries, 1783. **68.**27 Edited by Mary Ransome. 1972.

Transcript, slightly modified, of the replies made by the clergy at the primary visitation of Bishop Barrington.

28. Wiltshire extents for debts, Edward I–Elizabeth I. Edited **68.**28 by Angela Conyers. 1973.

Abstracts of the extents or descriptions, with valuations, of the goods of defaulting debtors who held property in Wiltshire, contained for the most part in classes C 131 and C 239 in the P.R.O., from 1306 to 1603. Glossary. Specimens, Latin, of the writs *capias, liberate, extendi facias, non omittas,* and *elegit* are given in the appendix; the procedures and circumstances involving their use are indicated in the introduction.

29. Abstracts of feet of fines relating to Wiltshire for the reign **68.**29 of Edward III. Edited by C. R. Elrington. 1974.

For earlier Wiltshire feet of fines see **67.**7 and **68.**1. The introduction analyses two characteristic docs. translated in full, and shows how the constituent parts might be modified to suit particular circumstances.

30. Abstracts of Wiltshire tithe apportionments. Edited by R. **68.**30 E. Sandell. 1975.

Agreements, Nov. 1836–Apr. 1844, and awards, Dec. 1838–May 1850, from the certified diocesan copies of apportionments made under the Tithe Commutation Act of 1836. The introduction briefly deals with tithe and tithe commutation in the county before 1836, the 1836 Act, and the progress of commutation under the Act.

31. Poverty in early-Stuart Salisbury. Edited by Paul Slack. **68.**31 1975.

Introductory account of the extent and complexity of the problem of poverty in the town, followed by transcripts of the register of passports for vagrants, 1598–1669, of surveys of the poor, 1625 and *c.* 1635, of a project for relief, *c.* 1613, of orders for the erection and government of the workhouse, 1623, and of orders for relief, 1626. Also, overseers' accounts, July–Dec. 1635, overseers' papers, 1635-6, and workhouse accounts, 1627-30. *A Declaration*, by John Ivie, alderman (London, 1661), providing 'a unique insight into urban government in the 17th century', is reprinted as an appendix.

32. **The subscription book of bishops Tounson and Davenant,**   **68.32**
1620–40. Edited by Barrie Williams. 1977.

English abstracts of subscriptions to the Thirty-nine Articles made by clergy when appointed to a benefice, ordained, or licensed to preach, supplemented from episcopal institution registers and exchequer registers of first fruits and tenths. Abstracts give the subscriber's name, his degree, college and university, and the nature of his benefice, ordination or licensing.

33. **Wiltshire gaol delivery and trailbaston trials, 1275–1306.**   **68.33**
Edited by Ralph B. Pugh. 1978.

English abstracts of all known records of Wiltshire gaol delivery and trailbaston trials for the period, with the extended Latin texts of two specimen entries. The methods of gaol delivery are described and the rolls analysed in the introduction.

34. **Lacock abbey charters. Edited by Kenneth H. Rogers.**   **68.34**
1979.

English abstracts of 476 docs., for the most part belonging to the 13th and 14th centuries, selected largely from the abbey's two cartularies and the holdings of the P.R.O.

35. **The cartulary of Bradenstoke priory. Edited by Vera C.**   **68.35**
M. London. 1979.

Calendar of the later of two 14th-century texts, with additions from the earlier text recording the foundation, in 1139, of the house of Augustinian canons, at first an offshoot of Cirencester abbey but independent from 1189. List of priors to 1539.

36. **Wiltshire coroners' bills, 1752–1796. Edited by R. F.**   **68.36**
Hunnisett. 1981.

Calendar of the claims presented to the justices at quarter sessions by the county coroners (one acting in ther northern part, one in the southern part) and by the coroners of the manor of Corsham and the borough of Wootton Bassett for payment of the inquest and travelling fees awarded to most coroners by the statute 25 Geo. II, c. 29, from 24 June 1752. The claims, or bills, certified on oath, list and summarize the inquests held in the period of the claim and 'are an unrivalled source for the activities of the eighteenth-century coroner and for the types of death which came within his jurisdiction, as well as throwing much incidental light on social and economic conditions'.

The introduction sets out the archival history and present arrangement of the Wiltshire bills and related docs.; examines the practice of particular coroners in regard to their claims; comments on the role of the justices; notes the boundaries between the two county jurisdictions, the northern producing the higher number of inquests, and the increasing strain on county coroners as the century advanced; and identifies the coroners and their suitability, Wiltshire possibly being unique in the 18th century in that all its country coroners had medical qualifications.

The vol. was presented to the president of the Society, R. B. Pugh, 'as an acknowledgement of his work on its behalf since its birth in 1937'. It includes an appreciation of Professor Pugh by C. R. Elrington, and a bibliography of his published writings, 1930-80, compiled by Susan M. Keeling.

37. The justicing notebook of William Hunt, 1744–1749. Edited by Elizabeth Crittall. 1982.   **68.37**

Transcript of the notebook kept by William Hunt (William Hunt Grubbe as he became towards the end of his life) of West Lavington, while he was a justice of the peace. Primarily a record of apprehending and conviction warrants (with the names of the poor to whom the resulting fines were paid), the notebook also lists some charitable payments to the poor and Hunt's expenses in attending sessions and meetings on justice business; its special interest is the record of his proceedings when acting outside quarter sessions, often alone, sometimes with another justice.

The introduction, after sketching Hunt's life (1696–1753) and character, describes his sphere of official activity (broadly the hundred of Swanborough and that of Potterne and Cannings), and draws from the notebook a summary account of the work during and out of sessions of 'a conscientious and reasonable justice', a commissioner for the land and window taxes, and a commissioner for recruiting. As a justice acting alone, his proceedings are shown to have embraced cases of assault, larceny, summary offences against property and the game laws, and numerous other matters.

A list of corrigenda to many preceding vols. in this series, compiled by Jane Freeman, is appended.

69. WORCESTERSHIRE HISTORICAL SOCIETY, NEW SERIES

[1] Miscellany I. 1960.   **69.44**

Rowland Aylwyn Wilson [1868–1959: a memoir]. By W. R. Buchanan-
Dunlop.

Evesham A, a Domesday text. Edited by P. H. Sawyer. [Transcript, Latin,
of one of two surveys in the cartulary of Evesham abbey, printed in
parallel beside the corresponding passages from Domesday book. The
editor concludes that his analytical consideration of the docs. confirms
the impression 'that Evesham A is based on an early stage of the
Domesday enquiry'.]

Swanimote rolls of Feckenham forest. Edited by R. H. Hilton. [Tran-
scripts, Latin, of rolls from 1496, 1499, 1502 and 1503 recording 'the
proceedings of courts administering the law of the forest in what was
left of one of the most important royal forests of the midlands' and
showing that the Feckenham swanimote of the late-15th century was
different from 'the swanimotes which operated as minor cogs in the
judicial system of the forest, with the forest eyre as the highest tribunal.
The upper regions of the system may have decayed. But at the local
level . . . the protection of the vert and the venison was still conducted
with vigour . . .'.]

Mortuary briefs. By N. R. Ker. [Descriptions and, where possible, transcripts, Latin, of the surviving briefs, nine of them in the library of
Worcester cathedral and all fourteen from the 15th or early-16th century, preceded by the regulations governing briefs and brief-bearers in
the 14th-century customary of St. Augustine's, Canterbury, and additional details from the records of other communities.]

An inventory of Hartlebury castle. Edited by P. C. Moore. [Transcript,
listing room by room the household goods and furniture at Hartlebury
and the old episcopal palace at Worcester, taken over from his predecessor by Bishop Richard Hurd in 1781 at a cost of £1472.]

Rectory Farm, Grafton Flyford, Worcestershire. By F. W. B. Charles. [A
report on the structure, based on a survey made in 1959, illustrated with
diagrams showing the main trusses.]

[2] Christopher Greenwood, country map-maker, and his   **69.45**
Worcestershire map of 1822. By J. B. Harley. 1962.

The introduction relates what is known of the career of this hitherto
neglected cartographer (he is frequently and erroneously named 'Charles'
in library catalogues and carto-bibliographical works); tells the story of
the map-making and map-publishing firm founded and directed by him
(it collapsed *c.* 1834); discusses his methods of field survey and triangu-

lation and the sales organization he developed; comments on the reliability of several features shown on the Worcestershire map (county, hundred and parish boundaries; woodland, parkland, heath and commons; industrial areas; navigable rivers and canals; and turnpike roads); and in the context of Worcestershire assesses the place of early 19th-century county maps in the historical study of an English county. An appendix contributed by Richard Newton describes the editions of Greenwood's 'one-inch' map. A second appendix lists chronologically the maps and other works produced by Greenwood and his partners. Four-sheet facsimile of the Worcestershire map in end pocket.

[3] The court rolls of the manor of Bromsgrove and King's **69.46** Norton, 1494–1504: a calendar. Prepared by A. F. C. Baber (A. F. C. Bourdillon). 1963.

Nine rolls, the matter of the separate rolls brought together into 12 sections, each section with an introduction, and the section for 'land pleas' limited to 17 cases of nine distinct types, the remaining 20 or so being briefly listed. Full transcript of the roll for 1494–5 (Latin) and of a customary of the manor (mainly English, partly Latin) put together in 1598.

The general introduction sketches the physical and economic circumstances of the manor, and in more detail considers the subject of ancient demesne and the implications for Bromsgrove: 'the fact of ancient demesne ... largely explains the many differences between these rolls and the court rolls of more normal manors. It also explains the very large number of land pleas, with their attendant obscurities, which constitute an important section of this calendar.'

Memoirs of James Frederick Parker (1878–1962), by G. E. S. Parker, and Harry Evers Palfrey (1875–1962), by H. Jack Haden.

4. A calendar of the register of Wolstan de Bransford, bishop **69.47** of Worcester, 1339–49. By R. M. Haines. 1966. [HMC JP 9]

Institutions to benefices and letters dimissory are excluded from the calendar: their essential details are given in tables at the end. Also given in tabular form are the appointments of heads of religious houses and licences for oratories. Other tables analyse licences for absence from benefices and the ordinations entered in the register (some are missing), omitting ordinations to the first tonsure. Full transcripts, Latin, of a number of the more interesting docs., particularly chantry endowments, are appended.

The introduction sets out the bishop's early life and priorate and treats of the extent and divisions of the diocese, the bishop's officers and 'familia', various aspects of Wolstan's administration, and assesses his achievement: 'one of the more conscientious bishops of the time'. Map.

5. Miscellany II. 1967. **69.48**

Probate inventories of Worcester tradesmen, 1545–1614. Edited by A. D. Dyer. [Transcripts of 21 unusually detailed inventories, each one representing a different occupation, chosen 'to give examples of the tools and stock of craftsmen and shopkeepers of the city' and 'to provide a representative cross-section of the contents of Worcester homes at different social and economic levels'. Glossary. Index.]

Henry Townshend's 'Notes of the office of a justice of peace', 1661–3. Edited by R. D. Hunt. [A selection of the notes made by Townshend in his interleaved copy of the 1661 edition of *The complete justice* 'to illustrate and expand the points of law and definitions of justices' duties'. Includes the relevant passages in *The complete justice*. Index.]

The Dougharty [also Doharty] family of Worcester, estate surveyors and mapmakers, 1700–60. By Brian S. Smith. [Includes a descriptive catalogue of the maps and surveys by John senior, Joseph, and John junior. Index.]

6. The state of the bishopric of Worcester, 1782–1808. Edited by Mary Ransome. 1968.

69.49

Transcript of the survey or 'state' which was compiled in the main from the replies by the parish clergy to the queries addressed to them at Bishop Hurd's triennial visitations, omitting its indexes. Analytical introduction.

7. A calendar of the register of Henry Wakefield, bishop of Worcester, 1375–95. By Warwick Paul Marett. 1972.

69.50

Includes transcripts, Latin, of a few particularly interesting items and, in an appendix, the Latin or French text of five wills in the register.

The introduction considers the compilation and contents of the register, sets out the state of the diocese as reflected in it, and sketches the bishop's antecedents and career. Appended is a transcript, Latin, of his will, dated 10 Mar., proved 27 Mar. 1395.

8. The chamber order book of Worcester, 1602–1650. Edited by Shelagh Bond. 1974.

69.51

Transcript of the register of acts and decisions by the governing body (or chamber) of the city. The main subjects of concern, as reflected in the register, are described in the introduction. Appendices list the members of the forty-eight and twenty-four; the bishops, deans and city preachers; the lord presidents in the marches of Wales; the members for the city in parliament (showing their wages and fees); and the royalist and parliamentary governors. Appendix II, a partial summary of the chamberlains' accounts, 1623–50, indicates the city's regular sources of income. Glossary.

Memoir of Shelagh Mary Bond (1926–73), by G. H. Martin.

9. A selection from the records of Philip Foley's Stour Valley iron works, 1668–74. Edited by R. G. Schafer. Pt. i. 1978.

69.52

Transcripts of (i) Philip Foley's stock and debts book for 1669, (ii) his summary of all his works' accounts for 1668–9, (iii) the accounts for Bustleholme slitting mill for the same years, and (iv) a group of agreements and accounts covering the business dealings between Philip and his uncle and associate Richard Foley for 1668–9.

The introduction sketches the development of the Foley organization from its foundation in the 1630s into a major iron producing system with sophisticated methods of manufacture, distribution, marketing, and control.

10. **Calendar of the register of Adam de Orleton, bishop of Worcester, 1327–1333. By R. M. Haines. 1979. [HMC JP 27]**   **69.53**

Made on the same general plan as the Bransford calendar (**69.**47 above), with modifications in detail. Thus, no entries in the register have been excluded from the calendar, and no full transcripts are appended. All tables as in Bransford, plus a summary itinerary indicating the bishop's activities and other events.

71. YORKSHIRE ARCHAEOLOGICAL SOCIETY, RECORD SERIES

121. Feet of fines for the county of York, from 1272 to 1300. **71.121**
Edited by F. H. Slingsby. 1956.
English abstracts. Contd. in **71.**127 below. For earlier fines see **71.**62, 67, 82.

122. Beverley corporation minute books, 1707–1835. Edited **71.122**
by K. A. MacMahon. 1958.
Memoranda books rather than minute books. Important entries calendared or *in extenso*, with summary notices of other entries selected for their 'significance and illustrative value'.

123. York minster fasti: being notes on the dignitaries, arch- **71.123**
deacons and prebendaries in the church of York prior to the
year 1307. Edited by Sir Charles Travis Clay. Vol. i. 1958.
Annotated lists of the holders of the four principal dignities and of the subdeanery and the five archdeaconries (York, Cleveland, the East Riding, Nottingham,and Richmond), with the Latin texts (English abstracts and notes) of 50 charters, mostly unprinted hitherto and all but one of them taken from the earliest extant register of the church (Cotton, Claudius B. iii), providing documentary evidence for the tenure of some of the dignities and archdeaconries and of several of the prebends. Contd. in the following.

124. York minster fasti ... Vol. ii. 1959. **71.124**
Annotated lists of the holders of the 36 prebends, a map showing the prebends, and 56 further charters from the same source. Appendices on the connexion of William of York with the prebends of Knaresborough and Ampleforth, and on the history of the church of Axminster and its connexion with the prebends of Grindale and Warthill.

125. Tudor treatises. Edited by A. G. Dickens. 1959. **71.125**
(i) Sir Francis Bigod's *A treatise concernyng impropriations of benefices* reprinted from one of the two known copies (London, *c.* 1535) with, in the editor's introduction, 'a brief recapitulation of the facts most necessary to an understanding of the text'; (ii) five short devotional treatises by Robert Parkyn (*d.* 1569) with, in the introduction, 'a rapid summary' of their contents and spiritual ancestry; (iii) 'The falle of religiouse howses, colleges, chantreys, hospitalls etc.', attributed 'with something like certainty' to Michael (not Cuthbert) Sherbrook, rector of Wickersley 1567–

1610, its main purpose being 'to justify the monasteries and to expose the selfishness and the social evils attendant upon their dissolution'.

126. A survey of the manor of Settrington. Edited by the late **71.126**
H. King and A. Harris. 1962.

Transcript, the Latin entries in English translation, of the 'exceptionally detailed survey carried out under the supervision of John Mansfield, Queen's surveyor in the North Riding' in March 1600, with one of its maps and its six summary tables.

127. Feet of fines for the county of York from 1300 to 1314. **71.127**
Edited by M. Roper. 1965.

Calendar of all the Yorkshire files and of all the Yorkshire items in the Divers Counties files, Court of Common Pleas (series I), in the P.R.O.

128. Letters of James Tate. Edited by L. P. Wenham. 1966. **71.128**

Transcripts of 124 letters, part of a voluminous and scattered correspondence, addressed to Mrs. Sarah Ottley, John Hutton, George Peacock, and Archdeacon Charles Wrangham by the Rev. James Tate (*d.* 1843), 'the Scholar of the North', master of Richmond school, Yorks., and subsequently a canon of St. Paul's.

129. Fasti parochiales. Vol. iii: Deanery of Dickering. Edited **71.129**
by N. A. H. Lawrance. 1967.

Annotated lists on the pattern of **71.**85, 107, continuing to 1662. Includes chantry chapels. Contd. in **71.**133 below.

130. Abstracts of Abbotside wills, 1552–1688. Edited by **71.130**
Hartley Thwaite. 1968.

Wills and administrations, bonds and inventories, of residents in the townships (later 'manors') of High and Low Abbotside, formerly called the manor of Wensleydale in the parish of Aysgarth, preserved for the most part among the records of the archdeaconry court of Richmond, then a part of the diocese of Chester. Glossary.

131. Court rolls of the manor of Acomb. Edited by Harold **71.131**
Richardson. Vol. 1. 1969.

English abstracts, May 1544–May 1761, with sketch plan of the manor. Concluded in **71.**137 below. Pagination is continous.

132. Bolton priory rentals and ministers' accounts, 1473– **71.132**
1539. Edited by Ian Kershaw. 1970.

English translation of three docs.: the rental of 1473 concerned only with estates in Craven, the dissolution inventory of 1539, and the ministers' accounts, 1538–9, constituting a rental of the priory's estates.

The introduction outlines the growth of the estate from 1120 and the development of rental income from 1286. Rents from the separate estates are set out in tabular form for selected years, beginning with 1297–8. Map.

133. Fasti parochiales. Vol. iv, being notes on the advowsons **71.133**
and pre-Reformation incumbents of the parishes in the deanry
of Craven. Edited by Norah K. M. Gurney and Sir Charles
Clay. 1971.

Appended, in English translation, are the preamble to the decree appro-
priating Gisbûrn church to Stainfield priory, 1338, and the agreement
between the abbot and convent of Cockersand and the vicar of Great
Mitton, 1438. Map.

134. Yorkshire probate inventories, 1542–1689. Edited by **71.134**
Peter C. D. Brears. 1972.

Transcripts of 44 inventories held by the Society (one undated) with brief
biographical introductions. The procedure is described and the articles in
the inventories are considered, group by group, under furniture, textiles,
cooking, tableware, brewing, dairying and transport. Three further inventories held by the Society, viz. of John Pawson (1576), Sir William Ingilby
(1617) and Sir William Middleton (1641), have been printed elsewhere.
Glossary.

135. Early Yorkshire families. Edited by Sir Charles Clay, **71.135**
with illustrative documents edited by Diana E. Greenway.
1973.

Notes relating to almost 100 'families descending in the male line or with
not more than one break due to marriage from an ancestor living before
the death of Henry I, and some at least of whose lands passed by inheritance to the reign of Edward I or later'. Pedigrees of Gospatric son of
Archil, the family of Vernoil, and ancestry of Vescy. The 17 illustrative
docs. (transcripts, Latin, of late 12th- and early 13th-century confirmations and gifts, with English summaries and note) relate mainly to lands
in Yorkshire held of the honour of Mowbray.

136. Constable of Everingham estate correspondence, 1726– **71.136**
43. Edited by Peter Roebuck. 1976.

Transcripts, shortened in part, of rather more than two-thirds of the
surviving correspondence between Sir Marmaduke Constable (*d.* 1746)
and Dom John Bede Potts, his chaplain and, from 1726 until Potts died in
1743, the supervisor of his estate and business affairs. The letters and
introduction together depict the Constable family's economy, developments in agriculture, and conditions generally on a medium-sized estate.
Map.

137. Court rolls of the manor of Acomb. Vol. 2. 1978. **71.137**

Includes rolls supplementary to the period covered in **71.131** above, so
that this edition comprises in reduced form all the known manorial records
of Acomb down to 1800 as well as those manorial docs. down to 1846
which were prepared for publication by the original editor. Additional
editorial work by Mrs. M. Stanley Price and John H. Harvey; the index
(in four sections) by John H. Watson.

138. York civic records. Vol. ix [1588–90]. Edited by Deborah **71.138**
Sutton. 1978.

Transcript, somewhat abridged, of York corportaion House book 30, continuing the edition begun in 71.98, the ms. described by Ann Ryecraft. In the introduction, a brief account of the Elizabethan corporation of York, its members and its work.

139. Leeds Friends' minute book, 1692 to 1712. Edited by   71.139
Jean and Russell Mortimer. 1980.

Transcript of the earliest minute book or book of record of Leeds preparative meeting, including the accounts for the poor, 1693–1712. Biographical notes on persons mentioned and, in the introduction, a summary description of organization and of the range of business recorded.

140. The Fountains abbey lease book. Edited by D. J. H.   71.140
Michelmore. 1981.

Annotated English abstracts of the 270 docs. copied into the lease book during the 1530s, the unusual or unique docs. presented in full if in English, in translation if originally in Latin. Leases from other sources are similarly presented in the appendix, together with a roll of the abbot's court for the lordships of Kilnsey, Litton and Malham held in Aug. 1534. A map and gazetteer of places referred to demonstrate that the estates did not form 'a solid block of land between the monastery and the Ribble'.

The introduction (nearly 70 pp.) treats of the characters and policies of the last three abbots and touches upon many aspects of land utilization (e.g. arable, meadow and pasture; woodland, mills, minerals and industry; dairy stock, milk yield, store cattle and draught oxen) as well as the nature of the tenancies, the status of the tenants, the personal service required of them, the manorial courts and customs, liveries, inheritance, and rights of dower.

72. YORKSHIRE ARCHAEOLOGICAL SOCIETY, RECORD SERIES, EXTRA SERIES

9. Early Yorkshire charters. Based on the manuscripts of the   **72.10**
late William Farrer and edited by Sir Charles Travis Clay.
Vol. xi: The Percy fee. 1963.

Transcripts, Latin, with English summaries and notes, 'bringing together all the available charters issued by the lords of the fee, especially in view of the witnesses'. Charters printed by Farrer are included in brief English summary but with witnesses listed in full. While surveying the work of others in this field and the sources accessible to them, the editor notes that 'many of Farrer's conclusions or suggestions would have been revised', and repeats his criticisms of the earlier edition of the Percy cartulary (see **41.**117), criticisms which this edition aims to meet. Two important corrections are made to the edition of the Sallay cartulary (**71.**87, 90).

The fee 'is an important example of a tenancy in chief of which the holders before the end of the twelfth century held under-tenancies of no less than six others'. In the sectional introductions are set out (i) a brief outline of the generations of the Percy family of the first line on branches of the family—of Dunsley, of Kildale, and of Bolton Percy— which can be traced to the 12th century or earlier, (ii) the lands of the fee in Yorkshire and Lincolnshire at the Domesday survey, (iii) charters issued by the lords of the fee, (iv) charters relating to the knights' fees held of the Percy tenancy in chief, (v) charters relating to demesne lands, and (vi) the considerable amount of land held of other tenancies in chief and spread over several counties. Pedigrees of Percy, lords of the fee, of Percy of Bolton Percy, of the descendants of Fulk son of Reinfrid, and of the Darel family.

10. Early Yorkshire charters. Vol. xii: The Tison fee. 1965.   **72.11**

Transcripts, Latin, with English summaries and notes, mainly concerned with the East Riding lands of Gilbert Tison, with the addition of material for some other lands of his tenancy in chief which became members of the honour of Mowbray, i.e. those in the West Riding, in Nottinghamshire, and in South Ferriby. Also considered are other lands in which the Tison family or families held an interest, in Northumberland and Gainsborough, Lincs. The final chapter examines the origins of the Constables of Flamborough, a family descending in the male line until the 17th century, distinct from that of Halsham and Burton Constable, and of 'undoubted descent from constables of Chester'. Other families on which notes are given include those of Anlaby, Gunby, Hay, Sancton, Spaldington and Salvain. Pedigrees of Tison, Salvain of Thorpe Salvin, and Constable of Flamborough. Map. Some corrections to earlier vols.

76. THORESBY SOCIETY, PUBLICATIONS

45. Documents relating to the manor and borough of Leeds, **76.46** 1066-1400. Edited by John Le Patourel. 1957.
English translations, accompanied for the most part by the Latin texts, of the Domesday entries; the borough charter of 1207; manorial extents, 1258, 1327, 1341, 1361; the yearly accounts of the keeper of rebels' lands in Yorkshire for the manor, 1322-7; reeve's accounts, 1356-7, 1373-4, 1383-4, 1399-1400; and extracts from accounts surviving from Queen Philippa's tenure of the manor.

46. The Thoresby miscellany. Vol. xiii. [1959-]1963. **76.47**
Medieval Leeds: Kirkstall abbey—the parish church—the medieval borough. By John Le Patourel. [Presidential addresses, 1952, 1953, 1954.]
New Grange, Kirkstall: its owners and occupants. By J. Sprittles.
A checklist of the correspondence of Ralph Thoresby. By Harold W. Jones. [Extracts from the same author's introduction to his list and indexes for close on 3,000 items, deposited in the library of the Yorkshire Archaeological Soc., and an alphabetical list of correspondents.]
Two hundred years of banking in Leeds. By H. Pemberton.
Leeds and the factory reform movement. By J. T. Ward.
Leeds leather industry in the nineteenth century. By W. G. Rimmer.
Working mens' cottages in Leeds, 1770-1840. By W. G. Rimmer. [With a contemporary calculation (12 Feb. 1832) showing that £1. 0s. 3d. was the 'least possible sum per week for which a man, his wife, and three children can obtain a sufficiency of food, clothing and other necessaries'.]
Leeds musical festivals [1858-1958]. By J. Sprittles.
Obituaries: Harry Pemberton [d. 1959]; George Edward Kirk [1886-1960], by R. J. Wood.
The building of Leeds town hall: a study in Victorian civic pride. By Asa Briggs.
Alfred Place Terminating Building Society, 1825-1843. By W. G. Rimmer.
Joseph Barker [1806-75] and The People, the true emigrant's guide. By Michael Brook.
William Hodgson's book. [Describes a ms. book compiled by a Leeds coachsmith between 1869 and 1875, containing notes on the family of his father, Benjamin, footman and coachman, and a chronicle of events public as well as private, Oct. 1813 to July 1875.]

47. Printed maps and plans of Leeds, 1711-1900. Compiled **76.48** by Kenneth J. Bonser and Harold Nichols. 1960.

Descriptive chronological catalogue with biographical and historical notes.

48. Kirkstall abbey excavations, 1955–1959. 1961. **76.49**

Reports by C. Vincent Bellamy, David Owen, and C. M. Mitchell; by Frank Rigg on masons' marks; by H. E. Jean Le Patourel on the pottery; by Michael L. Ryder on the animal bones. Earlier reports in **76.44**.

49. Pontefract priory excavations, 1957–1961. By C. Vincent Bellamy. 1965. **76.50**

Includes a report on the medieval pottery by Mrs. Le Patourel (with a contribution by J. G. Hurst), and a report on the animal remains by M. L. Ryder. Maps, plans, drawings, sections, masons' marks, etc. in separate folder.

50. The Thoresby miscellany. Vol. xiv. [1966–]1968. **76.51**

Leeds Quaker meeting: a history [1650–1962] based on the minute books of the Society of Friends in Leeds. By Wilfrid Allott.

A note on Leeds wills, 1539–1561. By Allister Lonsdale. [Showing, by examples from **76.19** and 27, how they reflect the changes taking place in religious beliefs and practices.]

Stourton Lodge, 1776 to April 1965. By Allister Lonsdale. [Apparently the last of the Yorkshire Roman Catholic mass houses, formerly at Ebor Lodge; not so used after 1804; demolished 1965.]

The evolution of Leeds to 1700. By W. G. Rimmer.

The industrial profile of Leeds, 1740–1840. By W. G. Rimmer.

Occupations in Leeds, 1841–1951. By W. G. Rimmer.

The postal history of Leeds. By H. C. Versey.

Futher notes upon Leeds church patronage in the eighteenth century. By R. J. Wood. [A poll during the contest for the appointment as vicar of Leeds in 1746; an account of the contest at Hunslet, 1746–9; and further details of the contest at Armley, 1761–6. See the article in **76.42** by the same.]

Obituary: Joseph Sprittles [d. 22 Mar. 1968.]

Index to the publications of the Thoresby Society, vols. 37–51 (1939–1968). Compiled by Mrs. G. C. F. Forster.

51. Kirkstall abbey excavations, 1960–1964. Reports by Elizabeth J. E. Pirie, H. E. J. Le Patourel, D. B. Whitehouse, J. Hurst, C. R. Robinson. 1967. **76.52**

52. Links with bygone Leeds. By Joseph Sprittles. 1969. **76.53**

Thirty short essays on the old buildings and traditions of Leeds, being the substance of talks given to local societies, together with 56 illustrative plates.

53. The Thoresby miscellany. Vol. xv. [1971–]1973. **76.54**

The Leeds churchwardens, 1828–1850. By Derek Fraser.

Poor law politics in Leeds, 1833–1855. By Derek Fraser.

The politics of Leeds water. By Derek Fraser.

Improvement in early Victorian Leeds. By Derek Fraser.

Thwaite mill, Hunslet, and Thomas Cheek Hewes. By Stuart B. Smith. [On the rebuilding of the mill in 1823. T. C. Hewes (1768-1832) founded the firm of Hewes and Wren, cotton machinery manufacturers and wheelwrights, pioneers in the application of wrought and cast iron. Includes plans of the millwork.]

Ebor House [Middleton Road, Leeds]. By Allister Lonsdale.

Extracts from the journals of John Deakin Heaton, M.D., of Claremont, Leeds [d. 1880]. Edited by Brian and Dorothy Payne. [Selected from his diaries and letters to cover aspects of his early family life or because of their relevance to the history of Leeds and some of its leading citizens. Pedigree showing related Heaton and Atkinson families.]

Kirkstall forge and monkish iron-making. By R. A. Mott. [Concludes that Kirkstall monks worked bloomeries at some distance from their house and that there were no ironworks on the abbey site until after the dissolution and perhaps not much earlier than 1600.]

The Venerable Edmund Sykes of Leeds, priest and martyr [executed 1587]. By George Bradley and Allister Lonsdale.

Wintoun Street [General] Baptist church, 1870-1895: a study in nineteenth-century church dissension. By R. J. Owen.

The rise of James Kitson: Trades Union and Mechanics Institution, Leeds, 1826-1851. By R. J. Morris.

The last monks of Kirkstall abbey. By Allister Lonsdale. [The pre-dissolution community and their subsequent careers, with a translation of the surrender deed and of the first pension list.]

John Smeaton [civil and mechanical engineer, 1724-92]. By C. A. Lupton.

Arthington nunnery. By C. A. Lupton.

54. The Thoresby miscellany. Vol. xvi. [1974-] 1979. **76.55**

The Irish in Leeds, 1851-1861. By T. Dillon. [A study of the peak years **76.55a** of Irish settlement in the township, the nature of the immigration, the area of settlement, and various demographic and environmental aspects of their presence.]

Spas, wells and springs of Leeds. By K. J. Bonser. **76.55b**

Christopher Wilkinson of Leeds and Maryland. By R. J. Wood. [Born **76.55c** 1663, became incumbent of Armley chapel in 1690 and was beneficed in Maryland from 1711 until his death in 1729.]

The autobiography of Robert Spurr [1801-69]. By Roger J. Owen. **76.55d**

The theatre in Hunslet Lane. By J. Copley. [Pt. 1: 1771-c.1860. Pt. 2: **76.55e** John Coleman's theatre, 1863-75.]

The Leeds gas strike, 1890. By H. Hendrick. **76.55f**

The Leeds Eye Dispensary [opened 1822, merged with Leeds General **76.55g** Infirmary in 1870]. By George Black.

City Square and Colonel Harding [lord mayor of Leeds, 1898-9, philan- **76.55h** thropist]. By George Black.

Wilson Armistead [1819-68] and the Leeds anti-slavery movement. By **76.55i** Irene E. Goodyear.

The Leeds Public Dispensary [founded 1824, closed 1971]. By S. T. **76.55j** Anning. [Includes a brief account of the dispensary movement. Appended lists of physicians, surgeons, dental surgeons, matrons, treasurers; statistics for income and expenditure, and for numbers of patients; table of larger legacies received and of receipts from the triennial musical festivals, 1874-1901; expenditure on leeches and on cod-liver oil.]

Leeds parish registers. Addenda [to **76.**25]: baptisms at St. Peter's, Apr. **76.**55*k* 26-30, 1775.

Profit, property interests, and public spirit: the provision of markets and **76.**55*l* commercial amenities in Leeds, 1822-29. By K. Grady. [Examines six enterprises: the Bazaar and Shambles, the South Market, the Free Market, the Central Market, the Commercial Buildings, and the Corn Exchange.]

The early years of the Yorkshire College. By P. H. J. H. Gosden. **76.**55*m* [Founded 1874, the College became an affiliated member of the Victoria University in 1887.]

The Baptist breach at Bramley. By Roger J. Owen. [Describes events **76.**55*n* leading to the formation of the break-away Second Baptist Church in 1878 and the reunion in 1972.]

Stank Hall barn, Leeds. Surveyed and written by Leeds University **76.**55*o* extra-mural class in Archaeology. Edited by H. E. Jean Le Patourel.

Obituary: Canon [Rowland John] Wood, 1885-1975. By John Le Pa- **76.**55*p* tourel. [With a list of Canon Wood's writings by John Wood.]

The early years of Leeds corporation. By G. C. F. Forster. [A lecture to **76.**55*q* mark (as do the two following papers) the 350th anniversary of the charter of incorporation, 1626.]

The corporation of Leeds in the eighteenth century. By R. G. Wilson. **76.**55*r*

The Leeds corporation, *c.* 1820-*c.* 1850. By Derek Fraser. **76.**55*s*

Holy Trinity church in the history of Leeds, 1727-1977. By G. C. F. **76.**55*t* Forster.

The architect of Holy Trinity church, Leeds. By W. J. Connor. [Suggests **76.**55*u* William Etty of York rather than William Halfpenny, otherwise known as Michael Hoare. Plates.]

The Leeds Savage Club and its origins. By George Black. **76.**55*v*

The 'wild Indian savages' in Leeds. By Colin G. Calloway. [An account **76.**55*w* of the rivalry between the *Leeds Mercury* and the *Leeds Intelligencer* as demonstrated in their coverage of the visit to Leeds of seven North American Indians in Apr. 1818.]

A Victorian city mission: the Unitarian contribution to social progress in **76.**55*x* Holbeck and New Wortley, 1844-78. By E. A. Elton.

A Yorkshire music critic in Germany and Austria in 1889. By P. S. **76.**55*y* Morrish. [Based on the travel diary of Herbert Thompson (*d.* 1945). A keen Wagnerian, his reports from Bayreuth for the *Yorkshire Post* were a scoop which the *Leeds Mercury* could not match. In the course of about six weeks he covered more than 1700 miles, chiefly by train, stopping at Wiesbaden, Munich, Salzburg, Vienna, Prague, Dresden, Leipzig and other music centres in addition to Bayreuth, sight-seeing and attending 18 performances of 14 operas, besides going to concerts and rehearsals.]

Obituary: His Honour Judge Allister Lonsdale, 1926-1977. By A.W. and **76.**55*z* F.W.

55. Leeds and the Oxford movement: a study in 'High **76.**56 Church' activity in the rural deaneries of Allerton, Armley, Headingley and Whitkirk in the diocese of Ripon. By Nigel Yates. 1975.

Aims 'to provide a detailed analysis of the parochial impact (or lack of impact) of the Oxford Movement in about a hundred parishes in and around Leeds, and to compare this impact with that in the nation as a whole, though ... this must still be largely a matter of assumption and guesswork'.

56. The Thoresby miscellany. Vol. xvii. [1979-] 1981.   76.57

'Fair befall the flax field': aspects of the history of the Boyle family and their flax business. By M. B. Boyle. [Follows the fortunes principally of three generations: James (1769-1815), his elder son Humphrey Bellamy (1794-1864), and Humphrey's son James (1835-1900). Deals in particular with the political interests and activities of Humphrey Bellamy Boyle, and gives some account of the establishment and development of the family firm, still in business within the field of natural fibres.]

The Yorkshire Ladies' Council of Education, 1871-91. By Isobel Jenkins. [Describes its origins, early work, administrative structure and membership; its involvement in the movement to improve the general education of middle-class women and girls and to spread information on health and hygiene, leading to its courses of instruction in cookery for working women and the establishment of the Yorkshire Training School of Cookery in 1875.]

Obituaries: Charles Athelstane Lupton, 1897-1977, by G. Woledge; Kenneth John Bonser, 1892-1976, by G. Woledge.

The Leeds workhouse under the old poor law, 1726-1834. By Philip Anderson. [An account of the origins of 'an excellent example of a provincial workhouse attempting to deal with the problems of destitution in the face of rapid urban growth and industrialisation', the evolution of its premises, its changing function and its administration. Treats in some detail of its officials (master, apothecaries, treasurer, etc.), the system of relief, the inmates, and the working of the apprenticeship system.]

The origins of gas in Leeds: the Leeds Gas Light Company, 1817-35. By A. Lockwood. [Describes the establishment, organization and commercial methods of the first gas company in Leeds; the opposition of the oil interests (who saw in the new source of light a threat to the whaling industry); the technical problems encountered in manufacture, distribution and marketing; and the possibly unusual nature of its financing.]

The Leeds Rational Recreation Society, 1852-9: 'music for the people' in a mid-Victorian city. By David Russell. [Traces the growth in Leeds of the 'people's concerts' movement as one response to the concern caused to moral reformers by the apparently strengthening link between working-class entertainment and the public house.]

William Vavasour: the squire of Weston, 1798-1833. By Mary Creaser. [An insight (derived from his eight unpublished diaries for the years 1798-1827, with some correspondence and related docs.) into the life and opinions of a country gentleman possessed of an ample competence, devoted for much of his time to the management of his estate, involved continually in the affairs of Weston and Askwith, and expected as a justice of the peace and a deputy lieutenant to be active in justiciary business.]

The Dewsbury riots [1739] and the Revd. Benjamin Ingham. By Beatrice

Scott. [Reprints the attack on Ingham by the vicar of Dewsbury, Thomas Bowman, as well as other public accusations, not as evidence that Ingham was instrumental in the riots, but to illustrate the animosity encountered by the early Methodists.]

Obituary: Frank Beckwith, 1904–1977 [with an annotated list of his writings, some of them unpublished], by Geoffrey Woledge.

PART 4
WELSH SOCIETIES

80. HISTORICAL SOCIETY OF THE CHURCH IN WALES

12. The journal of the Historical Society of the Church in   **80.10**
Wales. Vol. vii. Edited by E. T. Davies. 1957.
The consistory courts in the diocese of St. David's, 1660–1858. By Walter
T. Morgan.
Royal briefs for the restoration of churches in Wales. By Gwynfryn
Richards. Pt. 2. [Contd. from **80.9**. Concluded in **80.11** below.]
Contest for a Radnorshire rectory [Presteigne] in the seventeenth century.
By W. H. Howse.
The Cowbridge diocesan library, 1711–1848. By Ewart Lewis. Pt. 2:
Some account of its career. [Contd. from **80.7**.]
Dylanwad Mudiad Rhydychen yng Nghymru. By D. Eifion Evans. 2:
Braslun o'i hanes a'i dwf yn yr esgobaethau: Esgobaeth Llandaf. [The
influence of the Oxford Movement in Wales: a sketch of its history and
growth in the dioceses: Llandaff. For previous pts. see **80.7**, 9. Contd.
in **80.11**, 13 below.]

13. The journal ... Vol. viii. Edited by E. T. Davies. 1958.   **80.11**
The excommunications in the Book of Llan Dav. By J. W. James.
Saint Winifred's well and chapel, Holywell. By David Thomas.
Royal briefs for the restoration of churches in Wales. Pt. 3: an examination
of the data. [In the appendices, a transcript of the Clocaenog register of
all monies collected by briefs, 1709–36, and an examination of the
responsiveness of Welsh parishes to briefs. The brief for the relief of
distressed protestants in Piedmont in 1658 raised £582. 9s. from 517
parishes. Other briefs were for protestants in Lithuania, 1661, the
redemption of Christians in Turkish slavery, 1669, the redemption of
captives at Algiers, 1692, and French protestant refugees, 1694.]
An examination of churchwardens' accounts and of some disputes concerning them before the consistory courts of St. David's. By Walter T.
Morgan.
Dylanwad Mudiad Rhydychen ... Esgobaeth Llanelwy [St. Asaph]. Esgobaeth Tyddewi [St. David's].

14. The journal ... Vol. ix. Edited by E. T. Davies. 1959.   **80.12**
The Book of Llandav: the church and see of Llandav and their critics. By
J. W. James.
Border priests [15th and 16th centuries, in Radnorshire]. By E. J. L. Cole.
St. Asaph episcopal acts, 1536–1558. By G. Milwyn Griffiths. [A digest,
for bishops Wharton and Goldwell, the items re-arranged.]

Cases of subtraction of church-rate before the consistory courts of St. David's. By Walter T. Morgan.

15. The journal ... Vol. x. Edited by E. T. Davies. 1960.   80.13

The election of David Martin, bishop of St. David's, in 1293-6. By W. Greenway.

Disciplinary cases against churchwardens in the consistory courts of St. David's. By Walter T. Morgan.

Bunsen's reviewer. By Owain W. Jones. [On Rowland Williams and the furore occasioned by his article on Bunsen's biblical researches in *Essays and reviews* in 1860.]

Papers and correspondence about the restoration [by John Seddon] of Llanbadarn Fawr parish church, Cardiganshire, 1862-1870. By Geoffrey Rees.

Dylanwad Mudiad Rhydychen ... 3: Y gymdeithas leygol. [The lay community.]

16. The journal ... Vol. xi. Edited by E. T. Davies. 1961.   80.14

An ecclesiastical precedent book from St. Asaph. By C. E. Welch. [Calendar of a 'remarkably fine volume originally consisting of 546 folios' of the early 17th century, at Chichester, compiled by an unidentified lawyer who possibly started in the diocese of St. Asaph in the 1580s, moved to Rochester diocese, then became a member of Doctors' Commons, and returned to St. Asaph.]

1662 and before. By J. W. James. [A study of the Savoy conference, Mar.-July 1661, the twenty years preceding it, the consequent Act of Uniformity, and of the numbers of ministers ejected in Wales in 1660-2 and 1642-52.]

A Pembrokeshire skeptic [John Owen, d. 1896]. By Owain W. Jones.

Disputes concerning seats in church before the consistory courts of St. David's. By Walter T. Morgan.

17. The journal ... Vol. xii. Edited by E. T. Davies. 1962.   80.15

Restoration St. Asaph: the episcopate of Bishop George Griffith, 1660-1666. By G. Milwyn Griffiths. Pt. 1. [Contd. in **80.16** below.]

The prosecution of nonconformists in the consistory courts of St. David's, 1661-88. By Walter T. Morgan.

Hynt a helynt Brutus y dychanwr. By D. Melvin Davies. 1: Y blynyddoedd cynnar, 1795-1818. [The life and times of David Owen ('Brutus' the satirist), d. 1866. 1: Early years. English précis. Contd. in **80.16-18** below.]

18. The journal ... Vol. xiii. Edited by E. T. Davies. 1963.   80.16

Rotoland, subprior of Aberconway, and the controversy over the see of Bangor, 1199-1204. By Rhŷs Williams Hays.

The Restoration in St. Asaph: the episcopate of Bishop George Griffith, 1660-1666. Pt. 2.

Thomas Davies, rector of Coity, 1769-1819. By R. W. D. Fenn. [Includes the titles of some 63 works in his library.]

St. Katharine's church, Milford Haven: a note on the memorial to Lord Nelson. By J. F. Rees.

Hynt a helynt Brutus y dychanwr. 2: Crwydro'n ddiafael, 1819–35. [His years of aimless wandering. English précis.]

19. The journal . . . Vol. xiv. Edited by E. T. Davies. 1964.   80.17

Medieval records relating to the diocese of St. David's. By Francis Jones. [English versions of the following, *sede vacante*: (i) the account of Bogo de Cnoville, keeper of the temporalities, 1200; (ii) an inventory of the goods of Thomas Beck, late bishop, 1293, showing *inter alia* that he farmed extensively, and giving values for his animals—he had 2,348 of many kinds—and cereals; (iii) an incomplete extent of the temporalities in 1327; (iv) a statement of the lands in England held by the late bishop David Martin; (v) a still briefer return of the value of the temporalities in 1350.]

Religious life in Monmouth, 1066–1536. By K. E. Kissack. [Concerned chiefly with the Benedictine priory of St. Mary, its lands and churches, to its dissolution.]

The case against Bishop Jones of St. Asaph [found guilty of simony and in 1701 suspended from his office for six months]. By Owain W. Jones.

Connop Thirlwall [bishop of St. David's 1840–74]: liberal Anglican. By Geoffrey Rees.

Hynt a helynt Brutus y dychanwr. 3: Golygy'r *Haul*—y cyfnod toreithiog, 1835–50. [As editor of *Yr Haul*—his most fruitful phase. English précis.]

20. The journal . . . Vol. xv. Edited by E. T. Davies. 1965.   80.18

The Augustinian priory of St. Kinmark near Chepstow. By L. A. S. Butler.

Richard Watson [bishop of Llandaff, 1782–1816]: a reappraisal. By R. W. D. Fenn.

Mid-Victorian introspection in Wales. By Owain W. Jones. [What was wrong with the Church in Wales?]

Hynt a helynt Brutus y dychanwr. 4: Golygu'r *Haul*—y cyfnod olaf, 1851–66. [As editor of *Yr Haul*—the final phase. English précis.]

21. The journal . . . Vol. xvi. Edited by E. T. Davies. 1966.   80.19

The lordship and manors of Dewsland. By Francis Jones. 1. [The area; the bishop as lord marcher; the lordships. Lists the knights' fees and some of the chief officers. Contd. in **80.**20–23 below.]

The church of St. Mary and all Saints, Conway. By Gwynfryn Richards. [Describes the foundation of the Cistercian abbey at Aberconway *c.* 1186, its removal to Maenan in 1284, and its patronage of the church at Conway. The post-dissolution history of the church is outlined, with extracts from the returns made at the bishop's visitation in 1749 and from miscellaneous papers shedding light on 18th-century practices that are no longer observed. Later restorations (some by Sir Gilbert Scott) are described, and some of its features, memorials and possessions are listed, as are also its identifiable vicars from 1303.]

Llandaff cathedral in the eighteenth and nineteenth centuries. By D. R. Buttress. [Adds to the account of the Georgian restoration given by E. T. Davies in **80.**9 and compares it with the restoration of 1840–70. Reprints two letters from *The Builder* (1850–1) and correspondence from *The Ecclesiologist* concerning John Pollard Seddon's design for

the new west front exhibited at the Royal Academy in 1859. Also a letter from Dante Gabriel Rossetti to Seddon, 1875, after the chapter had refused him permission to overpaint one panel of his triptych.]
The church in industrial Rhymney, 1800–1855. By Islwyn Jenkins. [On work and wages, and the parish church built by the Rhymney Iron Company, Lodwick Edwards (d. 1855) its first incumbent.]

22. The journal ... Vol. xvii. Edited by E. T. Davies. 1967. **80.**20

The lordship and manors of Dewsland. 2: The episcopal manors.
The Welsh Book of Common Prayer. By R. Geraint Gruffydd. [Discusses the attribution of its authorship to Bishop Richard Davies, and states the 'much stronger case' for ascribing it to William Salesbury, d.? 1584.]
The Welsh Psalter, 1567. By Gwilym H. Jones. [A companion-piece to the preceding article, favouring William Salesbury as the translator and examining his technique.]

23. The journal ... Vol. xviii. Edited by E. T. Davies. 1968. **80.**21

Districts of the ancient Welsh *llannau*. By T. Thornley Jones. [A consideration of places with names incorporating or beginning 'llan', showing that their number in ancient Wales 'must have been very great', that they 'tend to be concentrated in groups', and that 'many of the names apply to considerable tracts of territory'.]
The lordship and manors of Dewsland. 3: The capitular manors and manors held by religious houses.
Bishop John Trevor II [d. 1410] of St. Asaph. By E. J. Jones.
A bishop of Bangor during the Glyn Dwr revolt: Richard Young [d. 1418]. By C. T. Allmand.
The mind of Robert Raikes. By Owain W. Jones. [Reflections on books in his library at Treberfydd, in the parish of Llangasty Talyllyn, and on the church and school rebuilt by him.]

24. The journal ... Vol. xix. Edited by E. T. Davies. 1969. **80.**22

Augustine's oak. By R. W. D. Fenn. [Considers the several sites claiming to be the place of Augustine's first meeting with the Celtic church in Britain and suggests as 'a more serious candidate' the oak in Abberley, Worcestershire. Bede's account of two meetings between Augustine and the British is seen as 'an expansion of a single incident' anterior to the confrontation at Chester, and the Chester affair 'becomes even more difficult to understand' if it is compared with the commencement of St. Birinus's work thirty years later amongst the West Saxons.]
The lordship and manors of Dewsland. 4: Lay manors. [Brimaston–Penmynydd *alias* Trerhos.]
The likeness of Bishop William Morgan. By T. J. Prichard. [An enquiry, strengthening the suspicion that no likeness of the bishop exists, certainly not in the memorials in Cardiff City Hall and St. Asaph, and not on the seal reputedly his in the P.R.O.]
Lay influence on religious life in Monmouth since the Reformation. By K. E. Kissack. [Instances of the way in which the establishment in Monmouth–clergy, magistrates, parish officers, and councilmen–and the lay rectors and patrons at Dixton influenced church affairs in the 18th and 19th centuries.]

25. The journal . . . Vol. xx. Edited by E. T. Davies. 1970. 80.23

The lordship and manors of Dewsland. 5: Lay manors. [Porth Clais–Whitchurch, with appended lists of manors as in *Menevia sacra* (for *c.* 1283) and the *Taylors Cussion* (for 1587–8).]
The origins of the nonconformist disestablishment campaign, 1830–1840. By R.Tudor Jones.
Welsh disestablishment and Welsh nationalism. By William B. George. [From the 1868 general election, tracing 'the transformation of Welsh radicalism into a genuine nationalist movement' which found expression in the motion for disestablishment introduced unsuccessfully by Lewis Llewellyn Dillwyn on 9 Mar. 1886.]

26. The journal . . . Vol. xxi. Edited by E. T. Davies. 1971. 80.24

The diocese of St. David's in the nineteenth century. By Walter T. Morgan. The unreformed church, pt. 1. [An enquiry into the financial structure of the church in the diocese, starting from the report of the Ecclesiastical Revenues Commission, 1835. Contd. in 80.25, 26 below. An appendix lists the tithe rent charges on parishes in the diocese, taken from the tithe commutation returns of 1887, and the stipends derived in 1833 from other preferments held by the cathedral prebendaries and the prebendaries of the collegiate church of Brecon.]
Bishop Green of Monmouth [the first bishop of the first diocese created after disestablishment, *d.* 1944]. By A. J. Edwards.

27. The journal . . . Vol. xxii. Edited by E. T. Davies. 1972. 80.25

St. Cynog's torc. By T. Thornley Jones.
The diocese of St. David's in the nineteenth century: the unreformed church, pt. 2. [Considers the administrative framework of the diocese and the condition of the church at parochial level, using the visitation returns of 1828.]
Bishop William Morgan's dispute with John Wynn of Gwydir in 1603–4 [over the appropriation of church property by laymen]. By J. Gwynfor Jones. [Includes transcripts of the extant correspondence (seven items).]

28. The journal . . . Vol. xxiii. Edited by E. T. Davies. 1973. 80.26

The distribution and proportion of Celtic and non-Celtic church dedications in Wales. By W. N. Yates.
The diocese of St. David's in the nineteenth century: the unreformed church, pt. 3. [Treats of the attitude of the bishops towards the Welsh language and culture, the provision of services in parishes with considerable English or Welsh minorities, the intrusion of English into parishes where services had previously been conducted entirely in Welsh, and the education and training of clergy able to carry out their duties efficiently in Welsh, the dominant language in the majority of parishes in diocese.]
The Reverend John Carne of Nash [*d.* 1798]. By John R. Guy. [Derived from his personal account books and diaries.]
Annals of a parish: the influence of the vicars on the life of the parish of Hay. By Geoffrey L. Fairs.

29. The journal ... Vol. xxiv. Edited by David Walker. 1974. **80.27**

Canon E. T. Davies. [Hon. editor, 1951–74. An appreciation, on his retirement.]

The episcopate of Richard, bishop of St. Asaph: a problem of twelfth-century chronology. By D. M. Smith. [Suggests that Richard was consecrated around the period 2 Feb.–1 Nov. 1141 and was succeeded by Bishop Gilbert in 1143.]

Gerald of Wales: a review of recent work. By David Walker.

The clergy in society in mid-Victorian South Wales. By Wilton D. Wills.

30. The journal ... Vol. xxv. Edited by David Walker. 1976. **80.28**

The diocese of St. David's from the end of the middle ages to the Methodist revival. By Glanmor Williams. [The substance of a lecture designed to outline 'some of the more interesting problems and possibilities facing those who are concerned to investigate the history of the diocese and also to indicate some of the more promising lines of inquiry which have recently been undertaken'.]

The 'popish plot' in Monmouth shire. By E. T. Davies. [A survey of the evidence for the number and distribution of papists and recusants in the county from c. 1570 to 1706, and of the 'subterfuge of occasional conformity', as a background to the events which led to the execution in 1679 of David Lewis *alias* Charles Baker, a Jesuit priest.]

A rent roll of the temporalities of the see of St. David's, 1685. By Francis Jones. [Transcript of a copy. The location of the original, a 'borrowed book' completed by Robert Lucy, registrar and receiver to the bishop, Laurence Womock, is unknown.]

Clandestine marriages in Wales [before Hardwicke's Marriage Act of 1753]. By R. Brown.

31. The journal ... Vol. xxvi. Edited by David Walker. 1979. **80.29**

Knights of the Holy Sepulchre. By Francis Jones. [On the origin and history of the Order, with brief biographical notices of 14 knights who were Welsh by descent and residence, 12 who were *advenae* settled in Wales, and 8 who belonged to border families. In all, the names of 48 knights in Britain in medieval times are know.]

Henry Rowlands, bishop of Bangor, 1598–1616. By J. Gwynfor Jones. [Includes a selection of his correspondence on ecclesiastical and other affairs.]

The education of the clergy in the diocese of Landaff, 1750–1866. By E. T. Davies.

The diocese of St. David's in the nineteenth century: a comment based on the life and career of the Rev. W. Seaton [rector of Lampeter Velfrey from 1830 until his death in 1851, to whom 'a considerable injustice' is said to have been done by W. T. Morgan's articles in **80.24–26** above]. By Peter M. S. Jones.

82. SOUTH WALES AND MONMOUTH RECORD SOCIETY, PUBLICATIONS

4. Edited by Henry John Randall and William Rees. 1957.   **82.4**

The accounts of the ministers for the lordships of Abergavenny, Grosmont and White Castle for the year 1256-1257. By A. J. Roderick and William Rees. Pt. iii: The lordship of Monmouth. [Transcript, Latin, with English translation. For previous pts. see **82.2, 3.**]

Records of the lordship of Senghenydd with the castle of Caerphilly (from the time of Edward I to Henry VIII). By William Rees. [Transcripts, Latin.]

The houses of the friars at Cardiff and Newport: the first financial accounts after the suppression, viz. for the year 1538-1539. By William Rees. [English translation, from P.R.O. Ministers' Accounts.]

Monmouthshire recusants in the reigns of Elizabeth and James I. By Frank H. Pugh. [A table of parish totals, 1581-1625, and nominal lists, with some biographical notes and two distribution maps.]

Sessions in eyre in a marcher lordship: a dispute between the earl of Worcester and his tenants of Gower and Kilvey in 1524. By T. B. Pugh and W. R. B. Robinson. [From Star Chamber Proceedings.]

The copper industry of Neath and Swansea: a record of a suit in the court of exchequer, 1723. Transcribed by D. Elwyn Gibbs. Edited by R. O. Roberts. [Pleadings and depositions in the action brought by John Phillips, chemist and metallurgist, claiming payment for his services and disbursements as a works manager in 1716-19 from Dr. John Lane of Bristol, physician and industrial entrepreneur.]

Rumney parish 1744-1854, as seen in the parish registers and account books. By D. Elywyn Williams.

Glamorgan men at the battle of Trafalgar. By J. F. W. Leigh.

Wreck de mer: rights of foreshore in Glamorgan. By William Rees. [Transcript of suit and rejoinder, from Star Chamber Proceedings, 1584-5.]

5. Edited by Henry John Randall and William Rees. 1963.   **82.5**

Diary of Lewis Weston Dillwyn. [Extracts, Oct. 1817-July 1852. Dillwyn, high sheriff of Glamorgan 1818 and Member of Parliament 1832-7, d. 1855. General introduction by H. J. Randall. Dillwyn as botanist, by H. A. Hyde. Dillwyn as zoologist, by Colin Matheson. Dillwyn and the Cambrian Pottery, by R. L. Charles. Pedigree of Dillwyn and list of Dillwyn's published works.]

PART 5
ADDENDA

86. BRISTOL AND GLOUCESTERSHIRE ARCHAEOLOGICAL SOCIETY, RECORDS SECTION

4. The registers of the church of St. Mary, Dymock, 1538– **86.4** 1790. Edited by Irvine Gray and J. E. Gethyn-Jones. 1960.

Baptisms, marriages, burials.

5. Guide to the parish records of the city of Bristol and the **86.5** county of Gloucester. Edited by Irvine Gray and Elizabeth Ralph. 1963.

6. The church book of St. Ewen's, Bristol, 1454–1584. Tran- **86.6** scribed and edited by Betty R. Masters and Elizabeth Ralph. 1967.

Transcripts, 1454–1518, of inventories of church goods, churchwardens' (proctors') accounts, lists of benefactors, etc., and a calendar of other memoranda, 1518–84. Also, transcript of copy accounts, 1547–84, and calendar of selected deeds, etc., c. 1256–1579. Glossary.

7. Cheltenham settlement examinations, 1815–1826. Edited **86.7** by Irvine Gray. 1969.

Abstracts. The introduction summarizes the law of settlement and indicates the range and use of settlement records.

8. Local government in Gloucestershire, 1775–1800: a study **86.8** of the justices of the peace. By Esther Moir. 1969.

9. Marriage allegations in the diocese of Gloucester. Edited **86.9** by Brian Frith. Vol. ii: 1681–1700. 1970.

Continues **86.2**.

10. The commission for ecclesiastical causes within the **86.10** dioceses of Bristol and Gloucester, 1574. Edited by F. D. Price. 1972.

Transcript, part Latin, part English (some lengthy formal Latin entries summarized in English), of 'what appears to be a virtually complete record of the Commission's acts [from the inaugural session on 14 Aug. 1574] until October 1576, several sessions held in October 1577, and a series of entries mainly concerned with a particular clerical offender between November 1581 and June 1582'. The cases recorded 'are all of Gloucestershire origin, just as were those before the Consistory Court (the diocese being coterminous with the shire)'.

The introduction (42 pp.) describes the task of the commission, its jurisdiction and powers, members and staff, its relations with the consistory court, its use of the agents of the local temporal as well as ecclesiastical authorities, its responsibility to the central government, its procedure, and the offences and offenders it dealt with.

11. **An ecclesiastical miscellany. 1976.**   **86.**11

A register of the churches of the monastery of St. Peter's, Gloucester. By David Walker. [Calendar of 179 miscellaneous docs. brought together at the end of the 14th century, of which 82 relate to the priory of Ewyas Harold.]

A survey of the diocese of Gloucester, 1603. Transcribed by Alicia C. Percival and edited by W. J. Sheils.

Wesleyan membership in Bristol, 1783. By John Kent. [Transcript of John Wesley's register of 790 members grouped by him into classes by proximity of residence, sex and occupation noted. Map.]

88. BANBURY HISTORICAL SOCIETY, RECORDS SECTION

1. Index to wills proved in the peculiar court of Banbury, **88.1** 1542–1858. Edited by J. S. W. Gibson. 1959.

Published jointly with the Oxfordshire Record Soc. and probably identical with the same title in **58.**40 above. Not seen.

2. Marriage register of Banbury. Pt. i: 1558–1724. Tran- **88.2** scribed by Mrs. N. Fillmore and Mrs. J. Pain. Edited by J. S. W. Gibson. 1960.

Abstract, presenting 'all the relevant information in the clearest possible way'. Contd. in the following and **88.**5. All vols. indexed by R. C. Couzens.

3. Marriage register of Banbury. Pt. ii: 1724–1790. Tran- **88.3** scribed by Mrs. N. Fillmore and J. S. W. Gibson. Edited by J. S. W. Gibson. 1961.

4. Clockmaking in Oxfordshire, 1400–1850. By C. F. C. Bee- **88.4** son. 1962.

A survey, alphabetically by parish, first of turret clocks, then of sundials and sand-glasses, followed by a biographical dictionary of 'some 320 apprentices, clockmakers, smiths and others concerned with the making and maintenance of clocks and watches', the names reclassified by places in the topographical list following the dictionary. Map and 48 plates. Published in association with the Antiquarian Horological Soc.

5. Marriage register of Banbury. Pt. iii: 1790–1837. Tran- **88.5** scribed and edited by J. S. W. Gibson. 1963.

6. South Newington churchwardens' accounts, 1553–1684. **88.6** Transcribed and edited by E. R. C. Brinkworth, with biblio- graphic descriptions by H. G. Pollard and D. M. Rogers. 1964.

The analytical introduction 'in the form of notes grouped under headings ... attempts to bring out the main points of interest and to explain some obscurities'.

7. Baptism and burial register of Banbury, Oxfordshire. Pt. i: **88.7** 1558–1653. Transcribed by Mrs. N. Fillmore. Edited by J. S. W. Gibson. [1966?]

Includes a description of the bindings of the two vols., by Paul Morgan.

In the appendices, (i) a list of wills of Banbury inhabitants, or of people holding land in Banbury, proved before the registers start in 1558, and after that date of those not appearing in the burials register, and (ii) abstracts of inscriptions relating to burials, virtually all the original monumental inscriptions inside the church having been destroyed when old St. Mary's was demolished in 1790. Map. Contd. in **88.**9, 16 below. All vols. indexed by R. C. Couzens, and all include references to wills or other testamentary docs. against the relevant burial entries.

8. A Victorian M.P. and his constituents: the correspondence **88.**8
of H. W. Tancred, 1841–1859. Edited by B. S. Trinder, with
a foreword by the Rt. Hon. Richard Crossman, M.P. 1969.

Transcripts. Never resident in the town, Tancred rarely visited more than twice a year the constituency which he represented from 1832 to 1858. The correspondence, addressed for the most part to John and William Munton, father and son, solicitors in Banbury and in turn Tancred's agents, 'throws light on many aspects of the relationship between the M.P. and his constituency which are of general interest'. The introduction summarizes (in 30 pp.) Tancred's life and unremarkable parliamentary career.

9. Baptism and burial register of Banbury, Oxfordshire. Pt. ii: **88.**9
1653–1723. Transcribed by Mrs. J. Pain. Edited by J. W. S.
Gibson. 1969.

Analytical introduction. Appendices as in **88.**7 above. Maps.

10. Shoemaker's window: recollections of Banbury in Oxford- **88.**10
shire before the railway age, by George Herbert, 1814–1902.
Edited by Christiana S. Cheney. Second edition, with a new
introduction and additional notes on the text by B. S. Trinder.
1971.

The autobiography and reminiscences of a shoemaker, giving 'an authentic picture of market town society', first published 1948 (Oxford). Map. Plates.

11. The Wigginton constables' book, 1691–1836. Edited by **88.**11
F. D. Price. 1971.

Transcript. The varying nature of the accounts 'reflects the striking changes which occurred in the life of the village during a period of major social upheaval'. The introduction describes these changes and their impact on the rôle of the constable in the government of Wigginton. Maps.

12. Parish accounts for the 'town' of Bodicote, Oxfordshire, **88.**12
1700–1822. Edited and annotated by J. H. Fearon. Based on
a transcription by C. W. Hurst. 1975.

Transcript. Loosely described as churchwardens' accounts, the accounts until the inclosure in 1768 are 'a complete set of village accounts for the churchwardens, surveyors, fieldsmen and constables'. After 1768 the accounts record only the churchwardens' transactions, but in more detail.

Analytical and explanatory notes. Lists of churchwardens and other officers. Map.

13. [In preparation.]   88.13

14. Banbury wills and inventories. Pt. ii: 1621–1650. Tran-   88.14
scribed, abstracted and edited by E. R. C. Brinkworth and J.
S. W. Gibson. 1976.

The indexes—of names, of trades, professions and offices, and of places—
are for the period 1591–1650. The abstracts for the years 1591–1620,
together with an analytical introduction, will presumably be in the as yet
(Jan. 1983) unpublished pt. i. Also in pt. ii are a glossary and a list of
Banbury inhabitants whose wills were proved in the prerogative court of
Canterbury, 1621–50.

15. Banbury corporation records: Tudor and Stuart. Calen-   88.15
dared, abstracted and edited by J. S. W. Gibson and E. R. C.
Brinkworth. 1977.

A detailed calendar of the book of accounts, 1555–1741, with additional
docs. relating either directly to the corporation or indirectly to the town,
these additional docs. also calendared (except for the translations and
abstracts of the town's charters) and inserted chronologically under the
mayoral year to which they relate. Includes numerous genealogical tables
showing the relationships between members of the corporation and, to a
lesser extent, with its officers. Lists of (i) the corporation under the first
charter, 1554–1607, (ii) the corporation under the second charter, 1608–
93, (iii) bailiffs and mayors, 1553–1700, (iv) chamberlains, wardens of the
town houses, bridgemasters, and auditors. Biographical notes (32 pp.).

16. Baptism register of Banbury, Oxfordshire. Pt. iii: 1723–   88.16
1812. Transcribed and edited by J. S. W. Gibson. 1978.

From the parish registers, with additional lists of baptisms (occasionally
including births) drawn from the registers kept by (i) Banbury monthly
meeting, Society of Friends, 1723–1812; (ii) Banbury independent or
congregational church, 1794–1806; (iii) Banbury independent church,
Countess of Huntingdon's Connexion, 1807–12; (iv) Banbury Methodist
church, 1805–13; (v) Bloxham, Milton and Banbury Presbyterian meeting, 1786–1812; and (vi) the Roman Catholic baptisms extracted by the
Rev. C. I. Bowen in 1876 from the journal kept by the Rev. P. J. Hersent,
1771–1812. Included in the last are Father Bowen's notes on Father
Hersent (d. 1833) and on the Catholic chapels which preceded the opening
of St. John's church, Banbury, in '1833 or therabouts'. Map.

17. Administrations and inventories of the archdeaconry of   88.17
Northampton. Pt. ii: 1711–1800. 1980.

Issued in conjunction with the British Record Soc. See 12.92 above.

18. [In preparation.]   88.18

19. Victorian Banbury. By Barrie Trinder. 1982.   **88.**19

A history, with map, plates, textual figures and 15 tables of statistical matter to illustrate population growth, the traffic on the main roads in the area, migration into Banbury from its hinterland and from places more remote, attendance at church services, the foundation of voluntary societies of many kinds, the occupational structure, and aspects of parliamentary elections.

89. BRITISH ACADEMY, ANGLO-SAXON CHARTERS*

1. **Charters of Rochester. Edited by A. Campbell. 1973.**   **89.1**
Transcripts, Latin or Old English, with brief English summaries. The introduction describes the archive (practically all the 37 docs. are contained in the *Textus Roffensis*), the estates dealt with by the charters, the authenticity of the charters, and their language. A concordance links this edition with the list in P. H. Sawyer, *Anglo-Saxon charters* (Royal Historical Soc., Guides and handbooks series, 1968), and with J. M. Kemble, *Codex diplomaticus aevi Saxonici* (1839–48), and W. de Gray Birch, *Cartularium Saxonicum* (1885–99). Indexes include a diplomatic index.

2. **Charters of Burton abbey. Edited by P. H. Sawyer. 1979.**   **89.2**
Transcripts, Latin or Old English, with brief English summaries and notes. Much of the introduction is concerned with Wulfric (later named Spot or Spott), the founder of the abbey; it includes a translation of his will (based on the published translation by Dorothy Whitelock), some consideration of the beneficiaries, identifications (some tentative) of the 80 estates bequeathed in the will, and an account of Wulfric and his family. Eight of the charters are seen as belonging to 'a group of texts, dated between 930 and 956, that are distinctive in being written, at least in part, in rhythmical and alliterative Latin'; the significance of the form is considered. The concordance (as in **89.1** above) is extended to include C. R. Hart, *The early charters of northern England and the north Midlands* (1975). Indexes include one of words and personal names used in boundary marks, a Latin glossary, and a diplomatic index. Plates illustrate Chrismons copied into the 13th-century Peniarth ms. 390 (National Library of Wales) and on the five charters in the William Salt Library at Stafford.

---

*The series aims to publish 'all pre-Conquest title-deeds known to have survived, that is, all documents relating to grants of lands and liberties, whoever their grantor or grantee, whatever their diplomatic form ..., whether written in Latin or the vernacular'. Records not comprised within these terms, such as professions of obedience, manumissions, acts of council, will be excluded. Originals and early copies will be reproduced 'as faithfully as is possible, without going to the extreme of "record type" and without following the manuscript in the use of capitals'. (Derived from the foreword by Professor C. R. Cheney in **89.1** above.)

90. BRITISH ACADEMY, ENGLISH EPISCOPAL ACTA*

1. Lincoln, 1067–1185. Edited by David M. Smith. 1980. **90.1**

The first vol. of a projected collection of Lincoln acta from the Conquest to Hugh of Wells. Transcripts, Latin, with brief English summaries, of all original acta, even if they have been printed elsewhere, and of all unpublished copies and transcripts where no originals survive. Copies which have been printed in satisfactory and easily accessible editions have been calendared, the witness-lists being retained in their original form. The textual and historical annotations include brief notes on the seals and sealing methods.

In accordance with the plan of the series, the introduction treats briefly of the five bishops and one bishop-elect of the see during the period, and also of the secular and domestic officials and of those clerical staff and advisers who formed the bishop's personal staff or *familia*. The form and nature of the acta are analysed and their seals described. An appendix sets out 'framework itineraries' of the bishops. Plates.

---

*The series aims 'to make readily available collections of English episcopal acta from the Conquest to a date in the thirteenth century, arranged diocese by diocese'. It will not provide 'detailed studies of the individual bishops' nor will it 'chronicle the administrative changes and developments in the bishoprics during their episcopates'. The introductions 'will aim to provide notes on the bishops and their households and on the contents and diplomatic of the acta'. (Derived from the editor's introduction in **90.1** above.)

91. CAMBRIDGE ANTIQUARIAN RECORDS SOCIETY

1. Letters to William Frend from the Reynolds family of Little Paxton, and John Hammond of Fenstanton, 1793–1814. Edited by Frida Knight. 1974.   **91.1**

Transcripts, with brief linking narrative. William Frend, mathematician and Unitarian, *d.* 1841. The letters recount the daily life of their time and express vigorous and unorthodox opinions on current events.

2. John Norden's survey of Barley, Hertfordshire, 1593–1603. Edited by J. C. Wilkerson. 1974.   **91.2**

Transcript, the Latin translated, with maps, a list of land owners, and a glossary of field names. The introduction touches briefly on the occupants and agricultural use of the land from pre-Domesday times to the mid-19th century.

3. The West Fields of Cambridge. Edited by Catherine P. Hall and J. R. Ravensdale. 1976.   **91.3**

Transcript, Latin, of the Corpus terrier, *c.* 1360, including all its marginalia. The ms., used as foundation both for Seebohm's *The English village community* and Maitland's *Township and borough*, remained largely neglected thereafter, with the consequence that 'a great deal of fierce academic controversy' had been 'waged wastefully and indecisively during the past twenty-five years'. Appended are topographical notes, English, based on the terrier of 1566 in St. John's College; transcripts, Latin, of two relevant charters, the earlier by William Mortimer to Adam Dunning (*c.* 1240), the other by Richard Dunning to Robert his son and wife Joan (1309); a note on trees; a glossary of field names; and tables showing the ownership in five areas of the West Fields.

The introduction (more than 80 pp.) has chapters devoted to the description of land (selions, gores, butts etc.; headlands, strips and doles etc.; balks great and small; furlongs; fields and seasons; enclosures); the map of the West Fields (topography and lay-out; place and field names etc.); origins, lordship and ownership; and the genesis of the Cambridge 'Backs'.

4. A Cambridgeshire gaol delivery roll, 1332–1334. Edited by Elisabeth G. Kimball. 1978.   **91.4**

Transcript, Latin, of the earliest roll for the county and town of Cambridge for which there is extant a kalendar or agenda of the business to be done at some of the sessions recorded on the roll.

The introduction, after describing the commissions (for county and town) and identifying the justices, considers the sessions, the offences (chiefly felonies), the personnel attending sessions, and the judicial process (including the various means by which accusations were brought against the persons arrested). Appended is a table giving the dates and places of gaol deliveries and assize sessions, with the names of the justices who sat, in the counties of the Norfolk circuit, June 1332—Sept. 1334, the information supplied by C. A. F. Meekings.

92. CATHOLIC RECORD SOCIETY, OCCASIONAL PUBLICATIONS

1. Returns of papists, 1767: diocese of Chester. Transcribed **92.1**
under the direction of E. S. Worral. Quarto, 1980.

Lists (497 in all) arranged under the 20 deaneries of the diocese. Map.
The returns were made in response to the request by the House of Lords
for 'as correct and complete lists as can be obtained of the papists, or
reputed papists . . . distinguishing their parishes, sexes, ages and occupations and how long they have been there resident'. 'If the Society's fi-
nances make it possible ever to publish the second volume, containing the
returns for the rest of the country, this will have the same format as the
first and will also be called an Occasional Publication.'

93. DERBYSHIRE ARCHAEOLOGICAL SOCIETY, RECORD SERIES

1. A calendar of the Shrewsbury papers in the Lambeth Palace **93.1**
library. Edited by E. G. W. Bill. 1966. [HMC JP 6]

Lambeth Palace library mss. 694–710, being the papers of the earls of
Shrewsbury, 15th century–1616. Few items earlier than 1538.

2. The cartulary of Dale abbey. Edited by Avrom Saltman. **93.2**
1967. [HMC JP 11]

Transcript, Latin, of the early 14th-century cartulary and supplementary
docs., with English abstracts. The introduction adds to the account of the
foundation given in *VCH Derbyshire* and H. M. Colvin, *The White Canons
in England*, treats of the founder's kin, surveys the possessions of the
abbey at the end of the 13th century, and draws from the charters various
sidelights on social and economic history.

3. The duchy of Lancaster's estates in Derbyshire, 1485– **93.3**
1540. Edited by I. S. W. Blanchard. 1971.

Extracts from duchy records, some transcribed, others in translation,
'chosen to illustrate disputes over pasture and common rights . . . and over
the duchy's attempts to profit from the commercial activity of the area',
with extracts from the minutes of the duchy council, from the reports of
the commissioners of improvement, the account of the bailiff of the High
Peak, 1491–2, and the account of the reeve of Duffield, 1493–4.

The introduction considers the estates, the changes in wool prices and
land rents, the alternating booms and slumps, the evidence of probate
inventories, and the rapid growth of pastoral activity between 1485 and
1520; it also relates the docs. to the hierarchical administrative structure
of the duchy and explains some of the interpretative difficulties.

4. A calendar of the Talbot papers in the College of Arms. **93.4**
Edited by G. R. Batho. 1971. [HMC JP 7]

Complementary to and covering much the same period as **93.1** above, and
'in themselves a rich record of a noble family's public service and private
living in the Tudor period'.

5. The church in Derbyshire in 1823–4: the parochial visita- **93.5**
tion of the Rev. Samuel Butler, archdeacon of Derby in the
diocese of Lichfield and Coventry. Edited by M. R. Austin.
1972.

Transcripts of the replies to the articles of inquiry, in alphabetical order by place-name. The introduction sketches the apprehension prevailing among the clergy in the 1820s, Butler's career and views as schoolmaster and cleric, the itinerary of his visitation, and Butler's own summary of his findings. Glossary of some ecclesiastical terms.

6. The cartulary of the Wakebridge chantries at Crich. Edited **93.6** by Avrom Saltman. 1976.

Transcript, Latin, with English summaries, of the cartulary compiled *c.*1369 at the behest of the founder, William of Wakebridge, and added to in a minor way in later years. Concerned in the main with the chantries at Crich (two) and Annesley, the parish church at Crich, and the chapels of Normanton and Wakebridge. In the introduction, a pedigree of the Wakebridge family, an outline of William's varied administrative career and (at greater length and drawn from the cartulary) an account of his observance of the steps needful for normal chantry foundation.

7. The Kniveton leiger. Edited ... by Avrom Saltman. 1977. **93.7** [HMC JP 24]

Transcript, Latin, with English summaries, of the early 14th-century register of title deeds and other evidences, beginning in the 13th century, of the Kniveton family relating to lands in Derbyshire, Staffordshire and Nottinghamshire, with supplementary docs. and genealogical tables of Kniveton, of the co-heiresses of Serlo de Grendon, and of the Meverels of Gayton.

94. DERBYSHIRE RECORD SOCIETY

1. Chesterfield wills and inventories, 1521–1603. Edited by   **94.1**
J. M. Bestall and D. V. Fowkes, with an introduction by
David Hey, a glossary by Rosemary Milward, and an index by
Barbara Bestall. 1977.
The wills calendared, the inventories presented in the standardized form
adopted by the Oxfordshire Record Soc. in **58.44** above. Analytical intro-
duction.

2. The diary of James Clegg of Chapel en le Frith, 1708–1755.   **94.2**
Edited by Vanessa S. Doe. Pt. 1 [1708–36]. 1978.
Transcript. James Clegg (1679–1755), dissenting minister, ordained in
1703, obtained a degree in medicine in 1729, and as preacher and doctor
was in demand over a wide area of Derbyshire, Cheshire, Lincolnshire
and Nottinghamshire. His diary, at first spasmodic and of a devotional
nature, developed into a regular daily record, from Dec. 1727, concerned
with his work for the ministry, his treatment of the sick, the state of the
weather and the crops, his reading, and his correspondence with religious
leaders in London and the provincial capitals. Genealogical tables for
Clegg of Shawfield in Rochdale, Champion of Edale, and of James Clegg's
family. Map of Chapel en le Frith and district, and of roads and trackways
in north Derbyshire. Contd. in the following and **94.5**. Pagination is
continuous.

3. The diary of James Clegg . . . Pt. 2 [1737–47]. 1979.   **94.3**

4. The building of Hardwick Hall. Edited by N. Durant and   **94.4**
Philip Riden. Pt. 1: The old hall, 1587–91. 1980.
The accounts transcribed and arranged to show wages paid to masons,
stone-getters, carpenters and others, payments for materials and in respect
of contracts for piece work, payments to wallers, and payments of quarterly wages. The design and progress of the work, and the present re-
bound state of the accounts, are described in the introduction. Total
payments to labourers (weekly from July 1587, fortnightly from Sept.
1590 to Jan. 1599) are set out in an appendix.

5. The diary of James Clegg . . . Pt. 3 [1748–55]. 1981.   **94.5**
Concluded, with the following appendices: autobiography of James Clegg;
letter to Edward Calamy, 1728; medical notes, Oct. 1729–1731; list of
contributors to the building of Chinley chapel, 1711; trustees of the chapel
in 1711 and chosen in 1728 and 1748; will of James Clegg, made in 1753;

will of Rev. John Ashe of Ashford in the Water, Bakewell, and probate inventory, 1735; extracts from the will of Thomas Cresswell senior, 1728; extracts from the will of Anne Cresswell, 1733; biographical notes on some of the many dissenting ministers mentioned in the diary; list of medicaments used by James Clegg, 1708-55. The cumulative index supersedes the indexes in the preceding pts.

6. **William Woolley's history of Derbyshire. Edited by Catherine Glover and Philip Riden. 1981.**   **94.6**

Transcript and index by Miss Glover, the preface and introduction by Mr. Riden. In end pocket, microfiche reproduction of the collections of Samuel Sanders of Little Ireton, on which Woolley relied heavily and which 'should be of particular value for parishes in the north of the county', Woolley's history being incomplete.

7. **Derbyshire hearth tax assessments, 1662-70. Edited by David G. Edwards with an introduction incorporating material by the late C. A. F. Meekings. 1982.**   **94.7**

The introduction sets out the nature and general history of the tax, describes the surviving records, and explains why the lists printed here are for 1670 (hundreds of High Peak, Morleston and Litchurch, Scarsdale, and Wirksworth) together with the 1662 or 1664 lists for Appletree and Repton and Gresley, supplemented by totals of names and hearths recorded in 1662, 1664 and 1670. Consideration is given to the administration of the tax and the range of records created in three periods, viz. 1662-4 under the sheriffs, 1664-5 under the first receivers, and 1669-74 under the second receivers. The lists are analysed.

95. DEVON AND CORNWALL RECORD SOCIETY, PUBLICATIONS, EXTRA SERIES

1. Exeter freemen, 1266–1967. Edited ... by Margery M. Rowe and Andrew M. Jackson. Foreword by W. G. Hoskins. 1973.

95.1

A list and index of 12,000 or so names 'compiled entirely from records among the official archives of the city', with an introduction dealing with the early history of the freedom, the numbers of admissions in medieval times, admission by purchase and the ordinances relating thereto, the obligations and economic aspects of the freedom, trade gilds and the freedom, developments due to parliamentary elections, freemen and mayoral elections, and the virtual extinction of freemen's privileges in 1835.

2. Guide to the parish and non-parochial registers of Devon and Cornwall, 1538–1837. Compiled with an introduction by Hugh Peskett. 1979.

95.2

Embraces the ancient diocese of Exeter, viz. the civil counties of Devon and Cornwall, the city of Exeter, and the Isles of Scilly. Offers information about population, civil and ecclesiastical jurisdictions, maps, and notes on the congregations, non-Anglican as well as Anglican. The wide-ranging introduction includes the history of parish registers, and sets out for every religious community of the area the particular features which should be taken into account when searching for or using its registers and records.

96. DORSET RECORD SOCIETY, PUBLICATIONS

1. Weymouth and Melcombe Regis minute book, 1625–1660. Edited by Maureen Weinstock. 1964.   **96.1**

   Transcript of part of minute book C, 'a mixture of council minutes, lists and surveys of different kinds, together with ... bye-laws or "Constitutions"'.

2. Witchcraft at Toner's Puddle, 19th c., from the diary of the Rev. William Ettrick. Edited by Christina Hole. 1964.   **96.2**

   Extracts, 1804–5, showing 'in a mind that might have been expected to be proof against them', the survival of traditions, suspicions and fears current two centuries before.

3. The Thomas Rackett papers, 17th [*sic*] to 19th centuries. Edited by H. S. L. Dewar. 1965.   **96.3**

   Transcripts of selected letters, several of them on antiquarian and theatrical subjects, addressed to the Rev. Thomas and Mrs. Rackett and others between 1754 and 1841. Among the writers are Mrs. Garrick, Dr. W. G. Maton (physician to Queen Charlotte), Charles Hatchett (chemist), Sir Richard Colt Hoare, John Knowles (of the Navy Office, biographer of Fuseli), and Mrs. Siddons.

4. The Dorset lay subsidy roll of 1332. Edited by A. D. Mills. 1971.   **96.4**

   Transcript, in a mixture of Latin, French and English, of the earliest surviving complete roll of its kind for Dorset, listing for the whole county those people who were assessed on their movables or personal property, with the amount at which each was assessed. Succinct introduction.

5. Two 17th century Dorset inventories. Edited by Lettice Ashley Cooper. 1974.   **96.5**

   Transcripts of inventories dated 7 May 1639 and 19 Dec. 1699 (with valuations) of the contents, room by room, of St. Giles's House, near Wimborne, Dorset, the property of Sir Anthony Ashley Cooper, 1st earl of Shaftesbury. Glossary.

6. The Dorset lay subsidy roll of 1327. Edited by Alexander R. Rumble. 1980.   **96.6**

   Transcript, Latin, of the 7399 assessments recoverable on the much damaged original doc.

97. ESSEX ARCHAEOLOGICAL SOCIETY

Feet of fines for Essex. 4 vols., 1899–1964. **97.1**

English abstracts, the abstracts for vols. iii–iv prepared by Robert Copp Fowler. The nature of a 'fine', its form and terminology are described in the introduction to vol. i, the editor observing that fines 'gradually ceased to afford the pleasing variety which characterised them in early times'. The changes are indicated in the preface to vol. ii.

i : 1182–1272. Edited by R. E. G. Kirk. (In pts., 1899–1910).
ii : 1272–1326. Edited by Ernest F. Kirk. (In pts., 1913–28).
iii: 1327–1422. Edited by Sidney Charles Ratcliff. Indexed by A. C. Wood, the slips ('something like 27,000') made by a professional archivist early in 1939 'at a cost of £26. 17. 6.' (In pts., 1929–49).
iv: 1423–1547. Edited by P. H. Reaney and Marc Fitch. (1964).

OCCASIONAL PUBLICATIONS

1. Cartularium prioratus de Colne. Transcribed and annotated by John L. Fisher. 1946. **97.2**

Latin, end of 12th century, edited with English abstracts and notes, a genealogical table of de Vere, and map of the parish of Earls Colne.

2. Guide to the Essex quarter sessions and other official records preserved in the Essex Record Office, Chelmsford. Prepared ... by F. G. Emmison, with a foreword by R. E. Negus. 1946. **97.3**

3. Essex sessions of the peace, 1351, 1371–1379. Edited ... by Elizabeth Chapin Furber. 1952. **97.4**

Transcripts, Latin, of records of indictments for felony and trespass (peace rolls). The introduction (69 pp. exclusive of its analytical appendices, among which are tables of prices and wages) sketches the general background to the rolls, between the Black Death of 1349 and the Great Revolt of 1381, and relates the course of the revolt in Essex. The commissions (not found on the rolls) are set out and their personnel considered, as also are the places and proceedings of the various sessions, the offences in the indictments, and their geographical distribution. An understanding of the results of the indictments is obtained 'by analysing them according to the men indicated rather than according to the indictments'. The 'palm for villainy' is awarded to Lord John Fitzwalter (*d.* 1361) who, with his followers, spread terror and destruction throughout the county: he and they (with one known exception) were fined. Transcripts, Latin, appended to the text, include (i) indictments before John de Sutton and others on the king's bench roll for Hilary 26 Edw. III, (ii) the account of the collection of the first year of the triennial grant of 1352 in Essex (Lay Subsidies 107/41), and (iii) indictments before Thomas de Mandeville and Robert Rikedon on the gaol delivery roll of 2-4 Rich. II.

98. HALIFAX ANTIQUARIAN SOCIETY, RECORD SERIES

1. Poll tax (lay subsidy), 2 Richard II (1379), parish of Halifax **98.1**
in the wapentake of Morley. Reprinted from *Yorkshire Archaeological Journal* (vol. 6), with notes on local returns. Also,
rental of Halifax and Heptonstall, 1439. By J. Lister and J. H.
Ogden. 1906. [85 pp.]

> The poll tax returns copiously annotated, and with further notes on the
> amount of tax paid by the townships; population; social status; surnames;
> trade and agriculture; housing; and artificers. The rental translated, with
> identifications.

2. The extent (or survey) of the graveships of Rastrick, Hip- **98.2**
perholme and Sowerby, 1309. Copied and translated by J.
Lister, with notes of identification by H. P. Kendall. 1914. [61
pp.]

3. The architecture of the church of St. John the Baptist, **98.3**
Halifax. Edited by Hugh P. Kendall. 1917. [21 pp.]

> Prints the descriptions read to the Society by Fairless Barber in 1876,
> with some notes on the setting-out by John Bilson, a schedule of masons'
> marks, drawings and photographic views, the whole ante-dating the res-
> toration of the building in 1878-9.

99. HARLEIAN SOCIETY, PUBLICATIONS, NEW SERIES

1. The register of the Temple church, London. Baptisms, **99.1**
1629–1853; marriages, 1628–1760. Transcribed by G. D.
Squibb. 1979.
With lists of masters and readers and an account of the post-medieval
monumental heraldry now or formerly in the church and churchyard. The
next marriage entry is dated 1865.

2. The visitation of Suffolk, 1561, made by William Hervey, **99.2**
Clarenceux king of arms. Transcribed and edited by Joan
Corder. Pt. 1. 1981.
Aims to reproduce the office copy 'in its entirety, *verbatim et literatim*',
with the addition of genealogical and heraldic notes. Welcoming this
approach, Sir Anthony Wagner writes in his foreword: 'In the past too
many so called editions of Visitation records have not really been editions
of these as documents in their own right at all, but mere extracts of their
genealogical content. This can be a double error, possibly as putting the
genealogical value too high and certainly as ignoring the historical value
of the contemporary record of an administrative operation. Miss Corder
does not make that mistake . . .' A map indicates the itinerary and approxi-
mate areas covered by Hervey, and the probable places of sitting, a public
rather than a private house more probably being preferred.

100. LONDON RECORD SOCIETY, PUBLICATIONS

1. London possessory assizes: a calendar. Edited by Helena M. Chew. 1965.   **100.1**

The record of assizes of novel disseisin and mort d'ancestor held before the sheriffs and coroner of London on various dates between 1340 and 1451, with additional individual pleas for the years 1317, 1380 and 1470, and seven for the period 1583-1603. The development of the action in London and of its scope are described in the introduction.

2. London inhabitants within the walls, 1695. Introduction by D. V. Glass. 1966.   **100.2**

An *index nominum* (prepared by many hands in the 1930s) based on the assessments upon births, marriages, burials, bachelors and childless widows made under the Act of 6 and 7 Wm. and Mary, c. 6, for eighty of the ninety-seven parishes within the walls, constituting 'in fact if not in name the first census of London inhabitants'. The introduction sets out the background and nature of the assessments and discusses their value for demographic studies.

3. London consistory court wills, 1492-1547. Edited by Ida Darlington. 1967.   **100.3**

The contents (wills and testaments) of register Palmer, 1492-1520, with some separate items (including inventories) 1507-47, the wills in English transcribed (omitting common form), wills wholly or partly in Latin translated. Other wills of this court and period are known. The brief analytical introduction includes a summary archival history of the probate records of the diocese.

4. Scriveners' Company common paper, 1357-1628, with a continuation to 1678. Edited by Francis W. Steer. 1968.   **100.4**

An haphazard combination of ordinances, memoranda, oaths on admission and lists of members, calendared in the main, with parts translated or transcribed, and supplemented from Bodleian ms. Rawlinson D 51. In the introduction the founding and early history of the company are described and the forms of oaths are analysed and illustrated.

5. London radicalism, 1830-1843: a selection from the papers of Francis Place. Edited by D. J. Rowe. 1970.   **100.5**

The introduction gives a brief account of Place's life and connections,

236

indicating the general direction of bias to be expected in his papers and the more obvious details of bias in the docs. selected. London radicalism is considered, and issue is taken with the 'artificial and forced view' that in the years 1831–2 England was near to revolution.

6. The London eyre of 1244. Edited by Helena M. Chew and 100.6 Martin Weinbaum. 1970.

Transcript, Latin, with English translation. The roll, 'a prime source for the study of customary law in London' and 'the oldest London document of its kind', is a copy of sessions of crown pleas, April–June 1244, and of a special inquest into purprestures Jan. 1246. Includes extracts, Latin, from London and Middlesex accounts in the pipe rolls, 29–37 Hen. III. Professor Weinbaum's introduction includes a contribution by C. A. F. Meekings to the section dealing with the eyre's financial issues.

7. The cartulary of Holy Trinity Aldgate. Edited by Gerald 100.7 A. J. Hodgett. 1971.

Compiled between 1425 and 1427. Calendar, with doubtful or particularly significant passages in full. Includes a transcript, Latin, of the opening *Historia*, from the foundation in 1108 to the death of the fourth prior in 1221, and a note on the illuminations by Francis Wormald. The brief introduction treats of the foundation and importance of the priory, its property and income, and the value of the cartulary for the social and economic history of medieval London.

8. The port and trade of early Elizabethan London: docu- 100.8 ments. Edited by Brian Dietz. 1972.

The port book kept by the controller of the subsidy of tonnage and poundage inwards, 1567–8, calendared so as 'to reproduce all the significant material in a simplified and systematic form'. The appendices include a list and valuation of imports, 1559–60 and 1565–6, transcripts of the survey of 1559 and of the summary account of the legal quays in 1584, notes on the quays, and (as a supplement to the six-part index) a descriptive list of commodities traded. Plan of the port.

The introduction describes the reforms instituted in the 1550s and 1560s by the marquis of Winchester as lord treasurer and assesses the effectiveness of the new multiple controls in preventing fraud by officials and smuggling by merchants. Figures for London's trade in the ten years 1558/9–1567/8 support the contention that while significant changes were occurring, the trading area was confined in the main to the ports of France, Spain and the Netherlands, the import trade with Amsterdam being still preeminent. The entries required to be made in the port books are described, as also are the problems of use and interpretation which arise.

9. The Spanish Company. By Pauline Croft. 1973. 100.9

Transcripts, calendared in part, of the register book, 1604–6, the book of oaths, acts and ordinances, written 1605, and the charter of 1605, with correspondence, petitions, and other docs. referred to in the register book.

The introduction, sketching the history of the first company (1530–85) and its revival (1604–6), summarily describes the political and mercantile relations between England and Spain, the differences between the company and the Merchant Adventurers and the Eastland merchants, the disputes with the outports, Mendoza's exploitation of the crisis caused by Drake, the 'irritating activities of a professional monopolist named William Tipper', the relations with Sir James Croft concerning the supply of sack to the royal household, the facilities and organization of the port of London, and the informal dissolution of the company as relations with Spain moved towards the Armada climax. Equally detailed is the narration of the revival of the company after 1600, the opposition from the outports, the company's plan to establish a network of consuls round the Iberian peninsula, and its decline as mercantile opinion turned against monopolies of every sort.

10. London assizes of nuisance, 1301–1431: a calendar. Edited   **100.10**
by Helena M. Chew and William Kellaway. 1973.

The introduction, after describing and, so far as is possible, dating the *assisa de edificiis* and the *lex de assisa*, sets out in some detail the procedure for assizes of nuisance in London and illustrates by elaborate references to the calendar the range of pleas heard and recorded in the nuisance rolls. Most of the pleas originated in disputes between neighbours about walls, gutters, windows, privies and paving, but others sought to correct public nuisances, among them purprestures or nuisances restricting free passage along the king's highway, streets, lanes, paths or waterways. Departures from the procedure normal to these assizes are noted.

11. Two Calvinistic Methodist chapels, 1743–1811: the Lon-   **100.11**
don Tabernacle and Spa Fields chapel. Edited by Edwin Welch. 1975.

Transcripts of the minutes of the Tabernacle (George Whitefield's Connexion), 1743–7, of the English Methodist Association, 1745–9, and of Northampton or Spa Fields chapel (Countess of Huntingdon's Connexion), 1778–1811, followed by the Fifteen Articles of the Countess of Huntingdon's Connexion, 1783, and the Plan of Association, 1790. The introduction distinguishes the many forms of Methodism and summarizes the history of the chapels.

12. The London eyre of 1276. Edited by Martin Weinbaum.   **100.12**
1976.

The roll of crown and civil pleas for the city of London held before the justices in eyre at the Tower, in English translation (somewhat shortened), together with a transcript, Latin, of the exchequer summons listing persons fined or amerced. The introduction describes and explains the procedures, analyses the docs., and 'outlines those features of London custom which are illustrated by the plea roll'.

13. The church in London, 1375–1392. By A. K. McHardy.   **100.13**
1977.

Calendars of (i) six clerical taxations, 1379–81, (ii) an assessment of ecclesiastical property in the city, 1392, and (iii) the *acta* of Bishop Courtenay, 1375–81, collected from a variety of sources to fill in part the gap left by the loss of his register. The introduction demonstrates the contribution made by the docs. towards a clearer picture of the diocese during Courtenay's episcopate.

14. **Committees for repeal of the Test and Corporation acts: minutes, 1786–90 and 1827–8. Edited by Thomas W. Davis. 1978.** 100.14

Minutes of two London committees of protestant dissenters, the minutes of the first (Edward Jeffries' committee) transcribed in full, and those parts of the second (the United committee) not printed in the *Test Act Reporter* likewise in full with summaries of the remainder.
The introduction describes the historical background and, in some detail, the two campaigns, the 'systematic and relatively complete' docs. showing 'how two early pressure groups operated ... to broaden the definition of religious toleration'. The docs. 'also illustrate the action of London pressure groups on national politics and provide an early model of reform tactics that was widely used in later campaigns'. Biographical notes on all members of the committees.

15. **Joshua Johnson's letterbook, 1771–1774: letters from a merchant in London to his partners in Maryland. Edited by Jacob M. Price. 1979.** 100.15

Approximately ninety per cent of the major part of the letters ('noteworthy for their detail, candour, and didactism'), with summary tables to help clarify Johnson's operations, and a glossary of the principal commercial terms. The firm (Wallace, Davidson & Johnson) imported linens, silks, cottons, woollen and other goods into Maryland, and consigned tobacco to London. The introduction describing the firm, its trade and financial policy, is adapted from the editor's contribution to *Essays ... presented to Dame Lucy Sutherland*, ed. A. Whiteman *et al.* (Oxford, 1973).

16. **London and Middlesex chantry certificate, 1548. Edited by C. J. Kitching. 1980.** 100.16

A calendar of the digest of the returns made by the city churches (including St. Paul's cathedral), the churches of Middlesex, and the city companies, with recourse to much supporting material, the foremost being the 'brief certificate' compiled by the commissioners for the guidance of those who later were to act upon their findings.
The introduction describes the differences between the Acts of 1545 and 1547, the differences between the commissions subsequently appointed, and the differences between their procedures. All the main elements of the individual entries are considered, viz. the donor, the purpose of the foundation, the source of income, the disbursements, the housling total, the clergy, and the school (if any). A study of the certificate for one church, St. Peter Paul's Wharf, and the complementary sources serves to 'stress the caution that is necessary' in interpreting the particulars given in the certificate 'and the need to consult as many other sources as possible'. A wider consideration of each section of the certificate identifies the issues on which it is illuminating and 'helps to redress the balance in its favour'. The omission from the certificate of certain minor churches, lesser city companies, former monastic churches, and other foundations

is tentatively explained. The entries for St. Paul's, for Middlesex and St. Stephen's Westminster, and for the city companies, are considered separately.

17. London politics, 1713-1717. Minutes of a Whig club, **100.17**
1714-1717, edited by H. Horwitz. London pollbooks, 1713, edited by W. A. Speck and W. A. Gray. 1981.

The minutes transcribed, with an introduction demonstrating their contribution towards 'an understanding of the complex, and largely unwritten political history of the City' and the light they cast on the national political scene. 'London pollbooks, 1713' conflates in a single alphabetical sequence the names and voting records of close on 7,000 voters given in two contemporary and partisan publications.

18. Parish fraternity register: fraternity of the Holy Trinity **100.18**
and SS. Fabian and Sebastian in the parish of St. Botolph without Aldersgate. Edited by Patricia Basing. 1982.

The records of the Trinity fraternity, from its foundation in 1377 to 1446, when it combined with the fraternity of SS. Fabian and Sebastian. Thereafter the records continue to about 1463, with miscellaneous entries until 1548. Rules, lists of members, and accounts, mainly in English, fully transcribed, as also have been the English entries in the cartulary of deeds from the 13th century; the remainder of the cartulary has been calendared.

The introduction, after describing the religious, charitable and economic aims of the medieval fraternities, and the circumstances which led to the guild certificates of 1388-9, sets out the history, nature, property and membership of the fraternities in St. Botolph's, and the mid-16th century dissolution.

101. ROYAL HISTORICAL SOCIETY, CAMDEN FOURTH SERIES

1. Camden miscellany. Vol. xxii. 1964. **101.1**

Charters of the earldom of Hereford, 1095–1201. Edited by David Walker. [Transcripts, Latin, of previously unpublished charters issued by the earls of Hereford and their family, drawn largely from the records of monastic houses, chief among them Llanthony Secunda by Gloucester, with a list of charters already in print.]

Indentures of retinue with John of Gaunt, duke of Lancaster, enrolled in chancery, 1367–1399. Edited by N. B. Lewis. [Transcripts, French, of enrolled exemplifications of indentures of service between the duke and a number of his retainers who secured confirmation of them from the reigning king, supplementary to the similar contracts in **33**.20, 21.]

Autobiographical memoir of Joseph Jewell, 1763–1846. Edited by Arthur Walter Slater. [Jewell, a partner in the firm of Howard, Jewell & Gibson, later known as Howards of Ilford Ltd., was a pioneer of the fine chemical industry in England. The introduction describes his early life and the development of his business activities. In the appendices, a list of his printed works, his patent specification for preparing medicinal calomel, an outline of the financial arrangements of the firm, and a transcript of the deed of co-partnership, 1813.]

2. Documents illustrating the rule of Walter de Wenlok, abbot of Westminster, 1283–1307. Edited by Barbara F. Harvey. 1965. **101.2**

Concerned particularly with the background to the quarrel between Wenlok and Prior Reginald de Hadham and other aspects of Wenlok's administration which are of more than local interest. Contains transcripts, Latin or French, of the surviving administrative writs etc. of the abbot and his officials; stewards' and receivers' accounts selected to illustrate financial reform; the major compositions or agreements regulating relations between the abbot and the convent and the division of lands and revenues between them; and Wenlok's household ordinances and livery list. The introduction includes an annotated list of officials, clerks and annuitants, and Wenlok's itinerary. Glossary.

3. The early correspondence of Richard Wood, 1831–1841. Edited by A. B. Cunningham. 1966. **101.3**

Transcripts, some in French, of the letters and reports written or received by the dragoman at Constantinople in the years leading to the signing of the Straits Convention, years in which 'Britain took up, at first hesitatingly but with increasing resolution, the cause of Turkish integrity'.

The introduction sets out Wood's origins and describes in some detail his relations with Lord Ponsonby, the ambassador, the missions he undertook and the many arduous negotiations he conducted, especially in Syria and the Lebanon. Includes his summary report and the longer report on 'the political and moral state of Syria', but not 'the dull and uninformative' report on the Pashalick of Baghdad. Also omitted (since its substance is to be found in his letters to Ponsonby) is the report on Kurdistan. Glossary.

4. **Letters from the English abbots to the chapter at Cîteaux,**   **101.4** **1442–1521. Edited by C. H. Talbot. 1967.**

Transcripts, Latin. The letters, all that survive 'of what must have been a complete dossier on all the Cistercian abbeys in Europe', are 'the sole material we have for judging the state of the Cistercians in England' during the 15th century.

The introduction summarizes this material, reflects on the burden borne by the abbot of Cîteaux, and concludes that although there was 'a departure from the vital and fundamental principles of the Rule' the picture of Cistercian life reflected in the letters 'is not as sombre as one might be led to expect' from the *comperta* made by the Henrician commissioners some 15 or 20 years later.

5. **The papers of George Wyatt, esquire, of Boxley Abbey in**   **101.5** **the county of Kent, son and heir of Sir Thomas Wyatt the younger. Edited by D. M. Loades. 1968.**

Transcripts of items selected from the Wyatt commonplace book, each with its own introduction: four by George Wyatt (1554–1624), viz. the introduction to his history in defence of Anne Boleyn (*c.* 1605), his treatise on the defence of Calais (1593), his treatise on the militia (*c.* 1590), and his letter of advice to Sir Francis Wyatt, governor of Virginia (1622), followed by four papers collected by him, viz. an anonymous chronicle and defence of the English reformation (*c.* 1604?), a treatise on the militia by Sir Thomas Wyatt the younger (1549), a defence of Sir Thomas the elder and Sir Thomas the younger against the accusations of Nicholas Sanders (*c.* 1595), and an account of the report by Prince Charles and the Duke of Buckingham to the committee of both Houses respecting the negotiations for a Spanish marriage (1624). In the appendices, a descriptive catalogue of the contents of the commonplace book, a pedigree of the family, a translation of the survey of Boxley manor from an early 18th-century copy of the original taken in 1554 upon the attainder of Sir Thomas the younger, and notes made in 1666 by Sir Francis Wyatt on the debt of £1000 due from Chas. I to him when governor of Virginia. In the introduction, an account of the family.

6. **Records of the trial of Walter Langeton, bishop of Coventry**   **101.6** **and Lichfield, 1307–1312. Edited by Alice Beardwood. 1969.**

Transcripts, Latin, of proceedings in the exchequer for the collection of

Langeton's debts, of the evidence given by John Langeton, and of the hearing of complaints against Langeton himself.

7. Camden miscellany. Vol. xxiii. [1970].   101.7

The accounts of John Balsall, purser of the *Trinity of Bristol*, 1480–1. Edited by T. F. Reddaway and Alwyn A. Ruddock. [Transcript. The introduction identifies the *Trinity* as one of the largest vessels of the port of Bristol, names her owners at this time, and treats of some of her pre-1480 voyages and cargoes. The winter voyage of 1480–1 was to Oran, with two stays at Huelva, where a donation was made to the Franciscan friary which was later to give strong support to Columbus. The editors conclude that the links between the *Trinity*, the friars of Sta Maria de la Rabida and the discoverer 'are suggestive of many things'.]

An anonymous parliamentary diary, 1705–6. Edited by W. A. Speck. [Transcript. Possibly kept by Henry Howard, Lord Walden, while he was in the Commons as knight of the shire for Essex. Appended is Sir John Packington's draft of the speech he delivered in the Commons on 'the Church in danger', 8 Dec. 1705. The introduction relates the diary to the business of the session.]

Leicester House politics, 1750–60, from the papers of John, second earl of Egmont. Edited by Aubrey N. Newman. [Transcripts, in full or in part, of 22 docs. concerned with the anticipated succession to the throne of Frederick, prince of Wales, the problems faced by the prince's supporters in this decade of political activity, and the events after the prince's death. The introductory summary includes 'a short undated memorandum drawn up by Egmont before he finally joined Frederick'.]

Parliamentary diaries of Nathaniel Ryder, 1764–7. Edited by P. D. G. Thomas. [Reports of debates in the Commons, the texts derived by K. L. Perrin from the original shorthand.]

[On the reverse of the title-page: *In memoriam* Thomas Fiddian Reddaway, treasurer of the Royal Historical Society 1949–1967.]

8. Documents illustrating the British conquest of Manila,   101.8
1762–1763. Edited by Nicholas P. Cushner. 1971.

Transcripts of docs. from various sources (with English abstracts of the Latin and Spanish), concluding with the claim for reimbursement submitted by the East India Company in June 1775. In the selecting, preference has been given to material from the Jesuit collection at San Cugat del Valles, outside Barcelona; the titles and general contents of the 17 files of that material are set out in the introduction.

9. Camden miscellany. Vol. xxiv. 1972.   101.9

Some documents relating to the disputed succession to the duchy of Brittany, 1341. Edited by Michael Jones. [Transcripts, French, of John de Montfort's case, and of subsidiary docs. in French and Latin. Among the points made by the editor are (i) that in the feudal law then current in northern France 'it would seem that Montfort's case was the stronger', (ii) that much that appears novel in Montfort's argument can be found in an earlier case, (iii) that in 14th-century France legal precedents counted for little if they contradicted the king's needs, and

(iv) that the *Somnium Viridarii* and the *Songe du Vergier* cannot be treated as independent authorities for the events of 1341.]
Documents relating to the Anglo-French negotiations of 1439. Edited by C. T. Allmand. [Transcripts, French and Latin, from several sources. Includes the anonymous French protocol, possibly by Robert Mallière, secretary to Charles VII, which complements and confirms the Latin protocol by Thomas Bekynton printed in vol. v of **1.26**. The docs. indicate, for this late stage of the war, the 'hardness of the French, who were determined to give away as little as possible', and 'the division of opinion among the English', some of whom saw in the claim to the French crown 'the main stumbling block in the way of a lasting peace'.]
John Benet's chronicle for the years 1400 to 1462. Edited by G. L. Harriss and M. A. Harriss. [Transcript of the concluding portion of the chronicle written into his commonplace book 'in homely and vernacular Latin' by the vicar of Harlington, Beds., within the years 1462–8. After describing the contents of the whole book ('more diverse and compendious than many others of its kind') and the stages of its compilation, the introduction notes the chronicle's borrowings in its pre-1440 section from such commonly-used sources as *The Brut* and the *Polychronicon* and its evident change after 1440 into an independent 'primary source for affairs seen and reported in the capital'. This leads to a consideration of whether and to what extent the vicar of Harlington was the author of the post-1440 section of the chronicle known by his name.]

10. Herefordshire militia assessments of 1663. Edited by M. A. Faraday. 1972.   **101.10**

Transcripts of estate valuations made by authority of the Militia Act of 1662, in alphabetical order of parishes within hundreds alphabetically, annotated 'to throw light on the dating of the returns and on the identification of individuals and their wealth and standing within their communities'. Included in the annotation are details of the largest charge to hearth tax in each parish on Lady Day 1664 and tabular statements of parish hearth tax returns for the same date. There is no valuation for the city of Hereford.

The introduction summarizes the Militia Acts of 1662 and 1663; describes and discusses the militia establishment maintained by the county, the methods of estate valuation, and the system of taxation by county quotas; prints in the form of a table a selection of Herefordshire hundred quotas for various taxations between 1636 and 1698; considers the social distribution of wealth in the county as shown by the valuations; and maintains that there is 'considerable value in comparing a hearth tax return with the militia valuations'.

11. The early correspondence of Jabez Bunting, 1820–1829. Edited by W. R. Ward. 1972.   **101.11**

Transcripts of 'everything of importance for domestic [Methodist] connexional policy for the period embracing Bunting's first two years as President [of the Wesleyan Conference], 1820 and 1828, and the years between'. The introduction describes the 'enormous' corpus of Bunting's correspondence, sets out the nature of Methodism in his time, and answers the question 'What kind of a man was he in fact?'.

12. Wentworth papers, 1597–1628. Edited by J. P. Cooper. 101.12
1973.

Transcripts of a selection from the papers from Wentworth Woodhouse, the main omissions from Wentworth's own papers being those concerned with the wardship of his nephews George and William Savile. Also omitted is most of his correspondence with his steward Richard Marris, Charles Greenwood, rector of Thornhill, and his servant and solicitor Peter Man about the details of the management of his estate and household. Another omission is Wentworth's long account of his first wife's last illness and death. Otherwise, and apart from the omission of a few letters seemingly trivial in content, the selection embraces most of Wentworth's correspondence and all his speeches until the end of 1628, with a very few letters from those of 1629 included for their complementary or parliamentary interest. The fragments of Sir George Radcliffe's life of Wentworth are appended. Papers printed by Knowler are listed and their contents noted, as are his misdatings and omissions. Virtually all the surviving papers of Sir William, Strafford's father, are included, followed by papers relating to the parliament of 1614 and, in chronological order, Wentworth's own papers.

In his introduction, the editor dissents in part from Dame Veronica Wedgwood's assessment of Sir William Wentworth; describes the importance of Court and Country as 'interdependent factors' in the parliamentary careers of Wentworth and his political rival Sir John Savile of Howley; notes Wentworth's 'predilection for complicated financial schemes', his self-assumed role as mediator between Court and Country, and the importance of Sir Arthur Ingram as his contact with the Court; and judges that Wentworth's political rhetoric 'was sufficiently vague and ambiguous in its assumptions ... to exculpate him from any charge of changing his political principles', whereas in his churchmanship 'the change is undeniable'. Genealogical tables showing Wentworth's and his mother's connexions.

13. Camden miscellany. Vol. xxv. 1974. 101.13

The letters of William, Lord Paget of Beaudesert, 1547–63. Edited by Barrett L. Beer and Sybil M. Jack. [An edition of all his known surviving letters of the period and of the most important papers relating to his political career, but excluding all materials pertaining to his household and landholdings. Letters never before printed are fully transcribed; all others are briefly calendared. A short selection of letters to Paget is appended.]

The parliamentary diary of John Clementson, 1770–1802. Edited by P. D. G. Thomas. [Transcript of a record of parliamentary practice and procedure compiled by the deputy serjeant at arms to the House of Commons, with a brief introductory note on Clementson's career, income, and official duties.]

Report on Bolivia, 1827, by Joseph Barclay Pentland. Edited by J. Valerie Fifer. [Transcript of chapters III–V of Pentland's report to the Foreign Office—'the first major description of Bolivia at a very early period in its history'—describing economic, commercial, and political conditions. Maps.]

14. Camden miscellany. Vol. xxvi. 1975.   101.14

Ordinances for the duchy of Lancaster. Edited by Sir Robert Somerville. [Transcript. Assigned to 1482 as their most probable date, the ordinances are concerned in the main to establish an efficient administration and to promote law and order, as well as with financial matters.] 'A breviat of the effectes devised for Wales', c. 1540–41. Edited by P. R. Roberts. [Transcript of one of several draft instruments outlining a new hierarchy of jurisdictions for Wales and defining relations between the courts.] 'The muster-master', by Gervase Markham. Edited by Charles L. Hamilton. [Transcript of a pamphlet, written c. 1630, on the muster-master in peace and war.] 'A book of all the several officers of the court of exchequer together with the names of the present officers, in whose gift, and how admitted, with a brief collection of the chief heads of what every officer usually doeth by vertue of his office according to the state of the exchequer at this day, January 1641', by Lawrence Squibb. Edited by William Hamilton Bryson. [Transcript of probably the earliest of sixteen known copies, with additions from later versions and, in the introduction, an account of the writer and of the collecting, collating and descent of the various mss.] The letters of Henry St. John to the earl of Orrery, 1709–1711. Edited by H. T. Dickinson. [Forty-three letters transcribed from letter-books, with references to ten others from the same source already in print, revealing 'much about St. John's growing determination to bring an end to the War of the Spanish Succession, about his activities as Secretary of State, and about the increasing friction between the allies as they manoeuvred to secure their own particular interests before peace was made with France'.]

15. Sidney ironworks accounts, 1541–1573. Edited by D. W.   101.15
Crossley. 1975.

Transcripts of selected annual summary accounts for the works at Robertsbridge and Panningridge, Sussex, annotated from the surviving forge and furnace books; of the furnace book for 1550 (the only surviving record for this year); the forge book for 1555 (a typical example); the first part of the Panningridge furnace book for 1543 (showing the building costs of an early blast furnace); Robertsbridge steelworks accounts, 1566 and 1566–7, and Glamorgan ironworks accounts, 1564–5 and 1567–8.

The introduction describes the sites and construction of the main works, and discusses their operation (the supply of ore, wood and charcoal; the form and cost of transport; the campaigns and yields; the costs of raw materials, wages and overheads) and profitability. The final ten years of the estate's interest in the industry are depicted as a period of diversification (into steelmaking) and retrenchment, 1563–73. Statistical tables serve to particularize the general presentation. Maps. Glossary.

16. The account-book of Beaulieu abbey. Edited by S. F.   101.16
Hockey. 1975.

Transcripts, Latin, from two mss. (they are described by P. D. A. Harvey), bringing together for a single year (probably 1269–70) the 'real, not artificial' accounts for the abbey's granges, manors, departments and workshops.

The introduction describes the various estates; inquires into the number and status of the personnel who controlled and manned the multifarious sections of the abbey's economy; sets out what crops were being grown (wool, wheat, barley, oats, rye, vetch, peas) and the yields for the year, the tithe and multure received, and the livestock kept (pigs, horses, cattle, sheep, poultry); reviews the thirty-one departmental and workshop accounts, indicating the crafts practised and the contribution made by each to the economy of the community; suggests that 'there was perhaps no vineyard as such', the grapes from the various plots possibly being served as fresh fruit; explains how all the different enterprises were integrated; and concludes by advising beginners in medieval accountancy to start with the account of the skinners, 'for it is exceptional': short, complete, and correct in all its arithmetic. Summary statistical tables throughout. Glossary. *Index verborum* and index of proper names.

17. Western circuit assize orders, 1629–1648: a calendar. Edited by J. S. Cockburn. 1976.　101.17

Occasional passages, as well as 23 orders 'of unusual interest or complexity', are printed in full in the original spelling. Index of persons and index of places.

18. Four English political tracts of the later middle ages. Edited by Jean-Philippe Genet. 1977.　101.18

Transcripts, the first (retaining the Middle English runic 'thorn' and 'yogh') and fourth in English, the second and third in Latin, of the *Tractatus de regibus*, the *De quadripartita regis specie*, the *Tractatus de regimine principum ad regem Henricum sextum*, and 'The III consideracions right necesserye to the good governaunce of a prince', each with its own introduction dealing with the ms., its contents, authorship and date, the *De regimine principum* supplied with an English summary and tables of quotations in it from biblical, classical, patristic and medieval sources.

The general introduction, starting from the premise that political theory 'is found in nearly all forms of literary work', dissents from the assumption that 'a particular type of political literature, concerned above all with the prince and his image', was the typical product of the Middle Ages in this field, and demonstrates the need for a new definition which will embrace 'the enormous bulk of literature ... lying beyond the borders of the *Fürstenspiegel* genre'. Several categories of that literature are then indicated, e.g. the *Miroirs au prince*, the political literature of the court, texts which show 'the influence of the pseudo-aristotelian *Secreta Secretorum*', politico-religious and politico-legal works, and the wide variety of means used by the 'ruling classes ... for the reshaping of political mentalities'. Lastly, the editor notes differences between England and France, e.g. the occurrence of numerous French works, including *Miroirs*, in English libraries, while the *Miroir* genre is generally under-represented in the political literature of England, and the existence in English political literature of several forms which have no parallel in France.

19. Proceedings of the Short Parliament of 1640. Edited by 101.19
Esther S. Cope in collaboration with Willson H. Coates. 1977.

Transcripts, from many sources and for both Houses, of journals, speeches, and petitions, the basic accounts taken from the Braye and Finch-Hatton/Harvard mss. Indirect accounts of proceedings, such as those in newsletters and diplomatic despatches, as well as speeches and petitions apparently not delivered, are cited, and there are lists of copies and versions of the major speeches and of the grievance voted in the Commons on 24 Apr. A comprehensive introduction to the sources (33 pp.) is included in the prefatory matter.

20. Heresy trials in the diocese of Norwich, 1428–31. Edited 101.20
by Norman P. Tanner. 1977.

Transcript, part English, part Latin, of a ms. now in Westminster Diocesan Archives recording the proceedings against 60 men and women, 'perhaps the most important record of heresy trials in the British Isles before the Reformation'.

The introduction deals with the trials, the beliefs of the defendants, and the defendants and lollardy. Appended are the relevant sections, Latin, of a Norwich Castle gaol delivery, 21 Feb. 1429, involving the defendants.

21. Edmund Ludlow, 'A voyce from the watch tower', part 101.21
five: 1660–1662. Edited by A. B. Worden. 1978.

Transcript of the fifth but first surviving part of the ms. on which Ludlow's posthumously published memoirs were based, with the concluding lines of the preceding part and a portion (1660–77) of Ludlow's own table of contents. The introduction (80 pp.) identifies the editor of the *Memoirs* and shows at some length that Ludlow's text was radically altered and abridged.

22. Camden miscellany. Vol. xxvii. 1979. 101.22

The disputed regency of the kingdom of Jerusalem, 1264/6 and 1268. Edited by P. W. Edbury. [Transcript, French, of the early 15th-century collection of materials in Codex Vaticanus latinus 4789, retaining the page and chapter numbers in Beugnot's *Documents relatifs* and noting the more important of the phrases and passages omitted by him. Genealogical table of the royal house of Jerusalem. The introduction sets out the claims of Hugh of Antioch-Lusignan (Hugh III) and Hugh of Brienne in the years 1264/6, the later claims of Hugh III and Maria of Antioch, and the complex formal pleading in which the claims and counter-claims were stated.]

George Rainsford's 'Ritratto d'Inghilterra' (1556). Edited by P. S. Donaldson. [Transcript, Italian, with English translation, of the 'portrait of the realm' composed by Rainsford expressly to supplement a treatise by Stephen Gardiner dealing with changes of dynasty in England, and appended by Rainsford to his own Italian translation of Gardiner's treatise (the 'Ragionamento') to form a composite work which was dedicated and presented to Philip II. The introduction identifies Rainsford and suggests that his translation of Gardiner's treatise (supporting Queen Mary's contention that Philip could rule in England) and the addition of an appendix (countering such of Gardiner's views as were no longer acceptable) formed part of the diplomatic effort being made in the spring of 1556 to induce Philip to return to England. Also considered are Rainsford's sources, the matters on which he and Gardiner agreed or differed, and his unusual economic views, e.g. his insistence that the price-increase was of great benefit to the nation as a whole.]

The letter-book of Thomas Bentham, bishop of Coventry and Lichfield. Edited by Rosemary O'Day and Joel Berlatsky. [Transcript. The letters, copied or paraphrased into the letter-book, span the period 20 June 1560–30 May 1561. They show the bishop's 'fumbling attempts to deal with the problems of an impecunious and large diocese', his dependence on his officials, the relationship between him and his chief clergy, his financial difficulties, the state of religious feeling in his diocese, the situation created by the return of the Marian exiles, and much else.]

23. The letters of the third Viscount Palmerston to Laurence and Elizabeth Sulivan, 1804-1863. Edited by Kenneth Bourne. 1979.   **101.23**

Most of the 380 items transcribed from the originals, with a small number from early 20th-century typescript copies. Letters previously printed have been summarized, with any necessary corrections and additions.

Little used by Bulwer and Ashley, and for the most part neglected by other writers, the letters provide 'interesting comments and details' for the major political crises of Palmerston's time, and 'with their wealth of comment on national affairs, parliamentary elections and the War Office' are of special importance for the period to 1837. They serve, moreover, 'as the record of Palmerston's principal adult friendship with a man'. The formation and course of his male friendships, and his relations with Sulivan and the Sulivan family, are the main theme of the introduction.

24. Documents illustrating the crisis of 1297-98 in England. Edited by Michael Prestwich. 1980.   **101.24**

Transcripts, French or Latin, of docs. from various classes of record, largely in the P.R.O., selected 'to illustrate, as far as possible, the salient problems that faced the English government' in the year from Feb. 1297 to Mar. 1298, Scottish affairs alone being almost totally excluded. In the appendix a transcript, Latin, of the section of the Hagnaby chronicle describing the events of 1297.

The docs. are described in the introduction (37 pp.) which then sets out Edward I's intentions; the opposition he encountered from the laity and the clergy; the functioning of central and local administration under the 'massive burden of work' resulting from the king's demands; the difficulty in calculating any definitive figures for royal income and expenditure; the use of propaganda by both the king and his opponents and the way in which the arguments proceeded; and the campaign in Flanders. The editor's final assessment is that the crisis 'sprang out of the immediate circumstances and needs of war, and was not the product of a widespread and fundamental dissatisfaction with the manner of the king's government'.

25. The diary of Edward Goschen, 1900–1914. Edited by   **101.25**
Christopher H. D. Howard. 1980.

Selected extracts, copious especially for Goschen's years as ambassador in
Vienna (1905–8) and in Berlin (1908–14), omitting much that is either
trivial or still private, a number of individuals mentioned in the diary
being alive when the editing was in hand. The introduction (61 pp.)
outlines Goschen's descent and life (1847–1924) and, by drawing on his
own correspondence as well as the letters and memoirs of others, describes
in some detail his work and achievements as a diplomat from his entry
into the service in 1869 until his departure from Berlin on 6 Aug. 1914.
The genesis of the *Daily Telegraph* 'interview' given by Wilhelm II, and
several questions raised in connexion with the phrase 'a scrap of paper',
attributed to Bethmann Hollweg by Goschen, are discussed in the appendices.

26. English suits before the Parlement of Paris, 1420–1436.   **101.26**
Edited by C. T. Allmand and C. A. J. Armstrong. 1982.

Transcripts of the records of 21 suits 'chosen to illustrate the historical
importance of certain aspects of the presence of the English in France',
the pleadings in French, the judgments in Latin, each suit with its own
explanatory introduction and comments. In an appendix are listed, with
brief particulars and references to the sources, over 80 civil suits concerning one or more Englishmen in northern France during the period of
Lancastrian rule, among them three suits before the Parlement of Poitiers.
Also appended are biographical details of English litigants, attention being
mainly directed to activities in France. Glossary.

The introduction shows how the Parlement, a lay court and 'the single
supreme court of the French monarchy' under the treaty of Troyes (1420),
'clung unswervingly to the letter of the treaty' yet functioned as an instru-
ment of Lancastrian rule, vigilantly opposing the exercise of autonomous
jurisdictions in other parts of the kingdom, restricting the franchise rights
of seignorial courts, and reducing clerical immunity to the minimum. The
sessions and procedure of the court are described, as also are the roles of
its officials and its records. Until the Valois reconquest of the capital in
Apr. 1436, the Paris Parlement 'like its opposite number in Poitiers,
though with more inherited authority ... maintained established legal
procedure, preserved the sovereign judicial power of the crown, and
fulfilled its duty to provide legal remedy for ... the king's subjects'.

27. The Devonshire diary: William Cavendish, fourth duke   **101.27**
of Devonshire, 'Memoranda on state of affairs', 1759–1762.
Edited by Peter D. Brown and Karl W. Schweizer. 1982.

Transcript, designed 'to make the text as readable as possible with a
minimum of alteration' and omitting the first 15 pp. of 'scattered notes on
political events, 1754–9, and thumb-nail sketches of Devonshire's contemporaries in the public world'.

Beginning with an outline history of the Cavendishes from the time of
Sir John, chief justice of the king's bench under Edw. III, the introduction
shows the political importance of the family *temp*. Geo. II and tells, with
recourse to Devonshire's memoranda, the story of events between Oct.

1760 and May 1762. Exclusively political, supremely objective, yet abounding in detail and revelation of character, the diary 'deepens rather than changes our understanding of the watershed implicit in the accession of George III'.

102. RUTLAND RECORD SOCIETY, RUTLAND RECORD SERIES

1. The county community under Henry VIII: the military 102.1 survey, 1522, and lay subsidy, 1524–5, for Rutland. Edited by Julian Cornwall. 1980.

For the survey or muster book the text transcribed, except for some repetitious matter, is that of the original return, its damaged parts to some extent supplied from an 18th-century copy. For the subsidy the text edited is that of the schedule for the first instalment supplemented from the second where the first is deficient. Short glossary of military terms.

Introducing his texts as part of the indispensable sources for English economic and social history in the 16th century, the editor sketches the recent growth of interest in the musters of 1522 (the subsidy rolls have been less neglected) and summarizes the early-Tudor need for a general reassessment of the country's wealth for fiscal purposes. The following pages set out the resort to new assessments under the pretext of holding musters, the procedure of the first survey in 1522, the loans raised on it, the assessments and subsidy agreed by the Commons in 1523, the subsequent procedure, and the resulting yield. Of the surviving surveys the Rutland example is the most thorough. Similar though briefer attention is given to the lay subsidy, 'the most comprehensive and realistic one levied in a period when truly effective taxation was seldom achieved'. In this edition the value of each doc. 'is immeasurably enhanced by the light shed on it by the other which offers an alternative view of the selfsame community'.

103. SOCIETY OF ANTIQUARIES
OF NEWCASTLE UPON TYNE, RECORD SERIES

1. The Northumberland lay subsidy roll of 1296. Edited in **103.1**
translation by Constance M. Fraser. 1968.

The introduction illustrates the limitations as well as the significance of
the roll, and comments upon Dr. F. Bradshaw's long article on it in
Archaeologia Aeliana, 3rd ser., vol. xiii (1916).

2. Monopoly on the Tyne, 1650–58: papers relating to Ralph **103.2**
Gardner. Edited by Roger Howell, Jr. 1978.

Transcripts of docs. connected with his attempts to break the monopoly
jurisdiction exercised by Newcastle over the main stretch of the river, and
the privileges which accrued from the monopoly to various town companies. Alleging harassment and illegal process against him, Gardner in 1653
petitioned parliament in terms which, had they been granted, would have
reduced the town's monopoly to naught. The story, drawn in part from
Gardner's *England's grievance discovered in relation to the coal-trade*
(1655), is briefly told in the context of Newcastle's prosperity, the town's
strenuous defence of privileges conferred on it by charter and statute, and
the suit brought against it by Thomas Cliffe in 1649. Papers associated
with Cliffe's case are among the docs. here transcribed.

104. SUFFOLK RECORDS SOCIETY

1. Suffolk farming in the nineteenth century. Edited by Joan **104.1**
Thirsk, assisted by Jean Imray. 1958.

The 'Redstone memorial volume', with a memoir of Vincent Burrough
Redstone (1853–1941) and Lilian Jane Redstone (1885–1955) by Norman
Scarfe.

Transcripts of a wide variety of docs. illustrating both the national and
the local history of agriculture and rural society, as well as the characteristics peculiar to Suffolk, grouped as to (i) routine husbandry, the farmer's
year, cropping on a farm at Playford, harvesting, sheep and cattle at the
Park Farm in Henham; (ii) agricultural improvement, enclosure, cabbages
and dairying in High Suffolk, crop improvement by selection, field drain-
age, control of animal diseases, the promotion of farming efficiency by
agricultural associations and by the development of implements, machinery and fertilizers, and improved availability of capital; (iii) agricultural
depression and crises; (iv) relations between landlords and tenants; (v) the
agricultural labourers, their lot in sickness and in health, the cottages
supplied by the earl of Stradbroke, cottages in 'open' and 'close' villages,
unemployment, the poor, children's employment on the land, the strike
and lock-out of 1874; (vi) marketing, the improved corn and cattle market
at Saxmundham, the coastal trade in farm produce; (vii) Suffolk farmers
at home and abroad (in New Zealand).

The introduction shows how the century 'that had opened with an
optimistic appraisal of Suffolk agriculture by Arthur Young ended with a
pessimistic and indeed despairing report by Wilson Fox'.

2. The Sibton abbey estates: select documents, 1325–1509. **104.2**
Edited by A. H. Denny. 1960.

Transcripts, Latin, of extents of demesne land, 1325, rent rolls of 1328
and 1484, and compoti of 1363–4 and 1508–9, with statistical analyses.
The introduction uses the docs. to give as general a picture as possible of
the abbey's economy and administration.

3. Suffolk and the great rebellion, 1640–1660. Edited by Alan **104.3**
Everitt. 1960 [1961].

Transcripts of docs. 'selected with the main objects of revealing the
characteristic features of the community of Suffolk, and of illustrating its
response to the Civil War and the impact of the war upon its administration, its society, its towns, and its villages'. Includes the Suffolk committee
book, 1641–5; select orders of the committee of Suffolk, 1644–52; correspondence, 1643–5, illustrating relations between the county and the East-

254

ern Association; John Weaver's account book of 1644 for the Association's regiments; docs. relating to the royalist risings of 1648 involving men from Exning and Newmarket; and docs. revealing the alienation of a major port (Ipswich) from its support of the parliamentary cause in the 'forties to its obstructive attitude in the 'fifties.

The introduction describes (i) the community of Suffolk during the war, (ii) the organization and functioning of the county committee (itself sprung from a committee of the gentry that 'had existed in all but name for upwards of fifty years before the Civil War') and the Eastern Association (including an assessment of the earl of Manchester), and (iii) the short-lived mood of victory followed by disillusionment. Concludes: 'Through all these changes of outlook and fortune the county continued to be guided by the same group of families [headed by the Barnardistons of Kedington] as in 1640.'

4. John Constable's correspondence. Edited ... by R. B. Beckett. [Vol. i:] The family at East Bergholt, 1807–1837. 1962. [HMC JP 3]   **104.4**

A brief account of the painter's parentage and family followed by transcripts of letters with linking narrative, the epilogue carried through to the late 1860s. Genealogical tables of the Constable, Watts, Gubbins, Archer-Burton and Allen families. Contd. in **104.**6, 8, 10, 11, 12, 14, 18 below.

5. The letter-book of William of Hoo, sacrist of Bury St. Edmunds, 1280–1294. Edited by Antonia Gransden. 1963.   **104.5**

Transcript, Latin, with English summaries, omitting the text of entries 'which are forms containing letters instead of the names of people and places ... unless the names can be supplied with fair certainty'. Listed in 1933 as the only book of its kind by a monastic obedientiary, it illustrates William's activities as sacrist, archdeacon and papal agent. Included in the introduction, in order to set the formulary or letter-book in its historical perspective, is a brief account of the abbey and of its importance at the time. Appendix of 26 additional illustrative docs.

6. John Constable's correspondence. [Vol.] ii: Early friends and Maria Bicknell (Mrs. Constable). 1964.   **104.6**

Letters, 1809–28, linked as in **104.**4 above, concerning the central relationship of his life, his love for Maria Bicknell and their marriage. The introduction covers Constable's relations with his friends (as distinct from his family) of the early days at East Bergholt, among them Mrs. Elizabeth Cobbold and J. T. Smith, Ann Taylor and Lucy Hurlock, John Dunthorne senior, and George Frost. Preliminary account of the Bicknells and the Rhuddes.

7. A dictionary of Suffolk arms. By Joan Corder. 1965.   **104.7**

An 'ordinary' or collection of arms arranged according to their design and their charges, with the names of the bearers attached. The alphabetical index of families allows the book to be used as an 'armory'. Foreword by Sir Anthony Wagner.

8. John Constable's correspondence. [Vol.] iii: The corres- **104.8**
pondence with C. R. Leslie, R.A. 1965.

Letters, 1826-37 and later, with linking narrative as before. Brief introduction.

9. Poor relief in Elizabethan Ipswich. Edited by John Webb. **104.9**
1966.

Docs. concerned in the main with the periods 1577-9 and 1596-8, among
them (i) the ordinances, 1588-9, of Henry Tooley's Foundation, with
accounts for 1577-8 and 1597-8; (ii) weekly payments to the poor in
Christ's Hospital, 1578-9, with the governors' accounts for 1580-1, 1586-
7 and 1596-7; (iii) a register of the poor, inmates of the Blackfriars, 1569-
83, showing the relief granted them and its source; (iv) poor rate assessments, 1574, and weekly payments to the poor, 1574, 1577-8; (v) plague
relief payments, 1579, 1585-6; (vi) a census of the poor, 1597, covering
nine of the twelve parishes. Appended are lists of wardens of the Tooley
Foundation, a table of its annual income and expenditure, similar lists for
Christ's Hospital, an analysis of poor rate assessments, 1577-8, and a table
of weekly outdoor relief payments for the same year.

The introduction describes the setting up, management and general
functioning of the Foundation and Hospital, as well as organized outdoor
relief, and concludes that 'Ipswich poor were comparatively well but-
tressed against the social and economic pressures of the age'.

10. John Constable's correspondence. [Vol.] iv: Patrons, **104.10**
dealers, and fellow artists. 1966.

Four chronological sequences, three as indicated on the title-page plus the
fourth, with David Lucas, Constable's engraver, each sequence with its
own introduction, the letters linked as before.

11. John Constable's correspondence. [Vol.] v: Various **104.11**
friends, with Charles Boner and the artist's children. 1967.

Four sequences—amateur artists, literary characters, other friends, and
Charles Boner and the Constable children—each sequence with its own
introduction, linked as before. Also, a list of Constable's descendants, and
three letters by Charles Golding Constable to the press.

12. John Constable's correspondence. [Vol.] vi: The Fishers. **104.12**
1968.

A new edition of the editor's *John Constable and the Fishers* (1952), cor-
recting mistakes and supplementing omissions, the grouping into chapters
abandoned in favour of the continuous narrative form common to the
preceding vols. Preface by Geoffrey Grigson.

13. The Suffolk committees for scandalous ministers, 1644- **104.13**
1646. Edited by Clive Holmes. 1970.

Transcript of the 'case book' recording the proceedings of the earl of
Manchester's two committees for Suffolk, with docs relating to cases
against William Keeble, rector of Ringshall, George Carter, rector of

Whatfield and Elmsett, and Maptid Violet, curate at Aldeburgh. Index of witnesses.

14. John Constable's discourses. Compiled and annotated by **104.14** R. B. Beckett. 1970.

The letterpress to *English Landscape*, the lectures on landscape, the address to Royal Academy students, and other writings, with a list of Constable's books and his pictures by other artists, a note and genealogical table on the Rhudde family (see **104.**6 above) contributed by Leslie Dow, and an appendix of additional letters and recent (1970) sales. This vol. seen through the press by Norman Scarfe.

15. The county of Suffolk, surveyed by Joseph Hodskinson, **104.15** of Arundel Street, Strand, London. Engraved and published by William Faden, geographer to the King, (successor to Mr. Jefferys) Charing Cross, August 14th, 1783. Edited by D. P. Dymond. Portfolio, 1972.

Photographic (scale reduced) edition in 12 sheets. The editor's introduction deals with the survey methods used, the scale and conventions, noteworthy differences between the county boundary *c.* 1780 and in 1970, the reliability and historical uses of the map, and the little that is known of Hodskinson's life. Ends with a list of his printed works and a preliminary list of his surveys, 1773–1822, excluding county maps.

16. The Ipswich recognizance rolls, 1294–1327: a calendar. **104.16** Edited by G. H. Martin. 1973.

The first 21 rolls of the series, the rolls being 'a record of conveyances of burgage tenements and the proof of testaments in the borough court'. List of bailiffs and coroners named in the rolls.

The introduction traces the evolution of the roll from the general record of business in the portmanmote, the new roll giving rise to a distinct series—the recognizance rolls—and creating by the middle of the 14th century a new court, the petty court of recognizances. In 1307 the roll attracted proofs of testaments. The rolls here calendared, though still 'an emergent record of transactions', their conventions 'not firmly established', nevertheless display 'a borough and port of the second rank ... at the full pitch of its first existence as a complex, self-conscious and self-documenting community'.

17. The field book of Walsham-le-Willows, 1577. Edited by **104.17** Kenneth Melton Dodd. 1974.

Transcripts of (i) the measured and descriptive survey (the field book) made for Sir Nicholas Bacon, (ii) the custumal of the manors of Walsham and Walsham Church House in the same year, and (iii) the perambulation, Latin.

The introduction, after sketching the pre-survey history of the manors, the probable methods of surveying recommended, and the probable procedure followed by the Walsham surveyors (John Hunt and one Amias, possibly Israel Amys), attempts to determine the acreages involved and whether a general pattern of land use existed. Table I shows the usage of the land of selected tenants, table II lists the tenants and their holdings in 1577 and 1581.

18. John Constable: further documents and correspondence. **104.18** Pt. 1: Documents, edited by Leslie Parris and Conal Shields. Pt. 2: Correspondence, edited by Ian Fleming-Williams. With a tribute to R. B. Beckett by Norman Scarfe. 1975.

In pt. 1, further lecture mss., over 20 pp. of book-titles additional to the list in **104.**14 above, and the whole of David Lucas's annotations in his copy of C. R. Leslie's *Memoirs* of the painter. Pt. 2 prints extracts from the diaries of Daniel Whalley and John Charles Constable, and more than 250 letters, arranged under headings and with linking narration as in preceding vols.

19. The chorography of Suffolk. Edited by Diarmaid Mac- **104.19** Culloch. 1976.

Transcript of a ms. history of Suffolk, now fragmented among at least six different ms. collections, which can be traced back 'with reasonable certainty' to the library of Sir Thomas Browne and identified as the counterpart of *The Chorography of Norfolk* edited by Mrs. Christobel Hood (Norwich, 1938) and ascribed by her to John Norden the elder.

The introduction describes the dismemberment of the ms. while it was in the possession of Peter Le Neve and subsequently Thomas Martin, dates it to *c.* 1605, analyses its primary and literary sources, rejects the attribution to the elder Norden, and agrees with the suggestion that Thomas Browne of Poringland near Norwich 'seems to fit the *internal* indications of the Chorographies very well'. The ms. 'provides a gazetteer of practically everyone of any importance in the Suffolk of 1600', contains 'much information of value on tithe and manor custom, ownership of land and the vicissitudes of markets and communities', and is 'a valuable supplement to the monumental and also monumentally slipshod published work of W. A. Copinger on the descent of Suffolk manors'.

20. A Suffolk bibliography. Compiled by A. V. Steward. **104.20** 1979.

A list of 8123 printed items, among them approximately 2,000 articles from 185 periodicals. Entries for books, articles and pamphlets omitted from the bibliography have been classified and deposited in the Suffolk Record Office.

21. The archives of the abbey of Bury St. Edmunds. Edited **104.21** by Rodney M. Thomson. 1980.

An account of the growth and development of the abbey archives, 1020–1539, followed by a descriptive catalogue of more than 1300 items: charters, court and account rolls, cartularies and registers, and the records of dependencies of the abbey. Includes lists of lost archival books and of 'modern' copies of lost records.

22. The Ipswich probate inventories, 1583–1631. Edited by **104.22** Michael Reed. 1981.

SUFFOLK RECORDS SOCIETY

Transcripts of the first 72 surviving probate inventories for inhabitants of Ipswich in the archives of the archdeaconry court of Suffolk and the consistory court of the diocese of Norwich. Brief analytical introduction. Glossary.

23. Boxford churchwardens' accounts, 1530-1561. Edited by Peter Northeast. 1982.   104.23

Transcript. Map.

24. A journal of excursions through the county of Suffolk, 1823-1844, [by] David Elisha Davy. Edited by John Blatchly. 1982.   104.24

Transcript, with introductory account of Davy's life and work. The excursions, 'in search of materials for a history of that county', resulted in the 170 volumes put together by Davy and now in the British Library.

259

105. SUFFOLK RECORDS SOCIETY, SUFFOLK CHARTERS*

1. **Leiston abbey cartulary and Butley priory charters. Edited by Richard Mortimer. 1979.**   **105.1**

Latin, with English summaries and notes. Docs. later than 1250 calendared in English. For Leiston, the early 13th-century register of deeds with some miscellaneous later additions and such originals as are known. For Butley, the surviving charters, nearly all hitherto unprinted, which relate to the foundation and the Suffolk possessions of the priory, and illustrate its connections with Leiston.

The introduction, concerned in the main with Leiston, considers the foundation and later history of each house, the donors (numerous genealogical tables), the two houses' churches, their temporal possessions, and in some detail the docs. themselves. Seals and sealing described by T. A. Heslop. Lists of abbots and priors to the dissolution. Maps.

2. **Blythburgh priory cartulary. Edited by Christopher Harper-Bill. Pt. 1. 1980.**   **105.2**

Latin, with English summaries and notes. Docs. later than 1250 calendared in English. Late 14th-century original, with early 15th-century additions. The scope of the introduction is indicated by the note to **105.1** above.

3. **Blythburgh priory cartulary. Pt. 2. 1981.**   **105.3**

Concludes the preceding, with corrections and index. Pagination is continuous.

5. **Stoke by Clare cartulary. Edited by Christopher Harper-Bill and Richard Mortimer. Pt. 1. 1982.**   **105.4**

Latin, with English summaries and notes. Contains the first 180 charters. 'It is intended that the remainder ... together with the Introduction and Index to the whole, will be contained in the next two volumes ...'

---

*A special series in which the Society proposes to print the whole of the pre-Reformation charter material relating to the county, including docs. relating to lands outside Suffolk if such docs. occur in Suffolk cartularies and/or Suffolk collections of original charters, in all cases preferring original charters, when extant, to cartulary texts. All docs. will be printed *in extenso* (and, so far as is practicable, whether they have been printed before or not) up to a date of *c.* 1250; beyond that date a full English abstract will generally be deemed sufficient. Docs. in Latin (or French or Anglo-Saxon) will have a brief English headnote, and all which require it a short footnote dealing with such essentials as date, the particulars of the doc. and seal in the cases of originals, and the location of previous editions. (Derived from the foreword by the general editor, R. Allen Brown, in the first vol. of the series.)

106. YORKSHIRE ARCHAEOLOGICAL SOCIETY, WAKEFIELD COURT ROLLS SERIES

1. The court rolls of the manor of Wakefield from October **106.1**
1639 to September 1640. Edited and calendared by C. M.
Fraser and Kenneth Emsley. 1977.

An abridged edition, in English, derived from the engrossed roll, chosen
from the almost uninterrupted run of Wakefield court rolls from 1326 to
1925 owned by the Society 'to illustrate the business of the manor courts
on the eve of the Civil War and to enable a comparison to be made with
the business of the West Riding Quarter Sessions, within whose jurisdiction Wakefield lay'.

The introduction describes the jurisdictions and procedure of Wakefield's two courts, the court baron (held every three weeks, and concerned
almost exclusively with land transfers) and court leet (held twice a year, at
four centres, for the regulation of community affairs at a local level). Rolls
from the fragmentary series from 1274 to 1326 are in **71.29** and the other
vols. there referred to.

2. The court roll of the manor of Wakefield from September **106.2**
1348 to September 1350. Edited and calendared by Helen M.
Jewell. 1981 [1982].

The rolls of the three-weekly court (court baron) at Wakefield for land
transactions and tenurial matters and civil pleas, and of the twice-yearly
court (tourn or leet) held variously at Wakefield, Halifax, Brighouse or
Rastrick, and Kirkburton for criminal cases and breaches of commercial
regulations.

The introduction explains that the rolls come from the period just after
the earl of Warenne's death (1347) when the estates had been granted to
Edmund of Langley, then aged six, son of Edw. III, custody and profits
being vested in Queen Philippa, and while the earl's widow, Joan of Bar,
survived and had dower rights. The church in Wakefield had also just
undergone a change of ownership, Wakefield and Dewsbury churches
having been granted in 1348 to the chapel of St. Stephen, Westminster,
which became rector. The sessions, the tenants and suitors, and the
procedures are described, as are the officers of the manor and the light
cast by the rolls on conditions in Wakefield during a period of abnormally
high mortality (no direct references to plague occur).

261

107. PEMBROKESHIRE RECORD SOCIETY
[PEMBROKESHIRE RECORD SERIES]

[1] Pembrokeshire life, 1572–1843: a selection of letters. Edited by B. E. and K. A. Howells. 1972.   **107.1**

Selected in the main from the mss. of Haverfordwest corporation, the mss. of the Church in Wales, and the holdings of the National Library of Wales, with others from the Bronwydd, Glansevern, Harcourt Powell, Lucas, Ottley, Owen and Colby, Picton Castle, Poyston, and Slebech mss.

[2] Elizabethan Pembrokeshire: the evidence of George Owen. Edited by Brian Howells. 1973.   **107.2**

Extracts from the published texts of Owen's *Description* and *The Taylors Cussion*, arranged to illustrate the peoples of the shire, economic life, the calendar, recreation, the shire and its localities, and government.

[3] The extent of Cemais, 1594. Edited by B. E. and K. A. Howells. 1977.   **107.3**

Transcript, the Latin in English translation. Cemais (Kemes, Kemeys), an ancient cantref, later a barony of the earldom of Pembroke, became a hundred of the county in 1536, its main town being Newport. George Owen, son of William Owen of Henllys, succeeded as its lord in 1574. Glossary.

PART 6

INDEX

USE OF THE INDEX

To facilitate reference to particular items the index makes use of the figures given in the right-hand margins: bold figures denote the section, ordinary figures after the full point denote the number of the item within the section; sections can be identified from the table of contents. In the case of works whose volumes or parts appear as separate items the index generally refers to the first volume or part; the location of subsequent volumes or parts is stated in the editorial note to the first unless they follow it in immediate sequence.

Commonly accepted abbreviations are used when appropriate to indicate county names, personal names, titles and designations of office or rank. Names of places come before names of persons, and titles of nobility in order of precedence come before surnames. The rank or office used to identify a person is generally the highest attained and may not be the same as that used in the item referred to. Names of editors and others concerned in the publication of items listed in this volume have not been indexed, nor does the index reflect the changes brought about by local government reorganization in England and Wales in 1974.

Abberley, Worcs., **80.**22
Abbotside, W. R. Yorks., **71.**130
Abbotsleigh, nr. Bristol, **42.**22
Aberconway, *see* Conway
Academies, **51.**24
Acapulco, treasure ship from, **28.**109
Accounting procedures, systems:
  Chester exchequer, **51.**28
  medieval, **48.**116, **58.**50, **101.**16
  royal household (Edw. I), **3.**90
  Wiltshire estates, **68.**14
Accounts, commercial and industrial:
  Foley ironworks, **69.**52
  John Isham, merchant, **55.**21
  Sidney ironworks, **101.**15
  John Smythe, merchant, **42.**28
  woad cultivation, **65.**31
Accounts, manorial:
  Bristol, St. Augustine's, **42.**22
  Cuxham, **58.**50
  Leeds, **76.**46
  Macclesfield, **51.**28
Accounts, monastic:
  Battle, **64.**67
  Beaulieu, **101.**16
  Harrold, **35.**49
  Newnham, **35.**49
  Norwich, **54.**41
  Sibton, **104.**2
  Westminster, **101.**2
Accounts, municipal:
  Banbury, **88.**15
  Bristol, **42.**24
  Norwich, **54.**39
  Oxford, **60.**15
  Worcester, **69.**51

Accounts, municipal—*cont.*:
  York, **41.**192
Accounts, personal:
  John Carne, **20.**26
  Sir Thos. Haggerston, **41.**180
  Thos. Heritage, **11.**13
  Giles Moore, **64.**70
  Gertrude Savile, **57.**24
  Peter Temple, **11.**13
Accounts, various:
  Bristol castle, **42.**34
  Canterbury *sede vacante*, **47.**21
  civil war, **47.**20, **62.**72, **104.**3
  coroners' bills, **68.**36
  dikereeves, **52.**71
  escheats etc. (Hen. III), **30.**82
  fraternity, **100.**18
  Merton College, **60.**18
  national revenue and expenditure, **3.**57
  poor relief, **104.**9
  regimental, **3.**57
  school, **65.**25
  ship's purser, **101.**7
  shipwrights, **41.**181
  treasurer of Scotland, **4.**4
  village officers, **88.**12
  wardrobe (Hen. III), **30.**82
  See also Administrators' accounts; Building accounts; Churchwardens' accounts; Customs, customs accounts; Estate accounts and papers; Fabric accounts; Farm accounts; Household accounts; Ministers' accounts
Achurch, John of, monk of Peterborough (14th cent.), **55.**20

Wodrofe, Wm. (fl. 1530), **60.**19
Wollaton, Notts., **57.**21
Wolsingham, co. Dur., **41.**183
Wolverhampton, Staffs., **62.**77
Wolverton family, **36.**18
Women's education, **76.**57
Womock, Laurence, bp. (*d.* 1686), **80.**28
Wood, Ben., privateer (fl. 1592), **20.**111
Wood, Sir Rich., at Constantinople (*d.* 1900), **101.**3
Wood, Rowland John (*d.* 1975), **76.**55*p*
Woodforde, James, of New College (*d.* 1803), **60.**21
Woodland, owned by:
  earl of Cardigan, **55.**24
  Devon monasteries, **40.**25
  Fountains abbey, **71.**140
Wood sales:
  Northamptonshire forests, **55.**23
  Peter Temple's estate, **11.**13
Wool:
  Beaulieu abbey, **101.**16
  prices (1485–1540), **93.**3
  in Peter Temple's accounts, **11.**13
Woollen drapers, Kingston-upon-Thames, **63.**29
Woollen industry, Lancashire, **51.**20
Woolley, Wm., of Darley Abbey (*d.* 1719), **94.**6
Woolwich, prison hulks at, **35.**49
Wootton Bassett, Wilts., **68.**36
Worcester, city of:
  cath. priory:
    cartulary, **30.**76
    portiforium, **25.**89
  chamberlains' accounts, **69.**51
  chamber order book, **69.**51
  Dougharty (Doharty) family, **69.**48
  M.P.s, **69.**51
  preachers, **69.**51
  probate inventories, **69.**48
Worcester, diocese of:
  archdeacons, **30.**76
  bps.' registers:
    (1327–33), **69.**53
    (1339–49), **69.**47
    (1375–95), **69.**50
  dissenting chapels, **62.**74
  estates of bpric., **3.**92*k*
  poor benefices (1707), **65.**27
  'state' of (1782–1808), **69.**49
  terriers, **65.**27
  under Bp. Bransford, **69.**47
  visitation articles (1585), **65.**27
  wills, in Bp. Wakefield's register, **69.**50
Worcester, earl of, *see* Somerset, Chas.
Worcestershire:
  Greenwood's map. **69.**45
  Oswaldslaw hundred, **30.**76
  plague in (1348–9), **3.**92*k*
  pleas (*temp.* John), **34.**83
Worcestershire Historical Soc., publications, new series, pp. 188–91

Workhouse accounts:
  Salisbury, **68.**31
  Wimbledon, **63.**26
Workhouse system, in Leeds, **76.**57
Worth, Rob., chancellor to Bp. Martival, **14.**68
Wrangham, Chas., archdeacon (fl. 1809–18), **71.**128
Wreck de mer, **82.**4
Wrest House, Beds., **35.**59
Wriothesley, Thos., earl of Southampton (*d.* 1667), **54.**45
Writs:
  early registers of, **34.**87
  for debts, **68.**28
  of computabitur, **3.**29
  of liberate, on exchequer rolls, **3.**29
  royal (11th–12th cent.), **34.**77
  sub pena (Edw. IV), **3.**92*p*
Writtle with Roxwell, peculiar of, **12.**78
Wulfric, later named Spot or Spott, founder of Burton abbey (*d. c.* 1003), **89.**2
Wulstan, Saint (*d.* 1095), **25.**89
Wyatt, Sir Francis, gov. of Virginia (*d.* 1644), **101.**5
Wyatt, Rich., of Surrey (*d.* 1813), **63.**31
Wyatt, Sir Thos., the elder (*d.* 1542), **101.**5
Wyatt, Sir Thos., the younger (*d.* 1554), **101.**5
Wyatt family, **101.**5
Wyclif, John, theologian (*d.* 1384), **60.**16*i*
Wycombe, *see* High Wycombe
Wye, liberty of, **3.**92*g*
Wyllis, Rob., identified with Rob. Joseph (*d.* 1569), **60.**19
Wynn, Sir John, of Gwydir (*d.* 1627), **80.**25

Yarmouth (Great Yarmouth), Norf., **54.**39
Year books:
  Edw. II (yr. 12), **34.**81
  London eyre (1321), **34.**85
  their language and its interpretation, **34.**81
Yermak Timofeyevich, cossack leader (*d.* 1585), **20.**146
Yesipov chronicle, **20.**146
York, archdeaconry of, **71.**123
York, city of:
  castle, recusant lists, **15.**53
  cathedral (minster):
    charters relating to, **71.**123, 124
    clergy and prebends (pre-1307), **71.**123
  chamberlains' accounts, **41.**192
  corporation (*temp.* Eliz. I), **71.**138
  historical monuments, **8.**12
  House book, **71.**138
  memorandum book, **41.**186
  pleas at (*temp.* John), **34.**83, 84

314

CORRECTIONS to *Texts and Calendars* (1958, 1978)

All the following corrections should be made in the original (1958) edition. Corrections made when the work was reprinted (1978) are distinguished by a preceding asterisk.

*p. viii, l. 7	*for* H.C. Hector *read* L.C. Hector
p. x	*for* Southampton Record Series *read* Southampton Records Series
p. 7, in **1**.24	*after* See also *insert* **3**.17 and
*p. 24, in **3**.41, col.**1**, l. 14	*for* pt. 3 *read* pt. 2
p. 27, in **3**.53	*delete* in progress *and amend punctuation*
p. 29, in **3**.57, l. 2	*for* xxvi *read* xxv *and for* 28 vols. in 52 *read* 29 vols. in 52
p. 30, in **3**.58	*for* 1728–30 *read* 1729–30, with one item from 1728 *and for* 1730–4 *read* 1731–4
p. 43, in **6**.9	*for* urbe *read* orbe *and for* 1858 *read* 1858–63
p. 44, in **6**.17	*for* chronicles *read* chronicle
p. 45, ll. 1–2	*delete* No more published.
p. 46, in **6**.27	*for* 1862–8 *read* 1862–6
p. 48, in **6**.32	*for* 1444–1450 *read* 1449–50
p. 51, in **6**.48	*for* Gaedhill *read* Gaedhil
p. 52, in **6**.54	*for* William A. Hennessy *read* William M. Hennessy
p. 53, in **6**.62	*for* 1314–1316 *read* 1311–1316
p. 54, in **6**.64	*for* 1338 *read* 1388
p. 55, in **6**.70	*for* 1878 read 1878–83
p. 59, in **6**.95	*for* Richard *read* Richards
p. 65, l. 3	*for* St. Catherine's *read* St. Catharine's
p. 106, in **12**.16	*delete* No more published *and insert* Also issued by the Scottish Record Soc. as its first publication and contd. to 1800 by the same editor as its publications 2 and 3 (6 pts. 1898–9)
p. 107, in **12**.20	*add* Also issued in 2 vols. by the Scottish Record Soc. as its publications 4 and 5 (1897–8).
p. 124, in **14**.38	*for* Ratcliffe *read* Ratcliff
p. 125	*delete last line*
p. 141, in **16**.8	*for* Orlèans *read* Orléans
p. 141, in **16**.15	*for* Saint *read* Sainte
p. 143, in **17**.2	*for* Nenni *read* Nennii
p. 143, in **17**.3	*for* monacho *read* monachi
p. 144, in **17**.11	*for* Heminford *read* Hemingford

p. 153, in **19**.37   *for* Goës *read* Goës's
p. 154, in **19**.41   *for* Verga *read* Vega
p. 156, in **19**.51   *after* Marpurg *insert* (Marburg)
p. 157, in **19**.59*b*   *after* with notes *insert* by C.H. Coote
p. 159, in **19**.78   *after* Stratfieldsay *insert* (sic)
p. 164, in **20**.9   *for* Tiexeira *read* Teixeira
p. 164, in **20**.11   *for* Spitzbergen (*twice*) *read* Spitsbergen *and insert comma* after Brugge
p. 164, in **20**.14   *for* Fernández de Quirós *read* Fernandez de Quiros
p. 164, in **20**.15   *for* Fernández de Quiros *read* Fernandez de Quiros
p. 168, in **20**.46   *after* Goa *change full point to comma*
p. 170, in **20**.64   *for* Quirós *read* Quiros *and after* council of state *insert* concerning Quiros, 1618,
p. 171, in **20**.69   *for* sumne *read* summe
p. 175, in **20**.104   *for Principal read Principall*
p. 176, in **21**.3   *for* land *read* lande
p. 216, in **28**.9   *for* 1896 *read* 1897
p. 224, in **28**.86   *for* Narborough *read* Narbrough
p. 225, in **28**.91,
  l. 15   *for* Pryse *read* Pryce
p. 246, in **31**.55,
  l. 7   *for* Stranford *read* Strangford
p. 255, in **32**.1   *for* 1891 *read* 1871
*p. 270, in **33**.53   *for* Russell *read* Fussell
p. 281, in **34**.42   *for* 1936 *read* 1926
*p. 289, in **35**.2,
  l. 2   *for* Lambert *read* Lambeth
p. 294, in **35**.25,
  l. 5   *for* registers *read* register
p. 294, in **35**.25,
  l. 10   *for* Cook *read* Crook
p. 305, in **40**.1   *for* Henry Alexander Fry *read* Edward Alexander Fry
p. 316, in **41**.49   *for* Scaife *read* Skaife
p. 317, in **41**.57   *for* Scaife *read* Skaife
p. 326, in **41**.125   *for* Pt. iii *read* Pt. ii
p. 335, in **43**.4   *for* 1896 *read* 1891
p. 342, in page
  heading   *for* RECORD *read* RECORDS
p. 371, in margin   *for* **46**.94 *read* **49**.94
p. 393, in **52**.38   *for* **53**.40, 44 *read* **52**.40, 44
p. 468, in **68**.11,
  l. 8   *for* jurers' *read* jurors'
p. 475, in **69**.43   *for* [1952- . In progress.] *read* Introduction by Mrs. Margaret O'Brien. 1952-7.
p. 520, in **80**.1   *for* Davis *read* Davies
p. 540, col. 1, l. 6
from foot   *for* Tewekesbury *read* Tewkesbury

318

*p. 544, col. 2, l. 7
from foot   *for* 60.58 *read* 62.58
p. 547, col. 2   *insert* Bekynton, Thos., *see* Beckington, Thos.
p. 548, col. 1, l. 6   *for* Bellinghausen *read* Bellingshausen
p. 550, col. 2   *for* Gloucester 7.46 *read* Gloucester 7.45
p. 553, col. 1, l. 3   *for* Richard *read* Ricart
p. 555, col. 1, l. 4
from foot   *for* Emanuel *read* Emmanuel
p. 555, col. 2, l. 8   *for* St. Catherine's *read* St. Catharine's
p. 556, col. 1, l. 12
from foot   *delete* , 14.55
p. 558, col. 2, l. 11
from foot   *for* Bates *read* Boste
p. 565, col. 1, l. 15
from foot   *for* Orlèans *read* Orléans
p. 567, col. 1, l. 24   *after* 1.24, *insert* 3.17,
p. 571, col. 1, l. 7   *for* lasgow *read* Glasgow
p. 571, col. 2   *for* Cumby, Wm. Pryse *read* Cumby, Wm. Pryce
p. 575, col. 1, l. 26   *for* 3.70 *read* 31.70
p. 577, col. 2, l. 30   *for* (1314–16) *read* (1311–16)
p. 577, col. 2, l. 35   *for* 42.21, 45, 162 *read* 41.21, 45, 162
p. 578, col. 2, l. 26   *for* register of testaments, 12.6 *read* register of testaments, 12.16
p. 579, col. 1   *for* Eglington *read* Eglinton
p. 581, col. 2   *for* Kippax, 67.33 *read* Kippax, 76.33
p. 583, col. 1, l. 33   *for* Ear *read* Earl
p. 585, col. 2   *insert* Gandavo, *see* Ghent, Simon of
p. 591, col. 1   *among* Hearth tax returns *insert* Surrey, 63.17
p. 598, col. 1   *under* Ireland, patent rolls *amend chronological order*, James I *to follow* Hen. VIII-Eliz.I
p. 599, col. 2, l. 30   *for* Earles Colne *read* Earls Colne
p. 603, col. 1, l. 24
from foot   *read* Lansdowne, Marquess of:
p. 603, col. 1, l. 23
from foot   *read* Bowood mss., 7.3, 6
p. 603, col. 1, l. 22
from foot   *read* Shelburne mss., 7.3,5,6
p. 605, col. 2, l. 2   *for* 6.23 *read* 6.24
p. 609, col. 1, l. 3   *delete* Bp. Frere on,
p. 610, col. 1   *among* London, French protestant churches *insert* Threadneedle St., 26.9, 21, 38
p. 610, col. 2, l. 5   *for* Towre *read* Tower
p. 610, col. 2   *for* Lonsdale, archdeaconry of *read* Lonsdale, deanery of
p. 611, col. 1,
l. 6 from foot   *for* 7.6 *read* 7.2
p. 615, col. 1,
l. 15 from foot   *for* 41.108 *read* 41.101

p. 618, col. 1   *for* More-Molineux *read* More-Molyneux
p. 630, col. 1, l. 10
from foot   *delete* , **14**.55
p. 632, col. 1   *for* Philippe IV *read* Philippe VI
p. 635, col. 2, l. 22
from foot   *for* Ptolomy (Ptolomaeus) *read* Ptolemy (Ptolemaeus)
p. 636, col. 1   *insert* Quiros, Pedro Fernandez de, **20**.14, 15, 64
p. 637, col. 2,
l. 9 from foot   *for* Guisbrough *read* Guisborough
p. 644, col. 2   *for* Serbo *read* Serlo
p. 647, col. 1   *for* Sneyd, Sir Walt. *read* Sneyd, Rev. Walt.
p. 647, col. 1   *for* Société Jersiase *read* Société Jersiaise
p. 647, col. 2   *for* Southampton Record Series *read* Southampton Records Series
p. 648, col. 2   *for* Spitzbergen *read* Spitsbergen (Spitzbergen)
p. 652, col. 2, l. 17
from foot   *for* 306–31 *read* 309–31
p. 654, col. 1,
l. 18 from foot   *for* appeal *read* repeal
p. 655, col. 1   *for* Tilbury, John of *read* Tilbury, Gervase of
p. 655, col. 2   *delete* Towneley Hall, co. Louth, **7**.31
     for Towneley Hall mss. *read* Townley Hall mss. *and amend alphabetical order*
p. 660, col. 1, l. 4   *for* Fernando de Quiros *read* Fernandez de Quiros
p. 661, col. 2   *insert* Waurin *see* Wavrin, John de
p. 666, col. 1   *insert* Wixamtree hundred, Beds., **35**.25

BOOKS NOT IN THE SOCIETY'S LIBRARY

The library of the Royal Historical Society does not at present (October 1983) include the following, some of which lie outside its scope. Full titles are given in the corresponding entries or sections of this volume. The list is supplementary to and does not replace the similar list in *T & C* 1958, 1978.

3. PUBLIC RECORD OFFICE
Calendar . . . of commissions on the dorses of the patent rolls. **3.**6

5. IRISH RECORD OFFICE
Calendar of the justiciary rolls, 1–7 Edw. III. **5.**3

8. HISTORICAL MONUMENTS COMMISSION (ENGLAND)
All vols. **8.**10–17

9. HISTORICAL MONUMENTS COMMISSION (WALES)
All vols. except Caenarvonshire, vol. i: East.

10. ALCUIN CLUB, COLLECTIONS
All vols. **10.**40–64

12. BRITISH RECORD SOCIETY, INDEX LIBRARY
All vols. **12.**77–92

21. HAKLUYT SOCIETY, EXTRA SERIES
All vols. **21.**4*a*–9

25. HENRY BRADSHAW SOCIETY
All vols. except **25.**88, 89, 90, 100.

37–39. CUMBERLAND AND WESTMORLAND ANTIQUARIAN AND ARCHAEOLOGICAL SOCIETY, EXTRA, RECORD AND TRACT SERIES
All vols. **37.**19–23, **38.**9, **39.**15–19

47. KENT ARCHAEOLOGICAL SOCIETY, KENT RECORDS
All vols. except **47.**20, 21.

BOOKS NOT IN THE SOCIETY'S LIBRARY

76. THORESBY SOCIETY

All vols.   **76**.46–57

80. HISTORICAL SOCIETY OF THE CHURCH IN WALES

All vols.   **80**.10–29

86. BRISTOL AND GLOUCESTERSHIRE ARCHAELOGICAL SOCIETY, RECORDS SECTION

All vols.   **86**.4–11

88. BANBURY HISTORICAL SOCIETY, RECORDS SECTION

All vols.   **88**.1–19

91. CAMBRIDGE ANTIQUARIAN RECORDS SOCIETY

All vols.   **91**.1–4

92. CATHOLIC RECORD SOCIETY, OCCASIONAL PUBLICATIONS

Returns of papists, 1767: diocese of Chester.   **92**.1

93. DERBYSHIRE ARCHAEOLOGICAL SOCIETY, RECORD SERIES

Duchy of Lancaster's estates in Derbyshire.   **93**.3

94. DERBYSHIRE RECORD SOCIETY

All vols.   **94**.1–7

96. DORSET RECORD SOCIETY

All vols, except **96**.4.

97. ESSEX ARCHAEOLOGICAL SOCIETY

Feet of fines, vol. iv (vol. iii imperfect).   **97**.1
Occasional publications, 1–3.   **97**.2–4

98. HALIFAX ANTIQUARIAN SOCIETY, RECORD SERIES

All vols.   **98**.1–3

102. RUTLAND RECORD SOCIETY

The country community under Henry VIII.   **102**.1

103. SOCIETY OF ANTIQUARIES OF NEWCASTLE UPON TYNE, RECORD SERIES

All vols.   **103**.1–2

106. YORKSHIRE ARCHAEOLOGICAL SOCIETY, WAKEFIELD COURT ROLL
SERIES

All vols.   106.1–2

107. PEMBROKESHIRE RECORD SOCIETY

All vols.   107.1–3